EFFECTIVE GRANT WRITING AND PROGRAM EVALUATION FOR HUMAN SERVICE PROFESSIONALS

EFFECTIVE GRANT WRITING AND PROGRAM EVALUATION FOR HUMAN SERVICE PROFESSIONALS

FRANCIS K. O. YUEN
KENNETH L. TERAO
ANNA MARIE SCHMIDT

WILEY

John Wiley & Sons. Inc.

Published by John Wiley & Sons, Inc., Hoboken, New Jersey.
Published simultaneously in Canada.

For general information on our other products and services please contact our Customer Care Department within the U.S. at (800) 762-2974, outside the United States at (317) 572-3993 or fax (317) 572-4002.

Wiley also publishes its books in a variety of electronic formats. Some content that appears in print may not be available in electronic books. For more information about Wiley products, visit our web site at www.wiley.com.

Library of Congress Cataloging-in-Publication Data:

Yuen, Francis K. O.
Effective grant writing and program evaluation for human service professionals / by Francis K.O. Yuen, Kenneth L. Terao, Anna Marie Schmidt.
   p. cm.

Includes bibliographical references and index.
 ISBN 978-0-470-46998-9 (pbk.)
   1. Proposal writing in human services. 2. Human services. 3. Proposal writing for grants. I. Terao, Kenneth L. II. Schmidt, Anna Marie. III. Title.
HV41.2.Y838 2009

658.15'224—dc22

10 9 8 7 6 5 4 3 2

To all dedicated and resourceful education, health, and human service professionals and volunteers, who with unflagging desire and commitment make a difference in our communities.

Contents

Acknowledgments

The authors would like to thank the contributors for their generosity in sharing their professional insights. Marquita Flemming, Senior Editor at Wiley, has been most supportive, considerate, flexible, and patient with us throughout the development of this book—thank you! We appreciate the editorial support of Kim A. Nir, Senior Production Editor; and Kathleen DeChants at Wiley; and Ginjer Clarke, copyeditor; as well as the initial editorial assistance of Meredith Linden, particularly on those last-minute turnarounds.

We are grateful for the inspiration, encouragement, critiques, and sharing of talents from the staff of Project STAR of JBS International Inc., Aguirre Division. Special recognition must go to the Project STAR training coaches, who have infused their training with creativity, energy, and humor, and who collectively have made it their mission to pull back the veil of mystery that enshrouds evaluation and ensure that it is both accessible and meaningful to program staff in the field. It is through their work with thousands of programs and training experiences that we have been able to field test much of the supportive material and interactive exercises. We want to express our appreciation to the Corporation for National and Community Service (CNCS) for their recognition and support of quality program planning and program evaluation. Some of the materials in this book are based on work supported for Project STAR of JBS International Inc., Aguirre Division by the CNCS under Grant No. 05TAHCA001. Appreciation is also extended to Chrystal Barranti who was a co-evaluator for several of the example projects used in this book.

Then, there are the hardworking human service professionals, who are social workers, public health workers, psychologists, community organizers, nurses, doctors, counselors, and administrators. They are affiliated with government agencies such as CNCS or are independent shoestring community organizations. Our shared learning experiences and their valuable feedback, candid discussion of challenges, and insightful guidance have shaped our ideas and approaches in writing this book. We are truly indebted to them.

With great affection and love, we acknowledge our spouses, Cindy Kellen-Yuen, Elizabeth Sheldon, and Bob Roat; and our children, Amanda Yuen, Emily Yuen, Eric Terao, Russell Terao, and Abby Roat. They have provided unconditional support during this writing adventure.

About the Authors

Francis K. O. Yuen, DSW, ACSW, is a Professor in the Division of Social Work at California State University, Sacramento. He has published widely in the areas of social work practice, children and families services, evaluation and grant writing, and human diversity. He has served in many capacities as human service agency administrator, principal investigator for government grant projects, grant writer and reviewer, and program evaluator for local, state, and international projects. He has also been an evaluation coach and trainer for the federal Corporation for National and Community Services and its grantees.

Kenneth L. Terao, MA, is a senior evaluation specialist with JBS International Inc., a social science research firm located in the San Francisco Bay Area. He has served as project director for a number of national contracts including Save the Children Inc., United Negro College Fund, American Diabetes Association, and federal Corporation for National and Community Service. He is an author and former administrator of educational prevention service projects for public and higher education, juvenile diversion projects, and public health projects.

Anna Marie Schmidt, MA, is an evaluation specialist with JBS International Inc., a social science research firm located in the San Francisco Bay Area. She has provided technical assistance and training in the area of performance measurement and evaluation to the federal Corporation for National and Community Service and its grantees. She has contributed to the development of Independent Living, train-the-trainer curriculum for Senior Corps programs. Ms. Schmidt has worked in Latin America in elementary and adult nonformal education and urban community development, and has also directed several projects for nonprofits.

About the Contributors

Edie L. Cook, PhD, is a senior evaluation researcher who has provided methodological assistance to universities and community-based organizations for nearly 20 years, including the University of Pittsburgh, PITT's Center for Public Health Practice, the Corporation for National and Community Service, the Mayo Clinic Psychiatry and Psychology Treatment Center, the University of Iowa, the U.S. General Accountability Office, and Cornell University. She is president of the Fox Chapel Area American Association of University Women and was recently named one of their 2009 Outstanding Women of the Year.

Adele James, MA, has spent more than 18 years working in the public sector, including 11 years in foundation grant making. Most recently, she served as a Program Officer for the California Endowment, the state's largest health foundation, where she managed the foundation's portfolio for its Community Health and Elimination of Disparities Goal for the 26-county Northern California Region. Prior to that, she was a Program Officer for The Women's Foundation based in San Francisco, where she managed three California-wide gender-based funds benefiting low-income women and girls.

D. Maurie Lung, MA, is a licensed Marriage Family Therapist and licensed Mental Health Counselor with almost 20 years of experience ranging from counseling, facilitation, and teaching to program management, curriculum development, and outcome evaluation. Currently, she is the owner of her own business as well as the Director of Performance Improvement for a national nonprofit. Her most recent endeavor is coauthoring the book, *Power of One: Adventure and Experiential Activities for One-on-One Counseling Sessions*.

Ann Mizoguchi, LCSW, is an Assistant Bureau Chief with the California Department of Social Services. She has 12 years of experience in administering grants. She was a former Division Chief at the Governor's Office of Criminal Justice Planning and Branch at the California Governor's Office of Emergency Services.

Elizabeth (Betsy) Sheldon, MA, is an Education Program Consultant in the Counseling, Student Support, and Service-Learning Office of the California Department of Education. She is responsible for working with local education agencies and other groups to increase the capacity of school mental health services in California. Ms. Sheldon worked as a manager at the California Department of Alcohol and Drug Programs overseeing federal grant programs, including the Safe and Drug Free Schools and Communities. She has also worked as a Project Manager for the Little Hoover Commission, a state oversight and accountability body.

Donna L. Yee, PhD, MSW, is the Chief Executive Officer at the Asian Community Center in Sacramento, California. She has more than 35 years of experience in long-term care. Before moving to Sacramento, her work at the National Pacific Asian Center on Aging and policy research at the Institute for Health Policy (Heller School, Brandeis University) focused on capacity building and Medicare access. Her health administration and clinical experience includes work at an 1,100-bed public chronic-care facility, On Lok Senior Health Services, and a home health agency in San Francisco.

EFFECTIVE GRANT WRITING AND PROGRAM EVALUATION FOR HUMAN SERVICE PROFESSIONALS

1

Introduction

Purpose of This Book

Human service professionals are dedicated people who want to serve the community and assist their clients in addressing various life challenges. They have been trained as social workers, public health educators, counselors, psychologists, nurses, teachers, community organizers, lawyers, and many other allied health and service workers. Alongside these professionals are the volunteers and grassroots individuals who understand and are concerned about their community and neighbors. These individuals are diverse in many aspects but are the same in that they engage themselves in services to improve the conditions that concern them. They understand that it takes resources to support the much-needed services they plan to deliver.

There are many needs in the community but very few resources. Jean, a youth counselor, is interested in bringing more resources to meet these needs and decides to take on the challenge of writing a grant proposal. Jean is confident she will do a good job. After all, she has many great program ideas, and she enjoys writing. Her agency director is very impressed and decides to send her to a well-known, one-day grant-writing training program from the local nonprofit development center. The director shows her some previous grant proposals and Internet resources. A coworker also agrees to work with Jean and edits her draft proposal.

Jeff, a program coordinator, is busy managing several service programs, experiencing many successes as well as challenges. He wants to spend more time in one great program increasing his clinical work with his clients. However, there is the program report he needs to complete. To prepare for that, he needs to collect and organize all of the program data to tell his story. He has so much to tell but does not know where to start or what to tell. His old social research methods and statistics books provide some hints, but he is still not sure how best to proceed.

Many human service practitioners begin their involvement in grant writing and program evaluation, voluntarily or involuntarily, through their assignments in a service agency. Some of them learn how to complete the tasks by diving in with both feet and hoping for a safe landing. Some attend specific workshops and training to get a head start. A few of the lucky ones are mentored by experienced colleagues. No matter how one learns the crafts of grant writing and program evaluation, there is no replacement for hands-on learning, mentoring, and a few useful reference guides.

The purpose of this book is to provide human service professionals and students with the knowledge and skills they could use to advance quality and accountable services to serve their clients and the communities in need. This is both a user-friendly and practical book, as well as an academic text backed by current literature. Specifically, it aims to help readers acquire the advanced knowledge and skills of grant writing and program evaluation. In turn, this will enhance their ability to obtain the proper and much-needed funding to deliver quality services and to demonstrate service results and accountability.

The Organization and Approaches Used for This Book

This grant-writing and program evaluation book follows a needs-driven, evidence-based, results-oriented, and client-centered perspective. "Beginning with the end in mind," "Keep it simple and sweet," and "Tell the stories" are some of the main aphorisms that drove the writing of this book. The general scheme for the structure, logic, and development for this book is presented in the Scheme for Effective Grant Writing and Program Evaluation for Human Service Professionals (Figure 1.1). This book is organized into three main logically connected sections.

The first section is the Four Key Components: (1) community and target population, (2) service providers, (3) funding sources, and (4) the craft of research and management evaluation. This section lays out the foundation knowledge essential to the grant-writing and program evaluation activities. The second section is the Grant Writing and Program Evaluation section. This section provides the skills and knowledge on

Figure 1.1 Scheme for Effective Grant Writing and Program Evaluation for Human Service Professionals

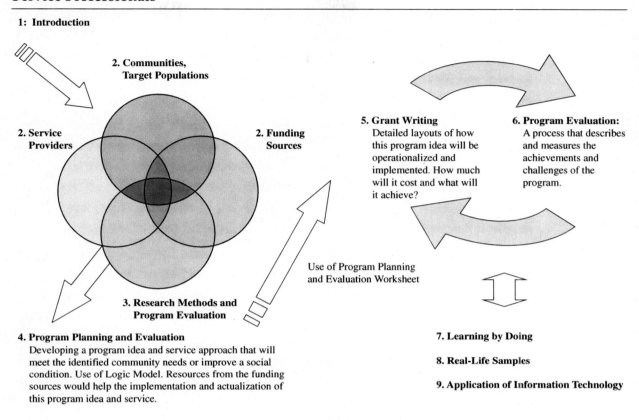

1: Introduction

2. Communities, Target Populations

2. Service Providers

2. Funding Sources

3. Research Methods and Program Evaluation

4. Program Planning and Evaluation
Developing a program idea and service approach that will meet the identified community needs or improve a social condition. Use of Logic Model. Resources from the funding sources would help the implementation and actualization of this program idea and service.

Use of Program Planning and Evaluation Worksheet

5. Grant Writing
Detailed layouts of how this program idea will be operationalized and implemented. How much will it cost and what will it achieve?

6. Program Evaluation:
A process that describes and measures the achievements and challenges of the program.

7. Learning by Doing

8. Real-Life Samples

9. Application of Information Technology

why and how to write grant proposals and conduct program evaluation. The final section is the Show and Tell: Learning by Doing and Real-Life Samples sections. Exercises and examples are included to facilitate more effective learning of grant proposal writing and program evaluation execution.

The authors view grant writing as a capacity-building macro practice in human services. It is not a stand-alone fund-seeking activity. The grant-writing effort should be driven by the needs of the community, guided by the mission of the service organization, and directed by the current research and literature. As to the program evaluation, it is an activity-driven and empowerment-oriented process. Grant writing and program evaluation are macro practice approaches for social change. This book targets practitioners who are program developers, program managers, program evaluators, and agency administrators. Graduate and undergraduate students in human services would also find this a very useful book for grant writing, program evaluation, data analysis, and social research methods.

Several special features are included to aid readers in getting hands-on experience and gaining insiders' insight into grant writing and program evaluation.

1. *Strength perspective and holistic orientation.* This book joins together grant writing and program evaluation. It integrates both professional practice and academic rigor. Readers will learn more than knowledge and skills in grant writing and program evaluation. They will learn the application of holistic and strength perspectives in the understanding, designing, implementing, and evaluating of human services. Service programs are client-centered and needs-driven, not agency-centered and funding-driven.

2. *Professional insights.* These are notes from practitioners who are grant writers, agency administrators, program managers from government agencies and foundations, as well as grant reviewers. These experienced practitioners offer their professional insights, insiders' look, and tips to the grant-writing and evaluation processes in short segments throughout the book. These straightforward practice wisdoms are survival guides for new and experienced practitioners alike.

3. *Samples, grant proposal, evaluation plan, and instruments.* These concrete examples give readers a sense of what the end products would be or should not be like. They serve as models for learning and practice. Guidelines and examples of instruments for data collection and analysis provide readers with a head start in setting their proposal and evaluation in place.

4. *Individual and group learning exercises.* Different learning exercises for developing and practicing grant-writing and evaluation skills are included in the appropriate sections of the book for hands-on learning. Most of these exercises have been developed and field-tested in training workshops conducted by the authors. Some of these exercises are organized to become a training module for a particular topic (e.g., writing effective objectives, identifying results, and developing appropriate data collection tools).

5. *Technology and other resources.* Internet and printed resources for grant writing and program evaluation are included throughout the book for quick reference and access to further studies.

Grant Writing and Program Evaluation: Outcomes and Evidence

How are grant proposal writing and program evaluation—two different functions—related? Simply speaking, many grant proposals are not considered to be complete unless they have included a strong program evaluation component. Many federal grant proposals, such as those for the Substance Abuse and Mental Health Services Administration (SAMHSA), would not be reviewed unless they had a clear program evaluation plan. For major funding sources, a grant proposal without a program evaluation piece is similar to a budget without the accounting.

Grant Proposal and Performance Measures

Since the early 1990s, many federal service grant applications have been "demonstration projects" that are quality service project proposals with a strong evaluation component. They are expected to be able to demonstrate the effectiveness, successes, and challenges of the projects. This emphasis on outcome-oriented programming and assessment put program evaluation and program planning together as two sides of a coin. Program evaluation is such an important element that some funding sources would set aside a certain percentage of the funded budget for program evaluation expenses.

The Corporation for National and Community Service (CNCS) was established as an independent federal agency when President Clinton signed the National and Community Service Trust Act of 1993. The CNCS "merged the work and staffs of two predecessor agencies, ACTION and the Commission on National and Community Service" (www.nationalservice.org/about/role_impact/history.asp). As the nation's largest grant maker, CNCS serves more than 4 million Americans through its National Service programs, Senior Corps, AmeriCorps, VISTA, NCCC (National Civilian Community Corps), and Learn and Serve America, and it supports millions more through a variety of other initiatives. It aims to improve lives through direct service (education, health, environment, human services, public safety) and building organizational capacity. In this way, CNCS strengthens communities and fosters civic engagement through service and volunteering (www.nationalservice.org/pdf/factsheet_cncs.pdf).

The National Service programs are required to do annual internal evaluation (performance measurement) and, therefore, must create project capacity for program evaluation. Program evaluation is part of the grant application, indicating the importance of a strong performance measure plan in its funding decisions.

All three authors of this book have many years of experience in human services and working with SAMHSA and CNCS programs at the local, state, and federal levels. We have seen many outstanding programs so well planned and sufficiently evaluated that they continue to improve. We have also witnessed the politics of funding in that the least deserving programs are poorly planned and disappointedly evaluated, if at all, and received the much-sought-after funding. Politics and other concerns aside, programs that produce results are the ones that receive board support and serve the needs of the community.

Evidence-Based Practice

Evidence-based medicine, or evidence-based practice (EBP) as it became known, offers a balance between professional judgment and current medical research. Scottish epidemiologist Archie Cochrane published his influential *Effectiveness and Efficiency: Random Reflections on Health Services* in 1972. Cochrane suggested the use of the most reliable information or the best evidence to guide health care services. He advocated the use of well-designed evaluations such as randomized controlled trials (RCT) to collect important evidences.

Gordon Guyatt and David Sackett of the McMaster University research group further developed the concepts and the practice of evidence-based medicine. They support the "conscientious, explicit and judicious use of current best evidence in making decisions about the care of individual patients" (Sackett, Rosenberg, Gray, Haynes, and Richardson, 1996, p. 72).

Established in 1993, the Cochrane Collaboration (www.cochrane.org) "is an international not-for-profit organization, providing up-to-date information about the effects of health care." It publishes its database of systematic reviews, clinical trials, and other high-quality studies in the Cochrane Library.

Different disciplines have also developed special studies and projects to explore how evidence-based practice could be applied to various disciplines. Johnson and Austin (2006) report that the "development of systematic reviews for the human services is still in its infancy but is growing largely due to the efforts of the Campbell Collaboration, a sibling of the Cochrane organization for research reviews in the social and behavioral sectors, criminology, and education" (p. 79).

Zlotnik (2007) reports that evidence-based practice is applicable both on an individual (micro) level as well as on the organizational and community (macro) levels. Although randomized controlled trials (RCT) is the ultimate standard for establishing evidence, social sciences and human services often find RCT not feasible. Zlotnik asserts that evidence from qualitative studies should also be considered. Many agencies find that it is difficult to fund basic program evaluation efforts; funding program evaluations that include RCT is certainly a stretch.

Without a program, there will be no evaluation. Without funding support and resources, there will be no program or service to meet community needs. Attaining and developing resources and funding are integral parts of human services. Evidence-based practice is more than direct service and evaluation; it is also about the use of the best evidence to advocate for funding and organizational support. Zlotnik (2007) further reflects that it is not enough to teach the evidence-based practice process, to undertake high-quality research, and to teach students to think critically. The human and social service communities should prepare students, faculty, and practitioners to be advocates for the funding, not just of the research, but of program funds as well so that services can be implemented in the way they were intended.

Grant writing and program evaluation are two interrelated parts of the whole. Their connection is illustrated in the scheme (see Figure 1.1). Understanding the needs of the service recipients, being informed by the best evidence collected, deciding on the appropriate interventions, focusing on the outcomes, and improving based on findings are all part of the process of ensuring that the best services are planned and delivered.

Defining Program and Program Planning

What Is a Program?

Program, in general, refers to a set of planned and purposive activities. Yuen and Terao (2003) define it as "a coordinated change effort that is theory based, goal-oriented, often time limited, target population-specific and activity driven" (p. 1).

Royse, Thyer, Padgett, and Logan (2006) view program as "an organized collection of activities designed to reach certain objectives . . . a series of planned actions designed to solve some problem . . . to have some kind of an impact on the program participants" (p. 5). Some have compared a program to a recipe. It has different ingredients with clear instructions or production procedures to bring about the end product. A service program has different components, interventions, or activities (ingredients); through a service delivery system or mechanism (instructions), particular end results (end products) are expected to be achieved.

There are different levels of program. At the organizational or community level, it may mean a set of coordinated service activities. At a more macro level, such as one at county, state, or federal government, it is used to refer to a social program that is the implementation of certain social or legislative policy.

What Is Program Planning?

Program planning is a need-based and goal-oriented process. It is "an organized process through which a set of coordinated activities or interventions is developed to address and facilitate change in some or all of the identified problems" (Yuen and Terao, 2003, p. 2). Program planning is a dynamic process that lays out strategies to meet identified needs. It involves the identification of needs and the development of goals, objectives, activities, and evaluation. "The [program planning] process presents the logic and the argument that justify the need, the significance, and the relevance of the proposed plan" (Yuen and Terao, 2003, p. 10).

Program planning and grant proposal writing are two closely related processes. "Program planning provides the process and the framework for the development of a service grant proposal. Grant proposal is a specific type of product of program planning. Both of them involve logical thinking and are objective driven" (Yuen and Terao, 2003, p. 11).

The Ethics and Secret Handshake of Grant Writing and Program Evaluation

Grant writing has evolved into an independent specialty and a specialized field of practice within established professions. The American Association of Grant Professionals (AAGP), "a nonprofit membership association, builds and supports an international community of grant professionals committed to serving the greater public good by practicing the highest ethical and professional standards" (http://grantprofessionals.org). AAGP is a national organization representing the needs and concerns of grant-writing professionals. It has an established code of ethics and organizes conferences and other events for its members. Grant writers from different disciplines, such as social work, sociology, psychology, public health, and public administration, participate in their own professional organizations and abide by the profession's standards and codes of ethics (e.g., National Association of Social Workers [NASW] Code of Ethics, www.socialworkers.org/pubs/Code/code.asp).

In addition to membership in their own professional organizations, many program evaluators join the American Evaluation Association (AEA). It is a "professional association of evaluators devoted to the application and exploration of program evaluation, personnel evaluation, technology, and many other forms of evaluation. Evaluation involves assessing the strengths and weaknesses of programs, policies, personnel, products, and organizations to improve their effectiveness" (www.eval.org/aboutus/organization/aboutus.asp). The evaluators are expected to follow the codes of ethics of their professional organizations, as well as those of the AEA.

Grant writing and program evaluation are not trivial tasks but professional activities that are altruistic, service-oriented, accountable, and ethical in practice. Also, they are not mysteries and full of secrets that only the fortunate few would know how to solve. The secret for grant writing and program evaluation is that there is no secret handshake or magic bullet. The only open secret is that applicants need to understand what the funding source wants and what the community needs are. They then develop a proposal that meets the needs of the community and matches the requirements of the funding organization. Innovativeness and creativity that bring about measurable results and accountable outcomes further distinguish an outstanding proposal from a good proposal.

Grant writing and program evaluation often differ for organizations of different sizes or with different capacities. Smaller or less established organizations may find that local or regional funding opportunities, such as local foundation, city, or county funding, are more appropriate for them. Larger or more established organizations may be more interested in seeking out major funding sources, such as state or federal multiyear funding. There is, however, no rule to say that smaller organizations should not seek out major grants from big funding sources. The simple factors for success in grant writing are knowing your organization, knowing your funding source, knowing your clients, and knowing your grant proposal. The only way to ensure getting funding support for your proposal is to submit one!

A good idea in your head is only a good idea; a good idea written in an organized and achievable format is a proposal; and an implemented good idea that meets the needs of clients is a successfully funded service program.

References

American Evaluation Association. About us. Retrieved January 11, 2009, from www.eval.org/aboutus/organization/aboutus.asp.

Cochrane, A. L. (1972). *Effectiveness and efficiency: Random reflections on Health*, (2nd ed.) London: Nuffield services, Provincial Hospitals Trust of health services.

Corporation for National and Community Service. About us and our program. Retrieved January 10, 2009, from www.nationalservice.org/about/role_impact/history.asp.

Corporation for National and Community Service. *Fact sheet*. Retrieved January 10, 2009, from www.nationalservice.org/pdf/factsheet_cncs.pdf.

Johnson, M., & Austin, M. (2006). Evidence-based practice in the social services. *Administration in Social Work (3) 3*, 75–104.

National Association of Social Workers. Code of ethics. Retrieved April 23, 2009, from www.social workers.org/pubs/Code/code.asp.

Royse, D., Thyer, B., Padgett, D., & Logan, T. K. (2006). *Program evaluation: An introduction* (4th ed.). Belmont, CA: Thomson Brooks/Cole.

Sackett, D. L., Rosenberg, W. M., Gray, J. A., Haynes, R. B., & Richardson, W. S. (1996). Evidence based medicine: What it is and what it isn't. *British Medical Journal 312*, 71–72.

The American Association of Grant Professionals. *Our mission*. Retrieved January 11, 2009, from http://grantprofessionals.org.

The Cochrane Collaboration. Retrieved January 11, 2009, from www.cochrane.org/docs/descrip.htm.

Yuen, F., & Terao, K. (2003). *Practical grant writing and program evaluation*. Pacific Grove, CA: Brooks/Cole–Thomson Learning.

Zlotnik, J. L. (2007). Evidence-based practice and social work education: a view from Washington. *Research on Social Work Practice (17) 5*, 625–629.

2

Community and Target Population, Service Providers, and Funding Sources

Community and target population, service providers, funding sources, and basic social research knowledge and skills are the four key components that form the basic framework for proposal writing and program evaluation in this book. Based on needs of the target populations in the community, a service provider seeking funding support from a funding source can employ basic social research methods to plan and evaluate the results of the program interventions. This chapter describes the first three components: community and target population, service providers, and funding sources. The following chapter will discuss the basic social research knowledge and skills.

The Good Idea Program

The Big Help Agency aims to use its newly funded Good Idea Program to improve racial relationships and facilitate economic recovery of the Shoestring community. Shoestring was once a growing town in the 1950s. Eighty-five percent of the residents were White, and the majority of them were employed by the only local industry, Comfort Shoe Factory. Since the closure of the factory in the late 1970s, the town and its residents have experienced economic hardship. Many residents moved out to the neighboring towns for better employment opportunities.

In the early 1980s, gentrification in the Upward City, 30 miles away, forced many African American families to move to Shoestring to find affordable housing. African Americans brought new lives to the town and opened up many new businesses and economic opportunities. Unfortunately, the growth was hindered by the recession of the 1980s and did not last. The expansion of several nearby towns, with the opening of a meatpacking plant in the 1990s, has not benefited Shoestring. In fact, the towns have diverted many of the economic investments from Shoestring. Currently, Shoestring does not have a bank or a major grocery store.

The arrivals of the Korean, Vietnamese, and Mexican immigrants since the mid-1990s have pumped new energy, as well as conflicts, into this community. Asian immigrants have taken over 60 percent of the local small businesses. However, according to the local residents, these business owners provide very few employment opportunities for the community, because "they only hire their own families." The only obvious growth of the community is the number of liquor and cigarette stores. Again, Asian immigrants own most of them. Hispanics are also competing with longtime residents for jobs at all levels. The influx of new immigrant families increases demands on the school system. Unfortunately, the local real estate and retail tax bases are not strong enough to support any increase in the school budget.

Many long-time residents feel they are displaced, and some, those who could, moved. New immigrant families are also slowly leaving Shoestring. Residents of all racial backgrounds grumble that they do not feel safe living in town. Older residents complain, "This is not the town I used to know anymore." They worry about the young people because there is too much violence in the homes and on the streets. Almost 30 percent of the elderly have been victims of crimes. Domestic violence and child abuse cases have been on the rise.

Recently, there were four incidents of suspicious burning and destruction of two African American churches, one synagogue, and one Metropolitan church. No one has claimed any responsibilities. Local youth problems have intensified due to the increase of ethnic gang groups, high dropout rates in schools, and the lack of employment opportunities. In the last couple of years, several major political figures dropped by to make speeches and held photo-ops with the few self-proclaimed ethnic community leaders. But so far, only empty and broken promises have been made.

You are a community social worker with the Good Idea Program for the Big Help Agency in the county. You are assigned to work with this community. What will you do? You are also the program manager and grant writer. What kinds of programs will you propose, and what kinds of funding sources will you look for?

What Is a Community?

There are many ways to define the construct of *community*: "Some focused on community as a geographical area; some on a group of people living in a particular place; and others which looked to community as an area of common life" (Smith, 2001). A community is a social system similar to an organism that is alive, organic, evolving, interactive, and dynamic. It is a collection of living entities sharing a common environment.

A community could be a settlement of people who are living in a particular geographic area or locality. This may be a city, a ranch, a neighborhood, or an apartment complex. A community, however, is not limited by physical boundaries. It could be defined by the shared values or cultural backgrounds that distinguish a group of people from others. People who share common religious beliefs or cultural backgrounds may consider themselves to belong to community although they live in different parts of the world.

A community could be formed based on a common purpose, interest, or characteristics. People are linked together because of their professions, work, schools, hobbies, or needs. Human service providers may consider themselves a community. A school is naturally and intentionally structured to provide students a sense of belonging and a community of learning. People who face a common life challenge or success, such as illness, addiction, or achievement, would also consider themselves part of a community. In human services, service recipients or target populations who have common issues are often referred to as a community.

A community is a social network that links people together. This network may be local and have limited boundaries, such as the business or educational communities. It could also be widespread and have no physical boundary, such as the virtual community over the Internet. The cyberspace social networks, such as the many chat rooms, blogs, and networking sites, provide a means for people to connect and relate in an unprecedented manner.

There are also communities within a community. People in a community share something in common, but there is diversity within the community. A student body in a university is a community. Within this community, there are many smaller communities, such as graduate students, undergraduate students, students of different majors, student clubs, sororities and fraternities, and on-campus and commuting students.

While a community is a dynamic and multifaceted social system, each community has common norms and functions. A community is organic in that it grows and dies. It has activities to help it sustain itself and allow it to continue to develop. Although it is a collective entity, the community as a whole is greater than the sum of its parts. A community has its own values, culture, norms and roles, functions, and purpose.

In order to better understand a community, one may have to explore the following questions. Together they provide the basic assessment of a community:

➤ Why is it a community? How is this community defined? Is it defined by its geographic location, its sociocultural significance, its nature and function as well as structure, or other characteristics?

➤ What are the community context, problems, assets, and strengths?

　➤ Population: diversity, socioeconomic status, types of households, educational level, etc.

　➤ Cultural values/norms/traditions/beliefs most emphasized and supported

　➤ Community resources, economic and political structure, and social issues. Who controls resources and power? What are the issues of power, influences, and leadership within the community? Who is considered a member or an outsider?

　➤ Are issues such as discrimination, neglect, or oppression a problem?

　➤ What are the community's strengths and limitations?

➤ What are the community needs? How are they defined?

　➤ What are the most urgent of the identified community needs?

　➤ Are there gaps between identified community needs/issues and resources?

　➤ Is data available to support identified community needs?

　➤ What are the linkages between service agencies and community needs?

As a human service provider with a local agency, which identified need(s) will you be able to address and why?

Macro Practice, Grant Writing, and Program Evaluations

Macro practice engages community and organization as the unit of intervention to promote positive changes. It is often referred to as *community practice*. Macro practice is a "professionally directed intervention designed to bring about planned change in organizations and communities. . . . (It) is built on theoretical foundations, proceeds within the framework of a practice model, and operates within the boundaries of professional values and ethics" (Netting, Kettner, and McMurtry, 1993, p. 3). It has many types and levels of practice approaches, such as community organizing, community development, social planning, social actions, policy, and administration. Macro practitioners perform many roles, including community organizer, program manager, program planner, agency administrator, program evaluator, and grant proposal writer.

Rubin and Rubin (2001) describe the mobilization model, social action model, and social production model. The *mobilization model* organizes people in the community to take collective actions, and the *social action model* uses planned and coordinated strategies to pressure the power structure for change. The *social production model* focuses on program planning, evaluation, fundraising, proposal writing, program implementation, and management.

The purpose of community work is "to work with communities experiencing disadvantages and enable them to collectively identify needs and rights, clarify objectives and take action to meet these within a democratic framework which respects the needs and rights of others" (Federation for Community Development Learning 2009). A grant proposal writer and program evaluator play a key role in the identification of needs, development of appropriate service programs, and monitoring of program performance and outcomes.

Target Populations and Needs

Many issues and needs exist in the community, thereby affecting its various populations. Human service providers are often called upon to serve the most vulnerable or at-risk populations with limited resources. For a program to be successful and effective, it is crucial for the program to clearly identify and have knowledge of the population it intends to serve. Simply speaking, a *target population* is the potential service recipients within the population in the community. Many factors contribute to why certain groups are being targeted for services. A common reason is that the target populations are in disadvantaged and risky situations such that their unmet needs would affect theirs and society's well-being.

What is a need and how is it defined? Need is different from but related to want. Children at the checkout counter in a grocery store may whine to have candy because they want it. Parents refuse to buy the candy because they believe the children do not need it. Many have used this common distinction: *need* is something we have to have to survive and cannot live without, whereas *want* is something we would like to have but is not entirely necessary. We need food and water to survive. We may want arts and music, but they are not required for survival. Need and want have intricate relationships and are not mutually exclusive. Need is fundamental and basic; want adds quality and values.

At times, need and want overlap. Would that be an enjoyment if you have your favorite foods and drinks in a nice environment with beautiful music in the background? An elderly woman who lives alone could have her basic nutritional needs met through the Meals on Wheels program, but she wants to maintain healthy human connections, so she attends activities and eats her meals in the elderly center. Human service providers deal with human needs that are often more complex than basic physiological needs. Maslow (1943) proposed the hierarchy of human needs that range from the basic physiological needs to safety and security, love, esteem, and self-actualization. Human needs are complicated and interwoven with an individual's unique quality and the social environments. It is, therefore, both the target population's and human service provider's responsibilities to identify and articulate what the needs are and how they are to be met.

Yuen and Terao (2003) explain the definitions of needs discussed by Mayer (1985) and Bradshaw (1997). Needs can be defined as four basic types: normative, felt, expressed, and comparative. These needs are not mutually exclusive. Human service providers may want to describe all of them to provide a better account of the needs for the target population.

"*Normative need* refers to conditions that are below the established social standards" (Yuen and Terao, pp. 12–13). Distribution of resources such as school lunch or after-school activity funding could be based on the number of students who are living in households below the national or local poverty line. Health disparity statistics or prevalence of a specific disease in a particular population also serves as an indicator for needs deviating from the norm. The neighborhood's more than average pedestrian-related traffic accidents point to the need for attention to traffic and pedestrian safety in the neighborhood.

"*Felt need* refers to the wants based on the individual's standards" (Yuen and Terao, p. 13). Bradshaw (1997) equated it with want. It is a matter of personal or collective preferences and choices. These needs are, however, meaningful and distinctive to the people who make the selection. For example, a frail elderly woman prefers to remain in her own home and receive home-help services instead of moving to a nursing home. In a severe budget-cut year, the school PTA supports the elimination of the school football team to keep the library open, because they believe the library is more vital to students' learning.

"*Expressed need* refers to attempts by the individuals to fulfill their needs" (Yuen and Terao, p. 13). Bradshaw (1997) equated it with the economic concept of demand. The out-of-control youth gang problems in a neighborhood have severely affected every aspect of life in a community. Residents brought the issue to the attention of the city leaders through the mass media and a letter-writing campaign. Several town hall meetings were organized to document complaints and solicit inputs. A community organizer also conducted a community survey and published a report on his findings. A documented felt need would become an expressed need that is also being referred to as a documented need. Community needs assessment or town hall meeting reports document expressed needs. U.S. Census reports provide a detailed description of a given community and a wealth of information of the documented needs. A simple way to establish expressed need for a human service agency is to use its waiting list. By putting their names on the waiting list, people express their need for such service and, obviously, the supply is less than the demand.

"*Comparative need* refers to the situation that an individual's condition is relatively worse off or less desirable than that of other people" (Yuen and Terao, p. 13). Children who live in drug- and gang-infested neighborhoods are more likely to be involved in the criminal justice system when they grow up, reflecting that they are more at risk than children from average neighborhoods. Families without health insurance coverage have more emergency room visits and longer hospital stays than those who have insurance, indicating they are comparatively less healthy and in more dire need.

Service Providers

Organizations that are recipients of the grants and contracts are responsible for the provision of the agreed-upon services. These organizations that utilize resources to deliver service programs to meet the needs of the community are the service providers. They include both private and public organizations. Many of them are commonly referred to as education, social, and human service organizations. They include social service agencies, mental health agencies, schools, private nonprofit organizations, local grassroots organizations, as well as government and public service authorities. Increasingly, for-profit organizations are represented among human service organizations. Guided by their missions, these service providers have particular areas of concern they want to address through their various programs, resources, and services. For example, Robison (2006) lists some of the major services provided to children and families:

Child care services: licensing, provider training and quality improvement, resource and referral, subsidies

Child support services: paternity establishment, child support enforcement

Child welfare services: child protective services, family-based services (family preservation, family reunification, respite care), emergency shelter care, foster care and other out-of-home placement, adoption, independent living

Disability services: early identification and intervention, specialized services for people with specific types of disabilities (the blind, the deaf and hearing impaired, developmentally disabled, physically disabled), rehabilitation services, vocational rehabilitation

Education: early childhood education, K–12, special education, adult education and training and literacy programs

Financial assistance: emergency cash assistance, general assistance, Temporary Assistance for Needy Families (TANF), eligibility determinations

Food assistance and nutrition programs: food stamps, food distribution for childcare providers, emergency assistance

Health care coverage: Medicaid, child health insurance, medical assistance, eligibility determinations

Health care services: prevention programs, maternal and child health programs, adolescent health programs, family planning, public health services

Housing assistance: rental subsidies, housing assistance, home energy assistance, weatherization programs, shelter and programs for the homeless

Juvenile corrections: delinquency prevention, in-home services, community programs, residential placement, probation services

Mental health services: prevention, child and adolescent mental health treatment, adult mental health treatment, family-focused services

Prevention programs: child abuse prevention, delinquency prevention, substance abuse prevention, teenage pregnancy prevention, parenting education, family support services

Substance abuse services: prevention, child and adolescent treatment, adult treatment, family-focused treatment

Welfare-to-work services: job training and assistance, workforce development services, services for employers, support services

Source: (www.ncsl.org/programs/cyf/hspubintro.htm#hsreorganize, pp. 3–4)

These organizations may have multimillion-dollar annual budgets; they could also be small operations that only have enough money to hire a part-time staff. Some of them are both granters and grantees of service funding, and some are strictly grantees who receive funding to support their operation and services. No matter what size or type of organizations they are, these organizations have the well-being of the target population as their main concern. Lewis, Lewis, Packard, and Souflée (2001) describe the purpose of human service programs:

> Human service programs deal with the personal and social development of individuals, families, and communities. Sometimes they enhance this development through the provision of direct services such as education, training, counseling, therapy, or casework. Often they work indirectly through consultation, advocacy, referral, information dissemination, community development, or social action. The ultimate purpose of these programs, regardless of methods used, is to enhance the well-being of clients or consumers. (p. 6)

Human service organizations perform various roles in the service delivery system. They are the service brokers that link resources including service funding to meet the needs of the community. They are also the advocates that promote the cause of the community and find ways to achieve community objectives. They are the organizers that gather and mobilize the community to meet identified needs. They are the administrators who manage funding, resources, and service. They are the evaluators who monitor programs, file reports, and identify ways for improvement. They are also, at the frontline, the direct service providers who deliver the service programs and activities.

The diversities of missions and capacities of service providers enable a service delivery system that could meet the diverse needs in the communities. In fact, the service providers are a unique and distinct community. Lewis, Lewis, Packard, and Souflée (2001) cite Taylor and Felten's (1993) assertions of the four key elements of organization. An organization is a transforming agency, an economic agency, a minisociety, and a collection of individuals. Human service providers assist their service recipients to transform and ameliorate their situations. The organization is an economic entity that operates with a budget and deals with many financial matters. Similar to a society but on a small scale, there are norms, roles, culture, and tradition for every organization. People with different talents and training come to the organization with their own set of values and beliefs. They bring their uniqueness and diversity to the organization and, ideally, work together and collectively to pursue the organization's mission.

In order to bring funding and resources to serve the needs of the target population, a community needs to have creditable service providers who could manage the funding, implement the service program, and act as the change agents. Funding sources fund human service organizations that have the capacities to perform the many demanding roles of service delivery. Funding sources do not fund individuals to provide services; they fund the organizations. Organizations are the key connection between the funding sources and the target populations. Effective ways to communicate with the funding source about the capacity of the organization are discussed in detail in Chapter 5, Grant Proposal Writing.

Professional Insight 2.1: Agency Administrator to Get Support for Service Projects
Donna L. Yee, PhD

Grants are only one of four common revenue strategies. Every organization has revenue strategies. For some, their funding is linked to the types of goods or services they provide to accomplish their mission. For others, how goods and services are funded reflect the skills and preferences of staff or volunteer leaders. An organization led by public-sector employees might look to grants and contracts, but one led by owners of small businesses might more easily rely on fees-for-service.

Among not-for-profit organizations, revenue strategies include fees-for-service, fundraising, contracts, and/or grants. Few organizations rely equally on all four strategies, and most rely on two or three to support operations. In other words, grants are not the only way to obtain revenue to cover organization costs. The following sections describe each of the common revenue strategies among nonprofits and provide some perspectives on the challenges of each strategy.

Fees-for-service include all revenue collected in return for services rendered, whether for the purchase of a product, a day of care provided to the beneficiary of an insurance plan, or an hour of care provided by a therapist. Whether the fee is based on what clients or consumers are willing to pay, the actual cost of providing the service,

(continued)

or what competitors charge for similar products and services, fees set a dollar value on what an organization produces. In many situations, clients are also consumers who "vote with their feet," using their dollars to let an organization know if they feel that products and services are a good value for their dollar and are satisfied with the organization's products and services. If revenue collected from fees is less than costs, the deficit is often offset by other revenue-generating activities.

Fundraising or fund development includes all donations (solicited and unsolicited) received from donors who support the mission and products or services of the organization. For tax-exempt nonprofit organizations, only the revenue net of dinner, raffle, or appeal costs become available for services. And unless an organization has the unusual fortune to get enough unsolicited funds to meet its needs, it costs money to raise this kind of revenue. Whether it is postage and printing of invitations and flyers, staff time to organize volunteers, rent for a hall, or the cost of food, a nonprofit's investment in fundraising as a means to an end can sometimes have a better long-term than a short-term return-on-investment. Fundraisers are often short on cash and long on broadening an organization's constituency, raising the organization's visibility, or building community capacity. If a fund development element to solicit supporters for larger and more serious gifts is not in place, this approach can be an acceptable stop-gap method to shore up deficits or enrich services, but not to meet significant operating deficits and salary obligations.

Contracts are activities undertaken in a defined manner as specified by a client/contractor for a set amount of money. The contract can be based on a cost per unit of service, with control on the amount of services to be provided, or the contract can be for work solely directed by the client. The client/contractor can be the government, a corporation, or an individual who determines the terms and conditions under which a nonprofit organization would receive payment. Contracts can be renewed annually and can be awarded on a competitive basis.

Alternately, grants are projects funded to achieve stated outcomes that provide the organization with some latitude in terms of what approaches are used to achieve the outcomes, and are often forgiving if all outcomes are not achieved. The grant maker often responds to a nonprofit organization's proposal to solve a broad problem or address a social issue. Grants awarded vary according to the interests and means of the grant maker (e.g., support of a conference, underwriting the launch of an innovative service intervention, support for core operating costs, or capital improvements). The outcomes sought may be as general as reducing poverty, improving quality of life, or improving access to health care, or as specific as a 50 percent increase in sustained enrollment among a target group of high school students, a 75 percent return of functional ability after suffering a stroke, or a 100 percent increase in employed persons.

Is any one strategy easier or more reliable than another? Every source of revenue requires a system of accountability, whether it is a minimum data set to justify fees for service; donor cultivation and stewardship to ensure that funds are appropriately used and adhere to donor gift restrictions; satisfactory contract performance is observed; and grant outcomes are achieved and address proposed goals and objectives. While some revenue strategies appear to lend themselves more easily to some settings over others, each strategy and combination of strategies has its own challenges. For example, art museums commonly charge entry fees, solicit memberships and donations, and obtain grants for specific shows or capital projects. Few rely on contracts with public- or private-sector organizations.

Some people mistakenly believe that grants are easy to obtain, or that "soft money" can easily be replenished. A social service agency that wants to launch a project over several years faces a dilemma when a one-year grant award means launching a project while actively searching for funds to support years two and three. Should the project get started? Should the grant be accepted? Can the organization afford to hire staff when there is a prospect that the organization may be unsuccessful at raising needed funds? Some Boards of Directors will only authorize a new program if staff has a plan and ensures ongoing efforts even if no follow-on grant is awarded. For young organizations with few staff, it may be impossible to both launch a new service and continue developing grants for funds.

Why not undertake all four revenue strategies? Most executives will admit that it is very difficult to use all revenue strategies equally for the following reasons:

1. The relationships required and approaches needed to sustain any one of these strategies require much commitment by the executive.

2. Each strategy requires different forms and formats of accountability: some are data intensive, some are relationship intensive, some require a lead person who is known in the right circles, and some require all forms in different strengths. For example, health facilities file an annual cost report when receiving government insurance payments to justify their rates; donors want visibility and to be convinced that their contributions result in meaningful outcomes; contractors want the most efficient price per unit of service or goods; and foundations want assurance that grantees commit to a share of cost or match their grant funds.

3. The record of revenues and expenses among different funds can be complex, especially if several sources are needed to ensure the viability of a one-service program. Organizations must show that expenses are legitimate and paid once. Why should the government pay for a service for which a family can pay out of pocket?

The aptitude of organization executives and their team to parlay and successfully deploy particular revenue strategies often determines which revenue strategies an organization uses.

How about reliance on just one of these strategies? In hard economic times when revenue is hard to grow, no matter the source, reliance on one strategy makes an organization vulnerable. When competition for scarce dollars for shelter, food, and clothing increases, even loyal customers are likely to "vote with their feet" and react to fee increases and specials. Even donors have downturns when their investments do not earn as expected. While we may argue that need and demand for mental health and other services increase during an economic downturn, it is hard to deny that fewer taxes collected result in smaller contracts and less support for community services.

Finally, grant makers (like donors) are very sensitive to market swings, even as gap-filling needs among nonprofit services are larger, and the competition among grant writers grows. In the years of the War on Poverty and Model Cities, grant writers used to submit two or three proposals for every grant received. During a downturn around 2009, many nonprofits and academic researchers submitted eight to twelve proposals for every grant received.

How about writing many proposals because it is difficult to tell what might be funded and because grant makers are interested in proposals on different issues? An organization could find itself with several grant awards that are unrelated. On the one hand, single-purpose grants are very focused, easy to execute, and easy to evaluate. Several projects or departments functioning as silos, alternately, could end up diluting energy needed to support the strategic growth of an organization. Too many boutique activities—and their champions inside the organization, competing for unrestricted resources of the organization—may distract an organization from its core services. Executives who can conceptually, strategically, and financially link boutique projects to core services and the organization's strategic plan are best able to integrate and sustain projects: taking what works to improve outcomes organization-wide, expanding the core through pilot projects, and growing the organization's constituency of clients and supporters.

These tips are meant to say that there are no easy answers to program development. Grant writing is one approach to revenue generation, and it needs to be linked with other revenue strategies.

Funding Sources

In seeking funding support for services, Miner and Miner (2003) discuss several common myths that nonprofit organizations harbor: *"People will fund my needs. Sponsors fund their needs, not yours. When writing proposals, you must show that you can become a change agent to solve a problem important to them"* (p. 4). A foster care agency may have a great need to provide more independent-living training classes for the youth who are about to age out of the foster care system. The funding source, however, is more interested in the results of facilitating the likelihood of a fulfilling and successful adulthood for these youth.

These results are in alignment with the funding source's mission and its current strategic plan. This successful adulthood could be achieved by many time-tested or new and innovative approaches. The independent-living skills training class may only be one of the many possible approaches. The agency believes the youth need these classes; therefore, it becomes the agency's needs. The funding source probably does not disagree with the need for such a class. However, it is more interested in meeting its own already-defined needs through its funding resources. Miner and Miner further assert the pitfall of *"Always plead poverty.* Pleading poverty is a poor grant strategy. Sponsors will not give you money just because you are poor, sponsors may conclude that you are poor because you lack good ideas, management, or community support" (p. 4).

Working beyond these myths, service providers may wonder where the funding support comes from. Where should they look? For health and human services, government agencies and foundations are the two main funding sources. Government funding sources represent public funding opportunities coming through local, city, and county agencies to the state and federal agencies. Foundations are private funding from various types of sources.

Governments at all levels are complex bureaucracies that have many agencies and departments. Their names and functions at times overlap each other; their structures are unclear to outsiders. It could be quite intimidating for anyone who is new to the system. This situation is the same for foundations or any other funding sources. Getting to know your funding sources is often the first step for service providers who plan to seek out support. This is a long-term relationship-building process that may not yield immediate results. It is easier for service providers to get to know local government offices; it is not that easy for them to know federal offices that have most of the major funding.

Government

Short of having some experienced professionals providing mentoring and connections, a relationship with federal agencies may well be started by going through a grant application process. It is also a good idea to start with agencies that have the same areas of concern as yours. Within the United States Department of Health and Human Services (DHHS) is the Substance Abuse and Mental Health Services Administration (SAMHSA). SAMHSA has several Centers and Offices: Center for Substance Abuse Prevention (CSAP), Center for Substance Abuse Treatment (CSAT), and Center for Mental Health Services (CMHS). Each of these centers has its own set of funding opportunities. A service provider should identify funding opportunities in line with the agency's mission and the needs of the community. CSAP may be a better funding source for an agency's interest in a school-based prevention program, and CSAT may be a more suitable choice for another agency's outpatient substance abuse treatment program.

Some of the federal funding is channeled down to state governments through formula or block grants (e.g., Violence Against Women Act funding, Community Development Block Grants). Each state has its own rules and procedures to distribute the funding. Service agencies may wish to find out how formula and block grants are distributed and solicit support from the appropriate state, county, or even city governments.

The Federal Register is one of the most comprehensive sources of information regarding new federal government funding opportunities, their rules and regulations, as well as their deadlines. It is available both in print and electronic formats. "Published by the Office of the Federal Register, National Archives and Records Administration (NARA), the Federal Register is the official daily publication for rules, proposed rules, and notices of Federal agencies and organizations, as well as executive orders and other presidential documents" (www.gpoaccess.gov/fr/index.html). Keeping track of funding activities through the Federal Register could provide up-to-date information to grant applicants or even early information, but it requires regular monitoring.

Grants.gov (http://grants.gov) is an excellent one-stop online location for finding federal government grants. "Today, Grants.gov is a central storehouse for information on over 1,000 grant programs and provides access to approximately $500 billion in annual awards" (http://grants.gov/aboutgrants/about_grants_gov.jsp).

The Catalog of Federal Domestic Assistance (CFDA) (http://cfda.gov) is another great source for finding federal support. "The CFDA provides a full listing of all Federal programs available to state and local governments (including the District of Columbia); Federally-recognized Indian tribal governments; territories (and possessions) of the United States; domestic public, quasi-public, and private profit and nonprofit organizations and institutions; specialized groups; and individuals" (http://cfda.gov).

In order to be successful in accessing federal fundings, service providers may wish to consider the following suggestions:

➤ Plan ahead. Service providers may need to visit department Web sites at the beginning of each program year. Many federal departments post the type of grants they plan to fund and may be released for the entire year on the Web site. This will allow the applicant agency to plan for and be prepared when the Requests for Proposals (RFPs) are released.

➤ If the agency misses the deadline for a particular grant opportunity for this year, the agency should still request and use the current RFP to prepare for the coming year. There will be changes, but the general framework will likely be very similar.

➤ All applicants for federal funding are required to obtain a Data Universal Numbering System (DUNS) number. It is a unique nine-digit identification number that is site-specific, so each location or branch of the agency would require one. Although in most situations it would not take too long to acquire the number, getting the registration done beforehand is always preferred.

➤ Understand types of requirements by department, state, county, or city funding. For example, in California, grant proposals for many state departments may require the applicant to prove there is a plan to subcontract, or attempt to find a subcontractor that is classified as a Disabled Vet–owned company. Understand the steps you will need to take to meet this requirement. Usually, this process takes several weeks. Again, plan ahead.

➤ Generally, grants are due four to six weeks after the federal department releases the RFP. In most cases, applicants will be allowed to submit questions, in writing, to the federal department for clarification of the RFP. Usually, this occurs within the first two weeks after release of the RFP. Responses to all questions are usually posted on the Web site.

➤ For some federal, state, county, and city RFPs, a bidders' meeting is held for interested applicants. This meeting discusses the RFP and allows applicants to ask questions. In a few cases, these bidders' meetings are mandatory if the applicant is interested in applying, but this is rare.

Having a fiscal plan for the agency and identifying possible government funding sources through online or library searches are the first steps. Similar to a program plan, an organization may need to have a fiscal plan that lays out its annual fiscal outlook and strategies to achieve stability and the ability to respond to community needs. In addition to grant support, many agencies seek government contracts (e.g., mental health services contract), and become partners in delivering services to meet community needs.

Professional Insight 2.2: Important Suggestions Related to State or Federal Grant Funds

Ann Mizoguchi, LCSW

Funding Sources and Eligibility Requirements Can Vary Considerably and Change Frequently

Aggregate this dynamic information into a single document, database, or other resource. Update it regularly and make it readily accessible. Encourage everyone to participate in its editorial process. You can structure it as a matrix within a collaborative spreadsheet, within an enterprise wiki, or in another centralized document management tool.

Funding Periods Are Typically Consistent but Vary by Agency

Become familiar with idiosyncratic funding cycles. They are unique to a federal, state, or even a local program's fiscal year. Remain especially aware of pivotal details, such as when Program Announcements, Program Kits, and Requests for Proposals (RFPs) or Requests for Applications (RFAs) are released, and their respective submission dates.

Maintain an Open Dialogue with Grant Administrators

Collaborate frequently with program managers. Seek their advice regarding the types of projects they may be interested in. Ask them to share their knowledge of other compatible programs and funding opportunities as well.

Maintain a Diverse Physical and Virtual Library of Important References Related to Not Only Grant Writing in General, but Unique to Your Population and Discipline

To get started, try the following search engine directories. For best results, enter the phrase "grant writing" (including the quotation marks is more precise because it informs the search engine to query as a phrase rather than the individual words):

The Open Directory Project: http://search.dmoz.org

The Google Directory: http://directory.google.com

The Yahoo Directory: http://dir.yahoo.com

Nonprofit Guides: www.npguides.org

Understand How Grants Are Developed

Some grants are awarded under the discretion of the administrator and are generally more flexible in the manner in which they are dispersed. Other grants may be provided to each state using a specific formula that includes a base amount and population unique to each state. Identify how state or federal governmental entities administer as well as distribute (e.g., task force, focus groups, town hall meetings, surveys, needs assessments, etc.) them. Participate in the community. Attend town hall meetings or focus groups and gather information like a seasoned reporter on the types and nuances of funds that are required. This will help you understand how they are distinct, so you are aware not only of what is available, but most importantly, what is appropriate. Review legislative, regulatory, and program requirements of the funding in which you are interested.

For more information, the Federal Register (www.gpoaccess.gov/fr/) is a daily publication that provides existing rules, rules under proposal, and public notices of federal funding opportunities and guidelines.

Obtain Historical Documentation That May Serve as a Model or Guideline

Ask the grantor for de-identified examples of prior applications that were especially successful or unique, or simply good exemplars of a well-executed submission.

Keep the Grantor's Intent and Your Scope Well Aligned

Be acutely aware of the grantor's intent and any unique or novel requirements. Although using templates can be efficient, do not get caught in this act by carelessly replicating a prior work or template or presuming familiarity with an administration's solicitation, because details can change substantially. Be attentive to details and remain agile or adaptive in preparing your submission. This also encourages you to critically appraise your prior work as well as to continue to improve upon it.

Explicitly Convey Any Innovative, Novel, Diverse, and Replicable Features of Your Proposal

Many grantors are especially interested in how a project is innovative, how it can be replicated, if it was coordinated with multiple disciplines and entities, what specific products will be produced, what strategies and outcomes will occur, how you presume what you propose will produce results, how underserved or unserved

(continued)

populations will be accessed and provided services, and so forth. They are also interested in demonstrated success with other programs and grant funds your agency administered in the past.

Consider Including a Formal Evaluation Component

There are several ways to perform an *objectivist* or *subjectivist* evaluation, and excellent books and online resources are available as guides. In general, understand the type and methods of performing a formal evaluation. Be prepared to identify which approach is appropriate, extra resources (e.g., subject-matter experts, human subjects review committee, survey instruments, analytical or statistical software), and expenses as well as the level of intrusion or impact the evaluation activity alone may have on the outcome (e.g., the Hawthorne Effect). Although most grantors will be interested in a well-performed, thorough, and objective analysis, the reality is that it could represent a significant portion of the overall cost and may require some creative editing to limit its scope but not its effectiveness and its exclusion altogether.

Demonstrate Ongoing Sustainability

Although this seems obvious, special attention to sustainability is often neglected or its importance not fully appreciated. Perhaps with the exception of a well-encapsulated research project, functional or operational and financial sustainability will be carefully reviewed. Brainstorm innovative as well as pragmatic methods to sustain funding beyond the described funding period, especially if the award could be staggered over a multiyear period (e.g., 100 percent funding provided the first year, 75 percent the second year, and 50 percent for the third and final year).

Keep informed about emerging but relevant trends, such as novel or innovative approaches to sustainability. Examples are new classifications or *labels* that are cognitively more intuitive to grantors as well as participants. These labels might relate to the impact on the environment (e.g., Is the project "green"?). Or they might encompass options to virtualize the organization to include geographically disparate experts and flexible schedules using Internet telephony and other communication tools, such as videoconferencing and Web-based collaborative documentation tools such as a secure wiki. Another example would be the goal of working toward almost zero waste in resources, overhead, or indirect costs.

Rating Forms Provide Excellent Guidance on Important Benchmarks

Rating forms used by the review panel for scoring your application bestow an unparalleled perspective. They provide essential insight into areas being rated and the variable weighting applied to different sections. Use this as a tool in designing your application. Elements are generally a justified *problem statement*, measurable and realistic *goals and objectives*, a sound *organizational profile*, corresponding detailed *budget*, and an intelligently designed *evaluation*.

Use meaningful information visualization methods such as timelines, logic models, or decision trees. However, include them only if they are carefully designed and they enhance overall understanding. Make sure the *target population* and *problem statement* are clearly justified using accurate and current data (properly structured citations to reputable sources are essential), and any accompanying statistical evaluation is relevant. Be certain your proposed services are unambiguous, comprehensive, cost effective, and achievable.

Prepare an Exemplary Application with Close Attention to Detail

This is critically important. Follow and cross-check all document preparation instructions. Do not exceed page limits, and make sure formatting (e.g., font size, spacing, margins) is well aligned with requirements. All elements described in the Application Kit must be included and completed, such as a signed and dated Memorandum(a) of Understanding, Certifications of Assurance of Compliance, and so forth. Even if you answered a question in one section of the application, if the same or similar question arises elsewhere, make sure you consistently address it again.

If a single individual is writing the application, good writing skills are essential. If written as a team effort, then identify at least one person as an editor or reviewer or even consider hiring a professional writer if the award is significant or important to your organization. The editor must review the entire application for consistency and continuity throughout. A collaborative document will appear obvious when the writing style and skill level vary among sections. This presents a significant risk for losing points in those areas that appear poorly written, unorganized, and disjointed. Likewise, identify someone with excellent fiscal skills to prepare a comprehensive budget with line-item detail and a well-crafted budget narrative that will appeal to an audience with a range of financial knowledge. The budget must be congruent, judicious, and realistic with the activities you propose.

Identify a Thoughtful and Objective Nonspecialist Who Is Not Hesitant to Be Critical to Review the Final Application

This individual should know nothing about the project and preferably nothing about the subject domain. A layperson should be able to understand the application's intent and feel like it is worthy to be funded.

Foundations

Foundations are one of the major sources of funding support for education, health, and human services. What are foundations, and what are their roles in funding and services? The Foundation Center (http://foundationcenter.org) provides the following description:

> A foundation is an entity that is established as a nonprofit corporation or a charitable trust, with a principal purpose of making grants to unrelated organizations or institutions or to individuals for scientific, educational, cultural, religious, or other charitable purposes. This broad definition encompasses two foundation types: private foundations and public foundations. The most common distinguishing characteristic of a private foundation is that most of its funds come from one source, whether an individual, a family, or a corporation. A public foundation, in contrast, normally receives its assets from multiple sources, which may include private foundations, individuals, government agencies, and fees for service. Moreover, a public foundation must continue to seek money from diverse sources in order to retain its public status (http://foundationcenter.org/getstarted/faqs/html/foundfun.html).

Foundations are nonprofit organizations with the tax-exempt 501(C)3 status. They are created to address general or specific social causes through the support from long-term investment of assets. Foundations normally do not provide direct service; instead, they provide funding and resources to organizations that deliver services. Based on the sources and sizes of funding, foundations could be private, public, or community based.

A private foundation has funding from a family, a corporation, or a smaller group of donors who want to support a particular social agenda. The Bill and Melinda Gates Foundation (www.gatesfoundation.org/Pages/home.aspx) is an example of such a foundation. Its specific focuses include promoting health care and reducing extreme poverty globally.

The Council on Foundations defines public foundations as "publicly supported nonprofit organizations and are predominantly funded by contributions from individuals, corporations, governmental units and private foundations. As distinguished from most public charities, public foundations focus more on grantmaking than on providing direct charitable services" (www.cof.org/learn/content.cfm?Item Number=550&navItemNumber=2748). Public foundations are also known as grantmaking public charities. The Women's Foundation of California (www.womens foundca.org) and the Vanguard Public Foundation (www.vanguardsf.org) are examples of public foundations.

Among public foundations, there are foundations that are primarily interested in supporting services in the geographic regions in which the foundations are located. These are community foundations. Most metropolitan cities or regions have their own community foundations. The Foundation Center (http://foundationcenter. org),the Council on Foundations (www.cof.org), and the Grantmanship Center (www. tgci.com) all provide comprehensive online information and linkages to identify appropriate foundation funding for service providers.

Similar to working with government funding, a new applicant agency will need to learn how to maneuver within the foundation system. Use the aforementioned Web sites to learn and identify potential foundations to which you would be interested in applying. Find out specifically what the identified foundations are interested in supporting. Check out eligibility, funding restrictions, geographic locations, timelines, and other details. Contact the foundation by phone or e-mail, identify a contact person, visit the foundation's local office, and start building a relationship. A productive working relationship with the foundation's program officer allows the agency to work with the office to further develop the program idea and identify suitable funding.

Professional Insight 2.3: Ten Tips on Successful Grant Seeking

Adele James, MA

Although there are no guarantees to securing funding when applying for a grant, understanding the application process and what a potential funder is looking for are critical pieces that can enhance the chances of success. The following 10 tips will assist you in approaching funders and provide key questions to keep in mind as you design your project:

1. *Do your homework.* Research the foundation you are applying to and read over materials on their program priorities *before* seeking an appointment with a staff person. This way, if you are able to make contact, the conversation can focus on more complex questions specific to your project and not answered by the foundation's public materials.

2. *Know your field.* Given the breadth of work covered by many foundation program staff members, they often depend on community organizations to assist them in keeping up with the latest developments in a field. Funders also want to know if your work is based on proven models accepted as industry standards. If a model does not exist, you should know the field well enough to talk about why your model provides added value and the gap that it fills.

3. *Know where you fit in the ecosystem.* Where do you fit in the continuum of local services? Are there others who provide similar services, or does your agency have a particular niche?

4. *Cultivate partnerships with other organizations.* Often the needs of the constituents served are very complex and require assistance from multiple agencies. Meeting all of these needs may not be possible for one agency. Knowing where you fit in the ecosystem is a good way to identify potential partners who can provide complementary services needed by your constituents.

5. *Keep the project focus on impact.* Many nonprofits come into existence in order to address challenges faced by community members. The new building, computers, or other equipment to be purchased with the grant are the tools that will help facilitate change and are not the final impact. Funders want to know what benefit will be experienced by those you serve or changes to the systems that may be the root of the problem experienced by your constituents.

6. *Do request funding for organizational development.* The Grantmaking School defines organizational development as the "tools, skills, and resources that enable a board and staff to run a nonprofit organization effectively" and encompasses the "practice of training, facilitating, leading and encouraging change in people and organizations to effect positive growth" *(Advanced Proposal Analysis for Grantmaker,* 2004). When requesting funding for a project, keep in mind the impact it might have from an organizational development standpoint, and be ready to articulate why addressing these needs are important in facilitating the implementation and sustainability of the project.

7. *Do request funding to support evaluation of your work.* Evaluations are not just something that should be done to satisfy funders. They can serve as a very important tool in validating the achievement of your project goals, and can provide valuable feedback toward strengthening your project.

8. *Get to know your funder.* These relationships are often underutilized by grantees who view foundation staff as primarily sources of funding. Foundation staff can be great resources on the latest research and evaluation specific to the foundation's priority areas. Given the bird's-eye view philanthropy can provide about a field of work, foundation staff may also be able to assist you in identifying who else in the philanthropy community has similar funding priorities, as well as potential local, state, and national partners.

9. *Cultivate working relationships with key decision makers.* Identify those individuals who do and/or can have influence on the funding, services, and policies that impact your organization. These include elected officials, representatives of government agencies, and the media. Stay on their radar, and make it a priority to periodically brief them about the work of your agency and projects that might be of particular interest to them. While these may not be relationships you need most immediately, it is important to build them so they exist when the need arises.

10. *Build your advocacy capacity.* More organizations are recognizing that in order to bring about fundamental changes in the lives of their constituents, they need to become involved in the policy and advocacy process. According to the Alliance for Justice, there are nine key indicators of advocacy capacity that organizations should consider: (1) decision-making structures; (2) advocacy agenda; (3) organizational commitment and resources for advocacy; (4) advocacy base; (5) advocacy partners; (6) advocacy targets; (7) media skills and infrastructure; (8) advocacy strategies; and (9) knowledge, skills, and systems to effectively implement strategies *(Build Your Advocacy Grantmaking,* 2005). Not all organizations will be able to have the full spectrum of these capacities, but participation in coalitions and working with other stakeholders who have similar aims to your organization can be another way of sharing and building advocacy capacity.

References

Advanced Proposal Analysis for Grantmakers, The Grantmaking School, Dorothy A. Johnson Center for Philanthropy and Nonprofit Leadership, Grand Valley State University, June 2004.

Build Your Advocacy Grantmaking, Alliance for Justice for the George Gund Foundation Evaluation of Advocacy Project, 2005.

References

Bradshaw, J. (1997). The concept of social need. In Gilbert, N., & Specht, H. (eds.). *Planning for social welfare issues, task, and models* (pp. 290–296). Englewood Cliffs, NJ: Prentice-Hall.

Council on Foundations. What is a public foundation? Retrieved April 30, 2009, from www.cof.org/learn/content.cfm?ItemNumber=550&navItemNumber=2748.

Federal Register (FR): Main Page. Retrieved April 29, 2009, fromwww.gpoaccess.gov/fr/index.html.

Federation for Community Development Learning, *Definition of Community Development Learning*. Retrieved January 5, 2009, from www.fcdl.org.uk/about/definition.htm.

Foundation Center. What is a foundation? Retrieved April 30, 2009, http://foundationcenter.org/getstarted/faqs/html/foundfun.html.

Grants.gov. *About grants.gov*. Retrieved April 29, 2009, from http://grants.gov/aboutgrants/about_grants_gov.jsp.

Grants.gov. *Find. Apply. Success*. Retrieved April 29, 2009, from http://grants.gov.

Lewis, J., Lewis, M., Packard, T., & Souflée, F. (2001). *Management of human service programs* (3rd ed.). Belmont, CA: Brooks/Cole.

Maslow, A.H. (1943). A theory of human motivation. *Psychological Review* 50(4), 370–396.

Mayer, R. (1985). *Policy and program planning: A development perspective*. Englewood Cliff, NJ: Prentice-Hall.

Miner, L., & Miner, J. (2003). *Proposal planning and writing* (3rd ed.). Westport, CT: Greenwood Press.

Netting, E., Kettner, P., & McMurtry, S. (1993). *Social work macro practice*. New York: Longman.

Robison, S. (2006). *State human services organization: strategies for improving results*. Washington, DC: National Conference of State Legislatures. Retrieved April 29, 2009, from www.ncsl.org/programs/cyf/hspubintro.htm#hsreorganize.

Rubin, H., & Rubin, I. (2001). *Community organizing and development* (3rd ed.). Needham Heights, MA: Allyn and Bacon.

Smith, M. K. (2001). "Community" in *The encyclopedia of informal education*, Retrieved January 5, 2009, from www.infed.org/community/community.htm.

Taylor, J.C. and Felten, D.F. (1993). *Performance by design: Sociotechnical systems in North America*, Englewood Cliffs, NJ: Prentice-Hall.

The Catalog of Federal Domestic Assistance. Retrieved April 29, 2009, from http://cfda.gov.

Yuen, F. K. O. & Terao, K. (2003). *Practical grant writing and program evaluation*. Pacific Grove, CA: Brooks/Cole–Thomson Learning.

3

Basic Research Methods and Program Evaluation

Data Collection and Instruments
Data Analysis
    Four Levels of Measurement
    Dependent and Independent Variables
Statistics
List of Tables
    Table 3.1: A General Outline of the Social Research Process
    Table 3.2: Comparison between Qualitative and Quantitative Research
    Table 3.3: Common Sampling Strategies
    Table 3.4: Data Collection Methods
    Table 3.5: Data Collection Methods and Instruments
    Table 3.6: Statistics and Levels of Measurement
    Table 3.7: Basic Statistics
    Table 3.8: Choosing the Appropriate Type of Statistics
List of Professional Insights
    Professional Insight 3.1: What Is "Self-Determination" All About?

Program Evaluation: A Practice of Social Research

Social research is a process of systematic inquiry of the social world through inductive and deductive reasoning. It uses logical and organized activities to explore, describe, and interpret social phenomena. The purpose is to accumulate dependable and unbiased data about the social reality. Social research uses various qualitative and quantitative study methods; it is both a science and an art. In human services, research activities help improve professional practice and services to clients, develop a knowledge base for the profession, and ensure the service's accountability to society.

Program evaluation is the practical application of social research methods to assess needs, examine progress, and measure the results of service programs. Program evaluations represent the practical application of social research to aid the planning, implementation, and decision making related to the programs. The sections of this chapter lay out the basics of social research, how they apply to program evaluation, and the details of conducting program evaluations as a part of evaluative research.

Table 3.1 lists the general outline of the social research process. It starts with the very important step of deciding the research questions and, thus, the appropriate hypotheses. A researcher then draws out the nature and designs of the research process. Specific research and data collection approaches or methods are planned, which include the associated data collection tools used to collect the appropriate information and data. Applying the proper data analysis technologies, including statistics and computer software such as SPSS, the researcher summarizes and applies the study findings to answer the research questions.

Table 3.1 A General Outline of the Social Research Process

1. Research Question (The Purpose, The Quest)
    - ➤ What do I want to know? Why am I doing this? Why do I care?
    - ➤ Is it ethical? Is it feasible? Can it be researched?
    - ➤ What has been done, and what do people already know (literature review)?
    - ➤ Variables, conceptual and operational definitions

2. Research Designs (The Framework, The Plan)
    - ➤ Qualitative or quantitative research designs; Inductive and deductive learning
    - ➤ Exploratory, descriptive, experimental, and evaluative designs
    - ➤ Validity and reliability
    - ➤ Causation and correlation
    - ➤ Sampling

3. Research/Data Collection Methods (Approaches, The Work)
    - ➤ Survey (Questionnaire, Interview)
    - ➤ Observation
    - ➤ Experiment, quasi-experimental study
    - ➤ Single-subject study, case study
    - ➤ Secondary data, focus group, expert interview, etc.

4. Data Collection Instruments (The Tools)
    - ➤ Questionnaire
    - ➤ Interview guide
    - ➤ Observational guide
    - ➤ Field notes and others

5. Data Analysis (The "CSI")
    - ➤ The inquiry
    - ➤ No hypothesis
    - ➤ Research hypothesis
    - ➤ Null hypothesis: Reject vs. fail to reject
    - ➤ Alternative hypothesis

    The objective and handy mathematical tools—Statistics

    - ➤ Categories: Parametric, non-parametric
    - ➤ Types: Presentation of data, descriptive, inferential
    - ➤ Some interesting terms:
        - ➤ Test of significance: Test of association, test of difference
        - ➤ Level of significance, confidence level, $p < .10$
        - ➤ Degree of freedom

6. Reporting Out (Dissemination of findings)

7. New Research Questions and Projects

Research Question

Developing a Research Question

Many researchers consider coming up with a good research question as being half the battle for a successful research project. In fact, identifying the right question to ask is itself a valid research question. One has to acknowledge that there is no single right research question; there are only good or appropriate research questions. There is also no single research question that could cover everyone's concerns and interests. A good research question should at least be clear, specific, researchable, relevant, and of significance to the researcher or society. "What is the correlation between spirituality and help-seeking behaviors among women in a rural community?" is probably a good research question. However, "Is eternal life reserved only for those who are religious?" is not a good researchable question for social scientists.

The quality of the research question affects the merits of the findings. Later in this chapter, in the discussions of various types of hypotheses, examples of research questions are further described. It is, however, important to ask a question that can be tested by the research process. Ask about people's attitudes toward recycling, but not about whether recycling increases one's chance for reincarnation. In most situations, try not to ask the obvious or dichotomized question that forces a simple yes-or-no answer. "What contributes to older adults' abilities to stay in their own homes and avoid premature institutionalization?" is better than "Is it better for older adults to stay in their own homes?"

Researchers may come up with research questions that are merely a result of professional curiosity. Over the course of one's practice, observation of certain unique patterns, trends, or even mysteries may become a basis for a research question. A human service provider may be interested in finding out what contributes to the ability of some of her clients coming from extremely high-risk environments to not only beat the odds but excel in their lives. Personal experience and history are often major sources of inspiration for research questions. A domestic violence survivor may be very interested in learning more about the effective helping process of working with children from families with a history of violence. Reporting or programmatic requirements, although at times unpleasant, could possibly be the key reasons for doing evaluative research such as program evaluation. The research questions may, therefore, be on the utilization, effectiveness, and efficiency of the program.

Ethical Considerations

Good research should also be ethical research when involving human subjects, particularly vulnerable populations such as children or other socially identifiable populations. There are several major ethical considerations in developing the research questions and their associated research designs. Among the ethical considerations are confidentiality, anonymity, voluntary participation, risks and benefits, and informed consent. In government agencies, universities, research institutions, or established organizations, a system is often in place to safely guide the ethical concerns of research. A main component of such a system is the use of the human subject review committee or the institutional review board (IRB). Within these organizations, all research projects are expected to seek review and approval from the proper IRBs before beginning the research process.

Confidentiality   Confidentiality is about how to treat data that is collected as classified information that would not be shared with entities that are inessential or indirectly related to the research. Confidentiality denotes researchers' respect of respondents' privacy and of the responses the respondents provide. While they are related topics, privacy is different from confidentiality. Privacy refers to one's rights and freedom to withhold information related to oneself from the public. Confidentiality refers to the trust and understanding that one's private or identifying information would be appropriately secured and not be improperly disclosed.

Confidentiality, however, is not an absolute standard. Human service providers need to share work-related information about the service recipients with the supervisors or the agencies. Researchers who are mandated reporters are required to report possible child abuse and neglect. Documentation and workers' knowledge of certain issues acquired through their research activities may be subjects for subpoena by the court. On the other hand, confidentiality is not always required for all research projects involving humans. For example, it does not apply to the observation of people's public behaviors in public places.

Section 301(d) of the Public Health Service Act, 42 U.S.C. §241(d), clearly states the requirements of confidentiality in research:

> The Secretary [of the Department of Health and Human Services] may authorize persons engaged in biomedical, behavioral, clinical, or other research (including research on mental health, and on the use and effect of alcohol and other psychoactive drugs) to protect the privacy of individuals who are the subject of such research by withholding from all persons not connected with the conduct of such research the names or other identifying characteristics of such individuals. Persons so authorized to protect the privacy of such individuals may not be compelled in any Federal, State, or local civil, criminal, administrative, legislative, or other proceedings to identify such individuals [Public Health Service Act 301(d), 42 U.S.C. §241(d), as amended by Public Law No. 100–607, Section 163 (November 4, 1988)]. (www.irb.arizona.edu/ investigator-information/certificate-confidentiality)

In addition to respecting the privacy of the respondents and minimizing unnecessary mishandling of data, researchers should be careful in deciding what information they want to collect. A simple rule is to ask only for information related to the research. (This topic is further elaborated later in Chapter 6, in the Table of Specifications.) If the age or marital status of the respondents is a variable that is essential or relevant to the study, then it should be included. If it is being asked just because the researchers think it may be interesting to know, then it is not an appropriate question. Researchers' personal curiosity is not a sufficient reason for the possible invasion of respondents' privacy.

Anonymity   Anonymity refers to the secrecy and protection of the identity of the respondents. The most common form of anonymity is that the researchers have no information about the identity of the respondents. Certain research methods, such as using large-scale mailed surveys with no respondents' names included, could make identifying the respondents almost impossible. An agency providing the researchers with copies of service records and documents that already have identifying information blacked out is another way to secure anonymity.

Another form of anonymity is within the data and the findings. Even though the researchers or the users already know who the respondents are, they cannot tell who provided what information. In many research situations, respondents are captive audiences or have prior contacts with the researchers. For example, a teacher should know the course evaluation data are only coming from the students enrolled in a particular class. There are also situations in which names or other identifying information is necessary for the study. For example, researchers of follow-up studies need to know who the respondents are in order to collect data from the same respondents. An agency may also wish to trace back to the respondents if victimization or the safety of the respondents are at stake. Usually, a third party, such as the agency administration or supervisors, would serve as a buffer or a clearinghouse. It will provide the study data to the researchers with no identifying information or with pseudonyms, which could simply be assigned numbers. In the meantime, it keeps a list of the respondents and their information including the pseudonyms in case tracing back is warranted.

Voluntary Participation   Participation in a research project including program evaluation should be voluntary. Potential respondents are free to participate without being concerned about any real or implied threat or inappropriate reward. Perhaps college students are asked to participate in a research project conducted by the course instructor before assigning the course grade. Although they are told participation is voluntary, they may be concerned that nonparticipation will affect their grades, because the instructor is noting who participates and who does not. In another class, the instructor gives extra points to students who participate. It is clear that students are under undue influence and are not voluntary participants in this instructor's study. It is also very likely that these instructors' data collection approaches would not be approved by the university's IRB.

Researchers certainly could promote and encourage participation by engaging in proper activities, such as emphasizing the importance of the research. They could also provide symbolic incentives to show their appreciation of respondents' participation. Some researchers attach a small gift certificate with the questionnaire; others may make a small donation to a charity for every completed participation.

Voluntary participation is emphasized during the initial participation in the study. It should be maintained after the study has begun. Participants are free to withdraw from the study or refuse to participate in any portion of the study at any time even after they have agreed to participate. Participants should be free of any fear that they would be penalized or lose a benefit for their discontinuation in the study.

Risks and Benefits Research activities aim to generate results that could benefit the respondents, the general population, and society. There is a possibility that respondents may face different levels of risk (e.g., experiencing discomfort or harm) because of their participation. The expectation is that the benefits are proportionate to or outweigh the risks that may be generated. Researchers should consider several major types of risks: physical (e.g., bodily harms), economic or financial (e.g., money, employment), psychological (e.g., trauma, fears, sadness), or social (e.g., social standing, embarrassment, stigma). The degree of risk could range from minimal to significant. Ideally, the research does not carry any risks and, if it does, the risks should be minimal and reasonable in relation to the benefits.

Minimal risk means that the probability and magnitude of harm or discomfort anticipated in the research are not greater in and of themselves than those ordinarily encountered in daily life or during the performance of routine physical or psychological examinations or tests 45 CFR 46.102(i)] (www.hhs.gov/ohrp/humansubjects/guidance/45cfr46.htm#46.102).

Precautions should be taken to minimize risks and provide appropriate coverage or remedy. The careful selection of study subjects, provision of resources or services, should the need arise, proper monitoring, and the use of trained personnel to carry out the research activities are some of the approaches that should be considered. Consultation with experts and the use of the IRB further enhance the proper assessment and management of the risks and benefits.

Informed Consent Informed consent includes two very distinct elements: informed and consent. Being *informed* means the participants are fully educated and have good knowledge of what they agree to do. *Consent* is their voluntary decision of agreeing to participate. Potential participants could be fully informed and decide not to consent to participate. Some might consent to participate. However, if they were not fully informed beforehand, the legitimacy of their consent is questionable.

Pedroni and Pimple (2001) discuss two notions of informed consent: moral sense and sociolegal sense. Under the moral sense, the informed consent transforms the person from merely being a subject in a study to being a competent and autonomous decision maker who is engaged in a cooperative activity. The sociolegal sense refers to the person who legally and socially agrees to the terms and is willing to participate in the study (http://poynter.indiana.edu/sas/res/ic.pdf).

As a written document, the informed consent form includes certain common elements. Many organizations have standard templates researchers could use. They usually include the following main items:

1. *Purpose of the study.* Describe the intent of the study and identify who the researchers are.

2. *General design and research procedures.* Describe the overall design of the research. Explain who the study subjects are and how many, how subjects will be recruited and sampled, what data collection instruments will be used, and how the data will be collected and analyzed.

3. *Risks and benefits.* Describe and explain the potential level of risks (i.e., physical, psychological, social, and economic) involved. What are the benefits of the study? What resources or assistance are available for participants, should the need arise?

4. *Compensation and incentive.* Make clear whether there will be compensation or incentive, if any, for participation. Describe what the incentives are (i.e., payment, token gift) and the terms.

5. *Voluntary participation and withdrawal.* Reiterate the voluntary nature of the participation and the right to withdraw at any time.

6. *Confidentiality and anonymity.* Explain how confidentiality will be protected and how anonymity, if any, will be achieved.

7. *Contact information.* If there are any questions, whom should the potential participants contact and at what phone number or at what e-mail?

8. *Printed name and signature.* Indicate one's informed understanding and willingness to participate.

Research Designs

A research design is the general plan and structure for the form of study used in achieving its intended research purpose. A research design could be categorized by whether it is inductive or deductive in nature and, therefore, whether it is a qualitative or quantitative type of study. It could also be presented in terms of its functions and structure as an exploratory, descriptive, experimental, or evaluative study.

While there are many discussions on the advantages and disadvantages of qualitative and quantitative research approaches, a program evaluator and staff need to learn the appropriate use of either approach. In fact, a mixed use of both approaches is often required to develop a better understanding of the subject matter. By nature, qualitative approaches are inductive reasoning and quantitative approaches are deductive reasoning.

Qualitative and Quantitative Research

It is not difficult to find materials related to the great debate between qualitative research and quantitative research. Trochim (2006) stated: "The heart of the

Table 3.2 Comparison between Qualitative and Quantitative Research

Qualitative	Quantitative
The challenges of program evaluation: A case study of a local nonprofit agency	*A pre- and post-study of the effectiveness of a parenting program for teens*
Perspectives on program evaluation: Interviews of program officers	*A cross-states study of the correlation between program evaluation outcomes and continuation of funding for a federal gang intervention program*
Does it really matter? An observational study of doing program evaluation by volunteer workers	
Discover, describe, interpret, and explicate	Measure, explain, and predict differences and relationships
Exploratory and descriptive	Descriptive, experimental, and explanatory
Research question, hypothesis, and theory generalization	Hypothesis and theory testing
More subjective and process-oriented	More objective and outcome-oriented
Inductive reasoning	Deductive reasoning
Analysis based on narrative, words, concepts, pictures, objects; dialectic and contextual	Analysis based on numbers and statistics; logical and context-free
Researcher is part of the research process. Researcher is the data collection tool	Researcher conducts the research but does not become part of the research.
Natural or less-controlled settings with suitable research design continues to unfold	Controlled experimental settings with predetermined research design
Limited ability for generalization; in-depth understanding of uniqueness and pattern	Greater ability for generalization, explanation, and prediction
Use instruments such as documents, observations, and interviews.	Use instruments such as tests, measures, and questionnaires.
Smaller sample	Larger sample

quantitative-qualitative debate is philosophical, not methodological" (The Qualitative Debate section, para. 21). Researchers have taken on a variety of positions on this debate. Some believe the two research methods cannot be mixed because of their epistemological differences. Some deem they could be used alternatively in conjunction with each other. Some consider mixed approaches to be acceptable. There are clear differences between these two approaches. The use of these two approaches is, therefore, up to the researchers to decide based on their philosophy, profession, training, and, most importantly, the purpose of the study. Table 3.2 compares the two approaches and provides a foundational understanding for further study.

Inductive and Deductive Learning

Inductive reasoning moves from specific to general, whereas deductive reasoning moves from general to specific. They represent two distinct ways to learn about our social world. In reality, we use both reasonings throughout our research projects and our daily lives. Together, they form a circle of learning that continues to evolve and advance. Yuen, Bein, and Lum (2006) explain the difference between inductive and deductive approaches to learning.

Arguments can be presented deductively or inductively. Moore (1998) explains the difference between deductive argument and inductive argument. She cites the old example of deductive reasoning that "All men are mortal.

Socrates is a man. Therefore, Socrates is mortal" (p. 5). A conclusion is drawn from the general premises. From a general truth, a conclusion for a specific situation is being drawn. The premises, in fact, contain more information than the conclusion, and the conclusion follows from the premises. In this situation, no matter how much more information is available on Socrates, he is still mortal, and the conclusion still stands. Deductive reasoning provides a more precise and confident assertion than that from inductive reasoning.

In an inductive argument example, individual specific situations are being used to make the generalization. "Socrates was mortal. Sappho was mortal. Cleopatra was mortal. Therefore, all people are mortal" (Moore, 1998, p. 6). The premises of three people's situations become the evidence and the basis for the conclusion that applies to all people. In this case, the conclusion bears more information than the premises. The conclusion could be altered as new information arises and is being incorporated. The inductive conclusion is more of the nature of probability, correlation, or contributory than that of a more causal determination of deductive reasoning.

Inductively, people can learn about situations and make generalizations through analogy and inductive generalization. Moore (1998) explains that learning through analogy involves the use of similar situations to comprehend a new or little-known situation. Using information from a member of a set to make a generalization to all members of that set is an inductive generalization. Inductive reasoning provides many avenues for the learning of diversity (Yuen, Lum & Bein, 2006, pp. 166–167).

Inductive and deductive approaches represent two ways to learn about our social world. The differences provide avenues for service programs and researchers to further our understanding and knowledge based on the nature and the need of the study.

Four Major Types of Research Designs

There are four major types of research designs: exploratory, descriptive, experimental, and evaluative (Atherton & Klemmack, 1982; Grinnell & Unrau, 2008; Royse, 2008; Yuen & Terao, 2003). Each is used for its ability to meet different purposes. At times, mixed designs are used to meet the unique needs of the study. A program evaluation may involve the use of exploratory study design, descriptive study design, experimental designs, or a combination.

Exploratory Designs

Exploratory studies help programs gain familiarity and develop a better understanding of a given question or situation in mind. They also help the program or the researcher to formulate more refined questions for future studies. Exploratory studies could involve a literature review, a needs assessment, a case study, a review of experience of selected examples, or interviews with individuals with different viewpoints.

For example, a community social worker has become aware that the lack of affordable housing in the community is a concern, and her agency is interested in starting a new service program targeting this concern. What should she do? Where should she start? A good way to start is to educate herself on this issue by studying the current literature. Reviews of professional and academic literature allow her to incorporate established knowledge to approach this issue. Local statistics, community reports, and news reporting provide her with an understanding from the perspectives of the local community. She may also want to seek input from knowledgeable individuals (i.e., local residents or people who are affected) through interviews, focus group discussions, or town hall meetings.

Incidentally, another local agency has just completed a community assessment exploratory study. The study results indicate that the targeted populations, although they contribute greatly to the local economy, are priced out of the local housing market both in ownership and in rental. Many of them are not aware of their options and ways to access support services to obtain stable housing. The agency staffs also find that the city is not in compliance with the affordable housing benchmark set from a prior legal settlement.

Based on these findings, this social worker designs a multilevel service and advocacy program. Informational workshops, personal coaches, and case managers are used to increase access and success in obtaining affordable housing. Intensive advocacy and legal activities are developed to ensure compliance from the city. These exploratory studies help identify the focus and the entry points for services and their development. Affordable housing in this community is a complicated issue, and many questions remain unanswered, awaiting further studies.

In research, exploratory studies do not necessarily have research hypotheses. Instead, they help generate more sophisticated or precise research questions and hypotheses for further studies. An exploratory study allows the researcher and service provider to define and further elaborate a general belief or suspicion with more refined questions. The aforementioned social worker may think affordable housing is a concern, but it is just hearsay until it is better defined by her exploratory studies. The results of her exploratory studies enable her to develop interventions and generate hypotheses for further studies on the relationships among affordable housing, community education, and advocacy.

Descriptive Designs

Descriptive studies provide in-depth information about a situation, its variables, or its characteristics. They also illustrate the relationships between two or more variables. A descriptive study is more specific in its scope and focus than an exploratory study. Based on Atherton and Klemmack's (1982) discussions, a descriptive study is different from an exploratory study in the following ways:

1. Attempts to secure a more representative sample and may involve comparison groups;

2. Uses more precise data-gathering methods; and

3. Provides clearer and more specific information on what is being studied.

There is no exact cutoff line to separate a descriptive study from an exploratory study. It is, therefore, a matter of the depth and the focus of the study (e.g., extent of the relationship between identified variables). A high school senior would engage in an exploratory study when he goes on an on-campus tour and orientation to learn more about the university. After the tour, he was able to ask precise questions about scholarship opportunities for a particular major from a counselor. He would also ask the college students about which professors to take for what courses. He was then studying the relationships between specific variables and doing a descriptive study.

Similarly, when a new community worker enters a community, he needs to talk to many people to explore and learn about the community. However, an experienced community worker could not only give the new worker a general introduction to the community, but she could also accurately describe the unique dynamics and relationships among the key elements existing in the community. A longtime resident could tell a newcomer which part of the community is safe, which part is unsafe, and exactly why.

The service provider who completed an exploratory study on affordable housing learned that there is a relationship between the number of hospitality and retail industries in the community and the demand for affordable housing. The exact nature of the relationship, therefore, is the target of her descriptive study. Through a survey of hospitality and retail industry workers and employers, she learns that there is a positive relationship between the two—more hospitality and retail jobs means more demands for affordable housing. Reviews of the local statistics also revealed that as the community attracts more businesses and becomes more affluent, the amount of affordable housing has decreased, although more workers are needed to staff these businesses. She is able to describe more precisely, and in more detail, the correlations through her descriptive studies. As a result, she is able to refine her service program to better address the identified situations.

Descriptive studies illustrate identified variables, their characteristics, and how they relate to or correlate with one another. A descriptive study could be a survey, a service utilization study, or a public opinion poll. Similar to all research activities, descriptive research designs need to pay attention to validity and reliability issues that are discussed later in this chapter.

A descriptive study could include a research hypothesis. A research hypothesis is an informed hunch or an educated guess. Using a simplistic way to conceptualize that, one could say it is a statement in the form of a research question. The research hypothesis for the research question of "Does participating in this parenting class increase parents' abilities to use positive parenting skills?" could be "Participating in this parenting class increases parents' positive parenting skills." A hypothesis describes the relationship between variables and provides a ground for empirical verifications. From a single research question, several research hypotheses could be derived. Hypotheses in descriptive research could take many forms (Atherton and Klemmack, 1982):

1. *X* has certain characteristics (p. 33).

   "Parents who neglect their children were themselves neglected."

   "Youth substance abusers often have a history of using tobacco and alcohol in their early teens."

2. *X* occurs more frequently than *Y* in a given population (p. 33).

   "Low income occurs more frequently than the lack of formal education in parents who neglect their children."

   "Hard work contributes more than luck in the success of one's education."

3. *X* is associated with *Y* in some important way (p. 33).

   "The greater the parental deprivation, the greater number of abusive incidents with their children."

   "Participants who attended more than 90 percent of the sessions have a significantly higher rate of success."

Human service providers would find exploratory and descriptive designs to be the most commonly used designs for their practice-based research or evaluation projects. The ease of these designs also allows them to be used by providers with various levels of training and preparation.

Experimental Designs

Experimental studies examine changes in the dependent variable (*Y*) based on changes in the independent variable (*X*). An experimental study is designed to assess causality or correlation among variables to the extent it is possible. Later in this chapter, the concepts of causality and correlation are further discussed. Experimental study can be conducted with one group or one participant only. A more rigorous design often involves the comparison between two or more groups.

Experimental studies are often useful in helping assess the effects of a given program model by comparing the difference in outcomes (i.e., dependent variable) between a group of people receiving intervention or services (i.e., independent variable) and those who did not receive any. The group that receives the intervention or services is called the experimental group, and the one that does not is called the control group.

Experimental designs involve the use of research hypotheses. The following are the few common forms of hypotheses (Atherton and Klemmack, 1982):

1. Contributory: *X* increases (or decreases) the likelihood of *Y*, but is only one of a number of factors (p. 38).

   "Hard work increases the likelihood of getting good grades."

   "Consistent family support contributes to the decrease of relapse among program participants who are in recovery."

2. Contingent: A condition may have a causative influence when X increases the likelihood of Y under certain circumstances in certain contingencies (p. 38).

   "Job placement services will decrease the number of people who are on the welfare roll when the economy is doing well."

   "Ex-foster care youth will more likely be successful in achieving independent living if they are paired up with mentors for at least two years after emancipation."

3. Alternative: Either X or Z increases the likelihood of Y (p. 38).

   "Changes in either parents' or their children's behaviors will lead to fewer child abuse incidents."

   "Improvement in either the instructor or the students' level of involvement would increase the educational outcomes of this class."

True experimental designs use experimental and control groups and involve sampling and randomization (i.e., random assignment and random sampling of participants). Validity and reliability are also issues that need to be seriously considered in the design of the experiment. The discussions on sampling, randomization, validity, and reliability are presented later in this chapter.

Some examples of the experimental designs:

   X—Administration of the independent variable (intervention/activity)

   O—Observation and measurement of the dependent variable (output, outcome/change)

   R—Randomization, i.e., random sampling or random assignment (participants are chosen/assigned equally by chance)

A. Pre-experimental designs *(No randomization)*

   1. One-shot case study/cross-sectional case study
      X   O   (X—tutoring, O—grade at post-test)

   2. One-group pre-test–post-test
      O_1 X O_2 (O_1—grade at pre-test, X—tutoring, O_2—grade at post-test)

   3. Static group comparison
      X   O   (experimental group—Receive tutoring)
      O   (control group—Not receive tutoring)

B. True experimental designs *(Involve randomization)*

   1. Cross-sectional survey
      R   X   O   (R—Randomization, X—tutoring, O—grade at post-test)

2. Pre-test–post-test control-group design

    R O_1 X O_2 (R—Randomization, O_1—grade at pre-test, X—tutoring, O_2—grade at post-test)

    R O_1 O_2

3. Post-test-only control-group design

    R   X   O   (R—Randomization, X—tutoring, O—grade at post-test)

    R   O

C. Quasi-experimental designs (*No randomization, multiple assessments of change*)

1. Basic time-series (longitudinal)

    X O_1 O_2 O_3 O_4

2. Nonequivalent comparison group pre-test–post-test

    O_1 X O_2

    O_1 O_2

3. Time-series quasi-experimental design/interrupted time-series

    O_1 O_2 O_3 O_4 X O_5 O_6 O_7 O_8

4. Multiple time-series design

    O_1 O_2 O_3 O_4 X O_5 O_6 O_7 O_8

    O_1 O_2 O_3 O_4 O_5 O_6 O_7 O_8

5. Single-subject design/the single-case study

Key terms: A (Baseline phase), B (Intervention phase/effects of the first intervention), C (Effects of the second intervention), D (Effects of the third intervention)

➤ B (Case study—what happens during the intervention period)

➤ AB (A—client's general performance before intervention, B—performance following intervention)

➤ ABA (A—performance without intervention, B—performance following intervention, A—performance without intervention)

➤ ABAB (A—performance without intervention, B—performance following intervention, A—performance without intervention, B—performance after returning to intervention)

➤ ABC (A—performance without intervention, B—performance following intervention, C—additional or the second intervention, e.g., individual counseling)

➤ ABCD (A—performance without intervention, B—performance following intervention, C—additional or the second intervention, D—effects of the third intervention, e.g., participating in a support group)

Evaluative Research Design

An evaluative research design involves the use of exploratory, descriptive, and experimental designs. It is the application of various research designs to study issues such as program performance, accountability, challenges, and improvement. It asks important questions: "Did the program achieve the goals it set out to achieve?" "How effective and efficient is the program?" "Should it be continued?" "Is it cost-effective?" "What changes are needed?"

Many names are used to describe the various types of evaluative research: process evaluation, outcome evaluation, progress evaluation, implementation evaluation, formative evaluation, and summative evaluation. A few of them are basically the same; they are named differently for their unique contexts and purposes of application. Most importantly, researchers distinguish two key forms of evaluative research: formative and summative evaluations.

Formative and Summative Evaluations

Formative evaluations monitor the progress of the program and study (i.e., whether it is on course). Some characterize formative evaluation as taking the temperature of the program. They are usually done while the program is being formulated or in progress. They generate information that could help validate, develop, and improve the program. Examples of a formative evaluation include needs assessment, process evaluation, case-conference, case study, and implementation evaluation.

Summative evaluations assess the end results of the program. The focus could be on the extent of goal attainment, challenges and successes, effectiveness and efficiency, as well as expected and unexpected outcomes. At the end, the merits of the program are examined. Examples of summative evaluation include cost analysis, outcome valuation, impact evaluation, and goal-attainment assessment.

Yuen and Terao (2003) use the flight of a commercial jetliner as an example to explain program evaluation and highlight its importance. A huge Boeing 747 was parked at the gate of an airport. Its front wheels rested on a small square box painted on the ground underneath the plane. With a detailed flight plan in hand, the pilots took the plane into the air and hours later landed at another airport several thousand miles away. It parked by the gate and again its front wheels rested on another small square box painted on the ground.

The passengers happily deplaned but they did not know that the plane was "off-course" most of the time. Many factors such as traffic, weather, and ground conditions made following the exact flight plan impossible. It was the pilots' consistent adjustments, guided by the well-developed flight plan, that made the trip a successful trip.

These pilots' professional performance is, in fact, not that different from what we do every day driving on the road. With the destination in mind, we determine the route and get on the road. We consistently evaluate the road conditions and adjust our driving accordingly. This ongoing monitoring and use of new information to assist our trip is an example of formative evaluation. Whether you arrive at your destination safely and on time just like those happily deplaned passengers is the summative evaluation.

Bob Stake, an evaluation theorist, is credited for saying, "When the cook tastes the soup, that's formative; when the guests taste the soup, that's summative." (http://jan.ucc.nau.edu/edtech/etc667/proposal/evaluation/summative_vs._formative.html). Formative evaluation provides information to the practitioners and participants, summative evaluation reports to the stakeholders, including the funders, organizations, clients, and community. We engage in evaluation, both formative and summative, in our everyday life.

A Mixed Approach

An evaluative research design (e.g., a program evaluation plan) may involve the use of exploratory study design, descriptive study design, and experimental design. The following is an example of an evaluative study with mixed designs.

A school-based service program conducts a needs assessment (exploratory study) and learns that the target students may benefit from intensive one-on-one tutoring in math and reading to improve their academic performance and sense of self-confidence. They do several surveys (descriptive study) using a questionnaire, observations, academic testing, and existing data to assess the intended change as well as the relationship between students' academic performance and self-confidence.

At the same time, a social work intern wants to apply a better-monitored and more focused assessment to a small number of students at her school site. She plans to study the likely effects of the interventions and the changes in performance at different times over a period of one semester (quasi-experimental studies, pre-experimental study). At a different school site, another group of students is identified by the student intern, their parents have given consent, and they are randomly assigned to participate in a controlled study (experimental study) of whether the use of peer-mentors makes a difference in their performance. Program staff are also interested in knowing whether the added individual counseling and/or support group services or the combinations of them help the participating students.

Findings from these studies facilitate the program to design and deliver interventions that are more effective. They also allow the program to be more accountable to the funding sources, the schools, the parents, and the students. Valuable findings help the program to prepare better grant proposals to continue the financial support for these needed programs.

Validity and Reliability

A driver's license is a valid identification to prove one's age, but it is not so for one's level of education. A rubber-band ruler probably is not the most reliable tool to measure one's height, because it will give varying results. *Validity* questions the

---

Professional Insight 3.1: What Is "Self-Determination" All About?

Edie L.. Cook, PhD

Researchers design evaluation studies involving people who have special needs of various kinds:

➤ Individuals who have been institutionalized or are currently in a treatment setting
➤ Individuals who use assistive technology in order to move around or communicate
➤ Mental health consumers who are a part of a wide system of care
➤ Individuals who have communication needs as a result of hearing, language, speech, or vision issues
➤ Individuals who are medically or chemically dependent
➤ Individuals who are geographically or culturally isolated

Although only some of us work *specifically* with special-needs populations, many or most of us are working or will work in projects that *include* individuals with special needs. How well do we plan for the participation of individuals with special needs when they are not our target population? Self-determination is an issue that should be salient to most of you, whether you are aware of the special needs in your population or not.

Simply put, *self-determination* means that people have the ability to:

➤ Control their own lives, including their participation in evaluation
➤ Reach goals they have set
➤ Take part fully in the world around them

Self-determination relates to autonomy, dignity, and individual choices being respected. The concept of self-determination has been written into federal law concerning medical care, and has been implemented as a public policy requirement in many states, but has not yet been formally endorsed as a right of participants in evaluation studies.

As self-determination is directly related to self-advocacy, in a general sense we have been prodded to think about and make explicit what we, as individuals, are getting out of our participation in grant writing, evaluation planning, or in a particular evaluation study. This is an ethical issue, because all too often participants report being exploited by evaluators, even evaluators who value their participation and include them in many phases of the project. Recently, the issue of compensation has become a hot topic, because of discrepancies between the compensation rates of paid evaluators, community participants, and program recipients and family members.

The concept of self-determination also has implications during the dissemination of evaluation results. Do participants have any say about what happens to the evaluation data? What about access to the results? Do they have any control over or input into how they are portrayed? At the American Evaluation Association, the question has been raised: Do we need Ethical Guidelines specific to individuals with special needs? And, if so, should we incorporate the concept of self-determination into our guidelines for evaluation? But whether the concept of self-determination is formalized as a guideline, we can consider its implication for designing our evaluation with care and consideration for all individuals of differing abilities.

---

appropriateness of the measure in producing the results, and *reliability* questions whether the same measure will produce the same results. Validity and reliability are two important measurement concepts in social research. Research activities that fail to achieve appropriate validity and reliability are merely busy work that produce defective results and lack credibility.

Validity

Validity refers to whether the measurement actually measures what it intends to measure. A simple bathroom scale is intended to measure one's weight but not one's height. Validity reflects the confidence in the truthfulness and the strength of the measurement and the conclusion. It begs the question of "Is it real? How real?" A Mexican grandma who also is a great cook comments that food from this one taqueria is very authentic. Her comments certainly carry more weight and respect than comments from someone who only has Mexican food from the chain taco joints. As one would likely point out, this authenticity assertion depends on the definition of *authentic* and how it is compared against another well-known local taqueria.

These are some good questions, and they can be answered by further understanding the concept of validity. There are several major types of validity:

➤ Face validity
➤ Content validity
➤ Criterion validity: concurrent validity and predictive validity
➤ Construct validity

Face Validity   Face validity refers to whether the measure appears to measure what it intends to measure. It asks questions such as "Does it look right?", "On the surface, does it reflect the intended concept?" and "Does it appear reasonable and capable of achieving its intention?" Face validity is the most basic and elementary type of validity. It only has limited strength and rigor, partly because it relies heavily on the perspectives and the selection of the authority who makes the judgment.

A new staff member just finished writing her case report for an initial assessment of a client. Before she submitted the report, she went to show it to a more experienced coworker. She asked the coworker to quickly look over the report to see if it looked all right. She wanted to know if the report appeared to be adequate. In another example, it seems to be appropriate to conclude that a handshake between two people when they meet is an indication of politeness and respect rather than an invitation for confrontation and argument. If it smells good, looks good, and sounds good, it probably is good. On the other hand, isn't it?

Content Validity   Content validity is about a measure's ability to assess the many aspects of a concept. According to the U.S. Department of Housing and Urban Development, a homeless person is "an individual who lacks a fixed, regular, and adequate nighttime residence" (www.hud.gov/homeless/definition.cfm). A measure that uses this definition to assess if someone is homeless would include individuals who sleep on the street or in a nighttime shelter, as well as those who do couch surfing in other people's homes, or live in their cars. An assessment would have low content validity if it does not adequately represent the various relevant aspects of a concept or variable.

Some researchers consider face validity as the simplest form of content validity. Similar to face validity, content validity relies on the input from experts and the experienced. It is more rigorous than face validity in that it aims to measure specific constructs and could be theory-based. A test paper on economic theories does not have the face validity to be used to assess college students' learning in an early childhood development class. The economic theories test paper also does not reflect the content being taught in the class. A valid test paper for this class should reflect the theories and knowledge included in this class and its intended learning outcomes.

Reviews of literature and other relevant studies are some of the most important steps in establishing the content validity of a study. They provide a knowledge-based foundation and framework for conceptualization and the development of the measurement.

Criterion Validity: Concurrent Validity and Predictive Validity   Criterion validity refers to how well the results of a measure correlate to established criteria or standards. It refers to the ability of a measure's results to predict the outcomes from another measure or in concrete events in the real word. Criterion validity is also known as concrete validity. It includes concurrent validity and predictive validity.

Concurrent validity is about how well one measure performs in comparison to another valid measure. If a new anxiety test can assess the degree of anxiety as accurately as that of a valid but older anxiety test, then this new one is said to have achieved a good concurrent validity. You have become a good cook when you are able to fix a Thanksgiving meal almost as great as that of your mother's!

Predictive validity refers to how one measure is able to predict the outcomes for another related measure. "Students who do well in the driving test in high school are believed to have fine driving records as adults" is an example of predictive validity. An ongoing argument among professors in graduate school is whether the Graduate Record Examination (GRE) really can predict one's success in graduate studies.

Construct Validity   Construct validity shows the extent to which a measure reflects or assesses a construct (i.e., the abstract underlying concept or idea, such as depression or intelligence). It is about whether a measure appraises a theoretical construct as it is hypothesized to assess. If self-esteem is theorized to consist of self-worth and self-image, then the measure of self-esteem has to reflect the traits of both self-worth and self-image. Self-pity may be a related concept but is not one of the aspects of self-esteem. A measure that assesses self-pity, therefore, does not have the construct validity for measuring the construct of self-esteem. There is a lack of agreement between the theoretical concept and the assessment measure.

A Validity Love Story   As a young woman in college, Jean met many people, including some interesting and eligible young men. Although she was not active in the dating scene, quite a few fine young men appeared to be the right type (face validity) for her. Jim stood out from the crowd. His views on life and everything else were very comparable to those of Jean. They also appeared to be rather complementary to each other. Based on their commonality and compatibility (content validity), they were considered a good match by their friends. Jim's qualities reminded Jean of her wonderful old boyfriend (concurrent validity), but Jim was even better.

Jean invited Jim home for Thanksgiving to meet her parents. Her parents gave her their approval of Jim. They agreed with Jean that Jim had all the good qualities (predictive validity) she (and they) was looking for. They got married not long afterward. Jean and Jim have been happily married for 50 years. They believe they are lucky to have found their soulmates. They made the right choice and picked someone who had the true and genuine qualities (construct validity) they were looking for in a life partner.

Internal and External Validity

Validity could also be divided into internal and external validity. *Internal validity* is the consideration of whether the independent variables are responsible for the results obtained. *External validity* concerns the generalizability of the study or to what extent the results of this study could be applied to other similar situations.

Threats to Internal Validity Internal validity questions whether the variables involved in the study bring about the results, or if there is something else (i.e., threats, alternative causes, alternative explanations, or confounding variables) that affected or threatened the results. Using various articulated research designs, researchers are to limit the effects of these threats to internal validity. This will allow them to study the real relationship to be studied. The following are several of the common threats to internal validity:

➤ *History*. Refers to outside events that affect the results of the study. The bad economy decreases the number of jobs in the market as well as the success rate of a job placement program. High prices for cigarettes decrease the amount of cigarettes purchases. The numbers for tobacco-related illness have been lowered, not because high-priced cigarettes are safer, but because people are consuming less tobacco. History does not refer to past events, but to events that happen during the course of the study.

➤ *Maturation*. Refers to the physiological changes of the participants that take place during the course of the study. People get tired after a while and children grow up. All of these may make them participate in the study differently.

➤ *Testing*. The implementation and the interaction of the testings or how the measures may affect the results of the study. Too-frequent tests, or when the post-test is too close to the pre-test, affect the performance of the participants.

➤ *Instrumental decay/instrumentation*. Deterioration of the data collection instrument. Over time, the spring for a scale may be less responsive, the prints of a repeatedly used test paper may become blurry, and even the test administrator may become tired.

➤ *Regression to the mean/statistical regression.* During repeated measures, people tend to move toward the mean score. If a study selects participants based on their extreme scores, it is possible that subsequent testing will produce scores that are more average than extreme. On the other hand, there is always a time of exception (e.g., the bad-hair day!). There is a statistical probability that data collection takes place during that exceptional point. The results may, therefore, be skewed. However, over time people do act normally (i.e., toward the mean).

➤ *Selection.* Preexisting differences between study subjects may interact with the independent variable and affect the outcomes of the study. Randomization may be able to minimize this initial selection problem, but randomization is not always feasible.

➤ *Experimental attrition/mortality.* The fact that study subjects, for whatever reasons, may drop out or decide to discontinue their participation in the study. Although it is referred to as mortality, it is not about participants dying; it is about their leaving the study. The loss of study subjects between measures may lead to inflated or inaccurate study results.

External validity is the ability to make generalizations from the study findings to another target population or setting. It is about the inference and applicability of findings from a specific study to a population beyond the sample. For example, several study findings have found that public announcements on TV and mailing of printed materials are effective in promoting the general population's participation in a census study in urban cities, but these findings may not be true for certain cultural minority groups or the rural populations. An experimental study finds that religious leaders are among the best spokespersons to promote participation in the census among Hispanics in Sacramento, California. A subsequent statewide study of Hispanics confirms the Sacramento study findings and its external validity.

Reliability

Reliability is the consistency and repeatability of a measure. A reliable measure is consistent such that it will produce the same results over repeated procedures. A reliable automobile will bring you to work every day without much trouble. A reliable employee will produce the same quality work day after day and assignment after assignment. Reliability is a concept that could be estimated statistically and through different methods. The following are several of the common types of reliability:

➤ *Internal consistency.* Refers to a correlation among related variables in a measure. It assesses whether related items from a questionnaire truly measure the same construct. Cronbach's alpha is a commonly used statistic to do the estimation.

➤ *Split-half or parallel forms reliability.* A measure is divided into two equivalent sets of items. The whole measure is used on the same group of people. The correlation of the results from the two equivalent sets is the estimate of the reliability of the measure. To achieve this reliability, a large number of items need to be developed. Often, it is not that feasible. Errors in assignment of items to form two equivalent forms is another difficulty.

➤ *Test–retest reliability.* The correlation of two administrations of the same measure to the same people. Theoretically, the two scores should be very close to each other. In practice, many factors may affect the likelihood of having similar outcomes.

➤ *Inter-rater reliability.* This refers to the correlation of the scores or findings between two or more independent raters or observers. This helps eliminate personal bias or random errors. The information is more reliable if two or more raters make the same observation or rating.

The Relationship between Validity and Reliability

Validity and reliability are two related but different concepts. Researchers always hope to develop studies that accurately measure what they want to measure (validity) and produce consistent or precise results over repeated procedures (reliability). Validity is about accuracy, and reliability is about precision. *Accuracy* refers to whether a measure hits the target and measures the right construct. *Precision* refers to producing the exact or very close hits time after time, even though they may be far off the target. Similar to playing darts, hitting the bull's-eye is accuracy, and repeatedly hitting the bull's-eye or consistently missing it to the left on the same spot is precision.

It is possible to have a measure that has low validity but high reliability. A common example is the bathroom scale example. A defective bathroom scale could consistently and precisely (reliability) indicate someone's weight as 100 pounds but fail to accurately (validity) tell the person's real weight of 150 pounds. Certainly, there are measures that have low validity and low reliability, although not much credible information would be produced. It is, however, not that possible to have a highly valid measure with low reliability. Measures low in reliability are very unlikely to produce valid measures. For example, it is difficult to believe one's words if that person has been repeatedly telling lies the whole time.

Causation and Correlation

The desire to seek out the causes and explanation has been the driving force behind the advancement of humankind and our existence. "Why" is a short word, but it has mighty power. Human service providers probably would like to know what causes a certain situation to happen and what causes a program to fail or succeed. One of the purposes for program evaluation is to assess which interventions have brought about the desirable outcomes. A straightforward causal relationship in social science is often not that easily achieved. Contributing variables correlated or associated with the desirable outcomes are equally important and more likely to be identified and studied.

Causation and correlation (and association) are two key concepts in the discussions of explanation. They are important for both program planning and evaluation. Program evaluation helps to explain what happened in the program, and program planning applies these explanations to designing programs. Yuen (2006) discusses different forms of explanations as they relate to causation and correlation in social work practice. This discussion is also applicable to other human service professionals.

Simplistically, people like answers that allow one to see a clear causation that a particular cause (e.g., reason, need) directly explains a particular change (e.g., effect, result). However, in most social work practice situations, the clear and clean answer of causation to the question "Why?" is not easy to obtain. Too many interrelated factors or conditions might have led to the presence of the client's current situation.

A *causal relation* can only be established in the presence of a "list of conditions which together are considered necessary and sufficient to explain the occurrence of the phenomenon in question" (Chafetz, 1978, p. 22). Chafetz further explains that "a *necessary explanation* is one in which the elements listed must be present to bring about the result in question" (p. 22). The presence of clouds is necessary to have any rainfall, but a cloud alone is not enough to cause rain. It is not possible to have rain under a clear blue sky, but it is possible to have a cloudy day with no rain in sight.

"A *sufficient explanation* is one in which the elements listed will always bring about the result in question" (Chafetz, p. 22). Always, a spoonful of cyanide is enough to kill a person if untreated. The presence of enough dosage of cyanide in a person's body can bring about death. Cyanide is a sufficient cause for death, but it is not necessary for anyone to have cyanide in order to die. While a cloud is a necessary but not sufficient condition for rainfall, cyanide is a sufficient but not necessary condition for death. Nevertheless, both are the important and key contributing factors that bring about the results in question.

Very often, social work practice could only be working with key contributing factors rather than the absolute root causes. These contributing factors are associated or correlated to the presence of the clients' current conditions. By making changes to the contributing factors and with the ultimate end outcomes in mind, social workers attempt to affect the likelihood of the attainment of the desirable results or the elimination of the undesirable results.

Medical doctors, supported by rigorous scientific testing and clinical studies, could pinpoint a particular virus, bacteria, or biological agent that causes a particular disease. Specific medical interventions are, therefore, used to eliminate or control the cause of the disease in the patient. Unlike medical doctors, social workers do not deal with causes of issues that behave like viruses or bacteria. They do not even necessarily know the exact causes for clients' situations and have the "magic pills" to cure the problem. Like medical professionals, social workers work with individuals, families, and communities to address issues and factors that affect their health and well-being. (Yuen, 2006, pp. 9–10)

Contributing factors that affect the likelihood of achieving the desirable outcomes probably are valuable and often more obtainable than the causal factors. Children who grow up in drug- and violence-infested communities have a higher likelihood of getting in trouble with the law when they become adults. The correlation between the community characteristics and legal involvement is a correlation that could be the focus for program planning and evaluation. It does not mean that a community with high drug and violence incidences causes its youth to become outlaws, or that children from this community are doomed to become criminals. Many successful youth from such communities have proven their resiliency and strength. It does, however, point out the correlation or the contributing risk and protective factors, which could possibly be the focus for interventions and their evaluation.

Correlation and Association

In the process of making claims about effecting change, there is a need to distinguish between causation (casual relation) and correlation (including association). Service programs are designed to bring about changes, but it is difficult, if not impossible, to claim that the program's intervention directly and solely caused the change. To establish causation, as discussed previously, both necessary and sufficient conditions have to be present. A correlation or association, however, is more likely to be established by service program than causality.

Association refers to two things changing together. Two people make a move at the same time. There is no information of how vigorous (e.g., fast/slow or strong/weak) they are and at what direction (e.g., left/right or positive/negative). Amy and John work together in the same office. It is not unusual to see both of them in the office at the same time, and it is not uncommon that one is in the office and the other is not. When someone is looking for Amy and does not find her, that person may ask John where Amy is. John may or may not know, but he is more likely than another person to know because they work together. If both of them are there, they would do their assignments separately or together. If one of them is not there, the other one needs to provide coverage to staff the office. As colleagues or associates, they are related to and affecting each other's work.

Whenever Amy enters the office, John follows into the office. If it happens enough times, people would connect Amy's presence in the office with the likelihood of John being in the office as well. While association only indicates that two things change together, correlation additionally indicates the strength (-1 to $+1$) and direction (i.e., positive and negative) of the association. When Amy is in the office, John also shows up in the office; they may have a positive correlation. If it happens all the time (100 percent or 100/100), the strength of the correlation will be +1.0. If it happens only 70 percent of the time, then the correlation will be +0.7. However, if 70 percent of the time, Amy comes in the office and John leaves, then they have a negative correlation of −0.7. If 100 percent of the time, when Amy is in the office, John is away from the office, they have a perfect −1 correlation.

Sometimes, Amy and John are both in the office, and sometimes they are not. There is not a clear link between one's presence and the other's presence or absence. A moderate correlation (both + and −) could range between 0.4 to 0.7. Any correlation less than 0.3 is a very weak one, and a 0.0 means a nonexisting correlation.

No matter what the correlation number is, one cannot tell whether Amy causes John to be in the office or John causes Amy to show up. All we can say is that if one sees Amy or John in the office, one may also likely (at different extent/strength) see the other one there (therefore, a positive correlation). Conversely, if one sees Amy or John in the office, it is (at different extent/strength) unlikely to see the other one there (therefore, a negative correlation).

Apply this discussion to a program evaluation situation. David's mother puts him in a tutoring program; she believes it will increase his likelihood of doing better in school. David's last report card showed he has been doing better since his enrollment in the tutoring program. In a way, David can say tutoring improves his academic performance. A program staff, however, cannot claim that tutoring directly and single-handedly causes David's improvement in school. It might, but it might not. No one could be completely certain whether it is because of the tutoring or because the family situation has improved because his mom just became employed full-time, or because he has the wonderful Mrs. Smith as his teacher this year. Program staff, however, could say there is a positive correlation between participating in the tutoring program and improved school performance. This by itself is an endorsement of the effectiveness of the tutoring program as a significant contributing factor.

Exploratory and descriptive researchers could provide data that test the correlation or association. The use of risk and protective factors in theory and in practice is based on the framework of correlation. Experimental research allows a researcher to identify the correlations as well as the possible causal relationships between variables. Although the absolute causation may be difficult to achieve, it is still a researcher's intention to find out why and how things happen.

Sampling

Sampling is a process of selecting study subjects. It employs probability theory and statistical methods to draw a *sample* (i.e., a portion, a subset, or a specimen) from the whole (i.e., population or class) for the study. The *population* is the target group the researcher is interested in studying. It could be a rather huge group, such as male college students in the state. Due to resources, cost, feasibility, and other reasons, the population may be unreachable or too large to conduct a census. The researcher may wish to consider a more feasible and accessible group of the population, such as male students at a local college. This accessible population is called the *sampling frame*. Out of this sampling frame, samples who become study subjects will be drawn.

Sampling could be categorized into nonprobability sampling and probability sampling. *Nonprobability sampling* does not involve the use of randomization, whereas *probability sampling* involves randomization. When a nonprobability sampling method is used, the results from studying the selected subset are snapshots of the sample and may have limited ability for generalization. However, if a probability sampling method is used, the results from the sample may have the ability to generalize to the population.

Randomization is a key concept in probability sampling. It includes both random sampling and random assignment. *Random sampling* refers to the units being randomly selected (i.e., each has an equal chance of being chosen and becoming a study subject). Drawing a name from the hat or picking the short straw are everyday examples of random sampling. *Random assignment* refers to the systematic and chance-based process of assigning the study subjects into different groups (i.e., the control group or the experimental group, group A or group B). Because random sampling encompasses the selection of subjects from the population, it is therefore more related to the concerns of the study's external validity (i.e., generalization to the population). Random assignment, however, is more concerned about issues related to internal validity (i.e., are two groups of equivalence to the point that they can be compared).

Randomization is a key feature for experimental research design. It is through random sampling or random assignment that a researcher could have confidence in claiming findings to be more trustworthy and valid.

Table 3.3 lists some of the common sampling strategies for both probability sampling and nonprobability sampling.

Probability Sampling (Random Sampling)

In random sampling, each case in the population has the same chance to be selected. If there are ten students in a class and the teacher wants to randomly select three to participate in a schoolwide survey, she writes each student's name on a separate piece of paper and places them all into a container. She mixes them up and draws

Table 3.3 Common Sampling Strategies

Probability Sampling (Random Sampling)	Nonprobability Sampling (Nonrandom Sampling)
Simple random sampling	Convenience sampling
Systematic random sampling	Snowball sampling
Stratified random sampling	Purposive sampling
Cluster random sampling	Quota sampling

names out one at a time. Each student should have an equal 10 percent (i.e., 1 out of 10) chance to be selected.

To ensure that everyone has the same 1/10 chance, any of the names picked are to be returned back to the container. There is a possibility that a student may be selected twice. If so, that student's opinion will be counted twice as if they are from two separate respondents. This is an example of *random sampling with replacement*. The values of the samples or observations are considered *independent*. Because of the replacement, each is being drawn from the same original population. The result of the first draw does not affect what the second draw will be. The covariance between two draws is zero. A *covariance* is a measure of how two values change together.

In another situation, the teacher is to give out prizes. Again, she puts names in a container and starts drawing names. However, she does not want the same students to get a prize more than one time. Therefore, she sets aside the names that are already drawn. This is a case of *random sampling without replacement*. Because there is no replacement, each of the drawings is from a slightly different or new population. The chance for the first student drawn in her class is 1/10, the next student is 1/9, and the next one is 1/8. Each sample or observation changes the probability of the others. The results of the first draw affects what the subsequent ones will be. They are, therefore, considered *dependent*, and the covariance between them is not zero.

The differences of these two approaches are of great interest to mathematicians. They are, however, not that significant for professionals who are mainly casual users of statistics. "In general, if the finite population is extremely large relative to n, then sampling without replacement is, for all intents and purposes, equivalent to sampling with replacement" (Panik, 2005, p. 301). In human services, because of small population and other limitations, random sampling without replacement is more feasible and is more commonly used.

Simple random sampling is the basic form of random sampling. Study subjects from the population are selected entirely by chance. If a program evaluator decides to draw 20 percent of the population as the sample for her study in a housing complex, she could randomly pick 20 names from the list of the 100 residents. Besides drawing names from the hat, selection of random samples could be achieved by using a random number table or by using a computer program to generate the random numbers.

Systematic random sampling is a simpler and less expensive way to draw a random sample than the simple random sampling method. It is the selection of samples from a population or sampling frame with a sampling interval. Once the sample size is determined, it will be used to divide the population and come up with the sampling interval. Starting with the randomly selected first element, additional elements will be selected at the increment of the sampling interval. For example, 120 client files are organized numerically from 001 to 120. The researcher wants to randomly select 20 of them for the study. The population is 120, sample size is 20, therefore the sampling interval is 6 (i.e., 120 ÷ 20 = 6). The researcher also randomly selects a starting point number, say, 4. As a result, the 20 samples will be 004, 010, 016, 022 . . . 106, 112, and 118. If the randomly selected starting point number is 15, then the samples will be 015, 021, 027 . . . 111, 117, 003, and 009.

Stratified random sampling draws samples that are representative of the different strata of the population. A *stratum* is a segment or category that shares a common characteristic (e.g., male and female, or instructors, students, and parents). A random sampling method is then used to draw a sufficient number of samples from each of the strata. If a researcher wants to know the effectiveness of the program including all parties involved, he may want to make sure he will have sufficient representations from the three strata: 10 administrators, 30 staff, and 100 clients. He may determine to use the stratified random sampling method to draw 20 percent from each of the strata to form the sample for his study: 2 administrators, 6 staff, and 20 clients. This approach is particularly useful to ensure participation from all segments of the population. This method is also more suitable for a homogeneous group.

Cluster random sampling is used to draw samples from natural groupings or existing structures, such as the county, city blocks, or schools. The population is divided into clusters. Samples of these clusters are randomly selected. Further sampling from these clusters would then be conducted as demanded by the study. For example, a community organizer could use cluster random sampling to develop a useful sample for her single-parent needs assessment. A random sample of 15 percent of all the clusters of the community is drawn by using city blocks, zip codes, or catchment areas. If this community has 200 city blocks, then 30 (15 percent of 200) of the randomly selected blocks will be identified. Single-parent households within these identified 30 city blocks will then be randomly selected to become potential study subjects.

She has many options to reach her desired number of samples. She could randomly draw samples from the 30 identified city blocks until the number reaches the target sample size. However, if she decides to survey 25 percent of these households, she could do so by randomly selecting 25 percent of the single-parent households in the identified 30 city blocks. Cluster sampling is less precise than the simple random sampling. It is, however, more feasible and suitable for heterogeneous populations. It is used by researchers, particularly in less accessible or organized areas, for surveying the impacts of natural disaster, poverty, or damages caused by war.

Nonprobability Sampling (Nonrandom Sampling)

Nonrandom sampling selects samples not on the basis of probability but on choice and judgment. The sample is biased, not representative of the population, and has limited ability to make generalizations. It is, however, a useful approach for gathering samples for exploratory and descriptive studies. It is also often employed for case selection for qualitative studies. If a program evaluator is merely interested in the efficacy of a program for its participants and not with the intention of making generalizations to other programs, nonrandom sampling is the appropriate and less expensive choice.

Convenience sampling is the use of accessible and readily available study subjects. They could be the current service recipients, coworkers, or whoever happens to be present at the time of data collection. It may be a wonderful idea to study the efficacy of cognitive behavioral therapy for female clients who are victims of domestic violence. Achieving a statewide random sample or gaining cooperation from other agencies may keep this study from ever happening. A study of eligible clients from the researcher and her colleagues' current caseload in her agency may be a reasonable, feasible, and practical alternative, however. Study results may not be generalized to agencies elsewhere in the United States, but they have much implication for the researcher's agency. The results could also be used for comparison with other similar studies.

Snowball sampling is developed through referral. It is particularly useful for studying hard-to-reach subjects. In a study of AIDS (Acquired Immune Deficiency Syndrome) in the early 1980s, stigma and taboo made reaching individuals with AIDS very difficult. A researcher completed a case interview with a person with AIDS and would ask the respondent to make a recommendation and contact for additional potential respondents. Similarly, the study of home remedy or folk medicine in the South among African Americans could have only been done by the referrals from the initial respondents. As the name implies, gathering respondents is just like building a snowball that starts with a small one and gets bigger as it begins to roll.

Purposive sampling selects samples that have the particular characteristics sought by the study. A service provider may be more interested in studying the effects of unemployment on grandparents who are raising grandchildren. Therefore, only such grandparents in the community will be selected for the study. Qualitative studies often use purposive sampling, seeking to reach respondents who have the characteristics and rich information about the subject matter (e.g., key informants or experts).

Quota sampling is the nonrandom equivalent of stratified random sampling. A set of quota is established for each of the strata or categories. Through convenience, snowball, purposive, or any of the nonrandom methods, study subjects in each stratum are recruited until the quota is filled. A study of the effectiveness of the "cold turkey" approach to quitting smoking may strive to recruit a sufficient number of individuals from groups that are "successful," "failed," and "still trying" in order to get a comprehensive picture of the issue.

Sample Size: How Many Is Needed?

Based on statistical principles, mathematicians have developed formulas to calculate the desirable sample size for random sampling. Program evaluators or professional human service practitioners may wish to consult these established methods if they are going to use random sampling for their evaluative studies.

The decision on sample size could be affected by the number of responses desired and the size requirements of the statistical analyses selected. For example, the average mailed questionnaire survey has a response rate of 20 to 30 percent. A researcher who wants to have 20 to 30 usable responses may need at least 100 potential respondents (samples).

The sample size also depends on the research questions and the statistics used. For chi-square analysis, it is desirable to have at least five cases for each of the cells in the table. A two-by-two table will, therefore, minimally require 20 cases, and still the chance of having a cell with less than five cases is great.

The general rule for determining the sample size is to try to obtain as large a sample as the research can afford. One also has to recognize that sampling is not necessary if the population is accessible and small enough to all be included in the study. Nonrandom sampling, while it has advantages to have a larger sample, is also limited by the biases it inherited. Because a nonrandom sample is intrinsically biased, more cases may merely mean more biases rather than more representation. It may be a better idea to draw two nonrandom samples or use the random assignment to create two samples for the results to be compared and contrasted.

In case study, it is not the number of the sample but the quality of the samples that is of more importance. For qualitative study, a smaller number may not mean something less desirable than a big number.

Data Collection and Instruments

The research questions and the associated research designs dictate the approaches and procedures for data collection as well as the instruments used. Details of the various data collection methods and instrument development issues are presented in Chapter 6, Program Evaluation. The concept of "beginning with the end in mind" is key to data collection. If the researcher wants to explore a particular research topic without any preconceived notions, he may adopt a more qualitative and inductive research design. His data collection instruments may just be his notebook and observation guide.

Another researcher may want to do a more controlled study in which a more elaborated experimental, quantitative, and deductive research design will be used. She may need to use tests and questionnaires, as well as other established tools to collect data suitable for advanced statistical analysis. Other than the research question, a researcher may want to consider the data sources from which she can obtain the data. From there, an appropriate data collection approach or method and its associated tools will be developed to gather the data. Tables 3.4 and 3.5 provide a summary of these various data collection methods and their associated instruments.

Table 3.4 Data Collection Methods

Pre–/Post–Standardized Tests	*Characteristics:* Preexisting tests with a large group of respondents. Tests are administered at two points in time (e.g., the beginning and end of activities).
	Advantages: They offer a rigorous, ready-made context for documenting improvement. They are widely accepted as credible evidence if appropriate for the activity. They may allow for comparison across programs or schools.
	Constraints: The tests may not be designed to measure the outcomes the program expects. They lose validity if changes in content, administration, or context occur.
Pre–/Post–Program–Based Tests	*Characteristics:* An alternative to standardized tests. National service programs can create such tests to document specific knowledge or performance, but they capture gains directly related to the consequences of national service program activities. These tests are administered at two or more points in time (e.g., the beginning, quarterly, and the end of activities).
	Advantages: The tests are widely accepted as credible evidence of accomplishments if they are directly related to the services provided. They must be administered to respondents both before their participation (a "pre-test") and upon the conclusion of their participation (a "post-test").
	Constraints: It is difficult to verify the degree to which the responses to test questions are an accurate representation of changes in knowledge or skills because of the program. They may not show changes in a consistent manner.
Logs or Tally Sheets	*Characteristics:* A log documents a participant's attendance or achievement, such as "acquisition of skills." It is especially appropriate for programs where it is difficult to identify exactly what will be learned at any point in time.
	Advantages: Logs are performance based. They accommodate a range of starting and ending points and are easy to complete.
	Constraints: Data are unreliable and invalid if observation/recording is not systematic. Logs should include specific questions or categories directly tied to the results and indicators to prompt the user.
Rubrics	*Characteristics:* Rubrics provide a detailed scale that can be used to measure performance. Rubrics are used either with other records, such as portfolios or written work, or with direct performance, such as conversation.
	Advantages: Rubrics can be used to measure a variety of abilities and behaviors. When well constructed, they are relatively easy to administer.
	Constraints: Developing a good rubric takes time. Off-the-shelf rubrics may be useful, but you need to match the rubric to the services you provide. The people administering the rubric must be thoroughly trained in its use.
Performance Ratings	*Characteristics:* Set of questions regarding the manner in which national service participants carry out their activities. The focus is on issues such as attitude and ability to carry out specific tasks.
	Advantages: Data collection can be integrated with regularly scheduled meetings with the supervisor, or accomplished through a supervisor questionnaire.
	Constraints: Rating for performance standards must be explicit and consistent. The rating process must be short and focused. Supervisors are unlikely to be able to assess the persistence of any traits observed outside the job site. It may be difficult to link to outcomes of participant development activities.
Interviews	*Characteristics:* Data are collected orally. The interviewer asks clearly defined, systematic questions. Usually questions are predetermined and limited to a specific topic. Sometimes there are additional questions asked to elicit a more detailed response.
	Advantages: The data demonstrate specific examples of the observed outcome of national service programs. Interviews allow for flexibility.
	Constraints: The interviewer must be skilled in the process of interviewing and conduct the interviews in a systematic manner to ensure unbiased results.

Surveys	*Characteristics:* The data are collected in a written format. Each respondent provides data on a set of clearly defined questions.
	Advantages: The data can be used to demonstrate specific examples of the observed outcome of national service programs.
	Constraints: It is difficult to balance specific and general questions and ensure that larger or unexpected issues are not missed. Survey instruments must be completed consistently to avoid biased results.
Focus Groups	*Characteristics:* A moderator guides a group discussion involving six to ten individuals representing specific stakeholders.
	Advantages: Focus groups provide specific, pertinent data. Group interaction can produce more information than individual interviews.
	Constraints: A specific set of skills is required of the focus group moderator. Data are difficult to summarize succinctly.
Plugging into Existing Information	*Characteristics:* Other sources have collected the existing data, often statistical in nature. This may range from student grade point averages to neighborhood crime statistics.
	Advantages: Existing rules are often perceived as being more reliable and less subject to bias than other kinds of data. It can be less burdensome than other methods and prevents duplicating data collection.
	Constraints: The usefulness depends on whether the program being evaluated can reasonably be expected to influence the data directly. A variety of factors typically influence these indicators, and they may change very slowly even if a national service program does have a great deal of impact on the problem being studied (e.g., crime statistics).

Data Analysis

In this section, some of the basic statistical analysis will be discussed. Data collection methods and instruments are discussed in other chapters in this book. Statistical analysis is an effective tool for grant writing and program evaluation. It helps tell the story through numbers with authority and clarity.

A concept is the basic unit of a phenomenon or theory. Each concept could become a variable. Each variable has many attributes or values. Based on the characteristics of these attributes, these variables could be categorized into four levels of measurement: nominal, ordinal, interval, and ratio. The level of measurement of a variable dictates the type of statistics that could be used for analysis.

Four Levels of Measurement

Nominal   A nominal variable is a categorical variable that has discrete values. The etymology for the word *nominal* is the Latin word "name." Different names refer to different people or objects. These values are mutually exclusive in that being in one category means not belonging to another category. At the same time, they are also inclusive in that each value includes all cases in its class. First graders and second graders are two complete sets of students. "First graders" is what all "first graders" are, and "first graders" cannot be "second graders" at the same time.

Table 3.5 Data Collection Methods and Instruments

Guiding Questions:

1. What do you want to find out? (Beginning with the end in mind)
2. What is available to you? (Data sources)
3. What types of data collection approach will you use? (Methods)
4. What types of tools do you need and how do you develop them? (Instruments: including indicators and targets)

	Questionnaire Survey	Interview Survey	Focus Group	Observation
Examples	≫ Needs assessment survey ≫ Satisfaction survey ≫ Pre/Post questionnaire	≫ Intake interview ≫ Exit interview ≫ Key informant interview	≫ End-of-the-year program impact focus group	≫ Home safety check ≫ Classroom behavior observation
Likely Data Source	≫ Service providers, volunteers, service recipients, general public, samples of groups, etc. ≫ Secondary data	≫ Secondary data ≫ Key informants ≫ Experts	≫ Key informants ≫ Experts	≫ Whatever was present ≫ Behaviors
Data Collection Methods	≫ Respondents are reached in person, by mail, by phone, or through Internet. ≫ On their own, they respond to the instruments (questionnaire) in their own words. ≫ Document what respondents put in writing.	≫ Respondents are reached in person, by mail, by phone, or through internet. ≫ The interviewer records the responses on to the instrument (interview guide). ≫ Document what interviewees say to the interviewer.	≫ A small group of respondents are recruited and meet through a structured group process in responding to a set of structured questions. ≫ Guided discussions ≫ Document what participants' express during the group process.	≫ Evaluator records behaviors observed and documents them on a record form or checklist. ≫ Observe the presence, frequency, duration, and strength of the happening. ≫ Document what people do.
Instruments	≫ Questionnaire	≫ Interview Guide	≫ Focus Group Discussion Guide	≫ Observation Record Form
Types of Results Assessed	≫ Output, intermediate, and end outcome	≫ Output, intermediate, and end outcome	≫ Intermediate and end outcome	≫ Intermediate and end outcome

Meals-on-Wheels and Home-Visiting program: An Example for Data Collection Methods and Instruments

1. Research Question: Does this Meals-on-Wheels and Home Visiting program increase elderly clients' ability to stay in their own homes?

2. Data Sources: Elderly clients, service providers, members, volunteers, and secondary data

3. Data Collection Methods:

   ➢ Volunteers will observe the well-being of the elderly by using the Home Safety Checklist. (Observation)

   ➢ They will also interview the elderly or the caregiver at the beginning and the end of the program year using the Stay-at-Home Interview Guide. (Interview)

   ➢ A sample of the volunteers will be selected to complete a Service Quality and Input Questionnaire at the sixth month of the program to identify ways to improve. (Questionnaire)

   ➢ Eight representatives from partner agencies and service recipients will participate in a Program Enhancement Focus Group meeting at the end of the program year to evaluate the overall outcome of the program and make suggestions for future directions. (Focus Group)

4. Instruments and Indicators Development:

   ➢ Home Safety Checklist (What items indicate the degree or the presence of safety in the home? e.g., adequate lighting, fire hazard, food, and medication, etc.)

   ➢ Stay-at-Home Interview Guide (Sample indicators: How many elderly report that they may need to reside in a nursing home if this program is not available to them. An elder who is not able to cook for himself, now has regular visits from his caregiver, etc.)

   ➢ Service Quality and Input Questionnaire (What constitutes quality service?)

   ➢ Program Enhancement Focus Group Discussion Guide (Indicator: Overall, what has happened to the targeted elderly because of this program?)

Variables such as gender, place of birth, social security number, or school attended are examples of nominal variables. Frequency distribution, counts, or percentages are common statistics used to describe and summarize these variables. A nominal variable is the most basic type of variable. In fact, by nature, all variables have the properties of being nominal variables.

Ordinal   This variable has a particular inherent order or ranking. In terms of level of education, being a high school student means one has more years of education than a grade-school student has. For shirt sizes, a large-size shirt is bigger than a medium-size one, which is bigger than a small-size shirt. For ordinal variables, the differences among its values are not constant (e.g., equal). The difference in the amount of soda between a large-size drink and a medium-size drink does not necessarily equal the difference between a medium-size drink and a small one. Similarly, the distances between "very helpful," "helpful," "neutral," "not helpful," and "not very helpful" are not equal. In addition to frequency distribution and percentage, ordinal-level variables could be summarized by statistics such as median and ranking.

Interval   An interval variable has a meaningful distance (i.e., constant or equal between its adjacent values). Today's average temperature is 75 degrees Fahrenheit, which is 10 degrees warmer than yesterday's 65-degree average. That 10-degree difference between 75 and 65 is the same difference as that between 65 and 55. Interval-level variables have the *arbitrary zero*, which is artificially created. The so-called zero-degree temperature is set differently and made for different temperature scales. Zero degrees Fahrenheit is not the same as zero degrees Celsius. Values of interval-level variables have the quantitative quality that would allow them to be used for more advanced and complex calculations.

Ratio   A ratio variable is an interval-level variable that has a *natural zero (absolute zero)*. Temperature has an arbitrary zero. A zero-degree temperature does not mean the absence of temperature. A person's age and height, number of participants, miles traveled, or dollar amount in a checking account are examples of ratio-level variables. It is possible to have an absolute zero number of participants and zero dollars in one's checking account. (Zero dollars means absolutely no money in the checking account, but it is not an indication of the absence of one's wealth, which includes more than money in the checking account.)

The existence of the natural zero allows these values to be calculated for their ratio—a meaningful fraction. Someone who is 40 years old is exactly twice the age of a 20-year-old. A program that has 90 participants has three times more people than another program with only 30 participants. A temperature of 60 degrees is, however, not twice as hot as 30 degrees, because temperature is only an interval variable, not a ratio.

Table 3.6 Statistics and Levels of Measurement

Statistics	Nominal	Ordinal	Interval	Ratio
Frequency, percentage, mode, presentation of data	Yes	Yes	Yes	Yes
Median, ranking, descriptive statistics	No	Yes	Yes	Yes
Addition, subtraction, mean, descriptive, inferential and other advanced statistics	No	No	Yes	Yes
Ratio, fraction	No	No	No	Yes

Interval/Ratio   In human services, researchers and program evaluators usually group interval and ratio levels into one category. The distinction between ratio and interval data is great for scientists, but the distinction is insignificant for most social science researches. As a result, it is common to consider only three levels of measurement: nominal, ordinal, and interval/ratio. Different levels of measurement possess different properties for statistical analysis. Table 3.6 summarizes the appropriate statistics for the four levels of measurement.

Ranking the Variables   Inherently, there is a ranking among these different levels of measurement. Potentials for statistical analysis are limited for nominal-level data, but the sky is the limit for ratio and interval-level variables. Researchers should use the highest allowable level of measurement for data analysis. However, there are times when lowering the level of measurement may create a better data set for analysis. For example, about 50 people of all age groups have provided their real ages for a study. The age distribution may be too spread out, so that the researchers regroup them into the categories of older adult, adult, and youth. As a result, the data for age have been changed from being at the ratio level to the ordinal or nominal level. These regroupings allow the researchers to better manage the data and be able to make comparisons across different age groups.

Dependent and Independent Variables

Variables within a theory or a service program are related to each other. Depending on their relationships and functions, they have many names. Among them are independent variable (e.g., the instigator, the intervention or treatment, and program activities) and dependent variable (the one that is affected or changed, expected changes, and outcomes). The dependent variable (X) is a function of the independent variable (Y). The formula to express this relationship is: $X = f(Y)$.

When a service provider believes the relationship with a trusted adult could contribute to the improvement of targeted children's self-confidence, mentoring will likely be included in the program design. In this program, mentoring is the independent variable, which is expected to improve the child's self-confidence level, the dependent variable.

Statistics

Data collection is only part of the story for research and program evaluation; data analysis is another key component. Statistical methods are often used to achieve this task for analysis. Statistics is a mathematical science that helps describe and summarize the features of the data that have been collected. Based on the data obtained, one could also make inferences and predictions about the topics being studied. In numbers and logics, statistics helps program staff and researchers tell their stories and provide a base for rational decision making. In program evaluation, statistics illustrates program activities and outcomes. It also helps measure the attainment of objectives.

Basically, statistics could be categorized into descriptive and inferential statistics. Descriptive statistics summarize and present data as what they are. Inferential statistics attempt to infer from the samples about the population, draw conclusions, give explanations, or make predictions. As a result, inferential statistics also involve normal curve distribution, samples, and randomization, experimental designs, and hypothesis testing. Table 3.7 summarizes some of the key components for both descriptive and inferential statistics.

One of the difficulties for practitioners who do not use statistics on a regular basis is to decide which statistics method is the most appropriate one. The research questions and the quality and characteristics of the data dictate which types of statistics are appropriate. Table 3.8 provides a framework for choosing the correct statistics for analysis.

Table 3.7 Basic Statistics

Descriptive Statistics

Descriptive statistics summarize, present, and describe data as what they are, but do not make hypothesis-related conclusions.

I. Presentation of Data
    Present the data as they are and their summaries

    A. Frequency distributions

        1. Absolute frequency distributions
        2. Percentage distributions

    B. Graphic presentation

        1. Bar graphs—nominal—height
        2. Histograms—interval & ratio—height & width
        3. Pie-charts—nominal to ratio—segments of the whole
        4. Frequency polygons—interval
        5. Scattergrams—interval & ratio – association

II. Measures of Central Tendency
    Summarizing the data or reporting on what attributes are "typical." They also provide a common denominator for comparing.

        1. Mode—tells which value(s) in the distribution of values is observed most frequently. It is the most "popular" value and is used for nominal or higher-level data.
        2. Median—divides any distribution of values into two equal parts or proportions. It is the "middle" point. It is least affected by extreme values and therefore is the most stable one. It is used for ordinal or higher-level data.
        3. Mean—is the sum of all the values of a variable divided by the number of values. It is the "average." It is affected by extreme scores and used for interval or ratio level data.

    We must consider reporting more than one measure of central tendency.

III. Measures of Dispersion (Variability)

The way in which values scatter themselves (the spread of distribution of values) around a measure of central tendency (mean, mode, or median).

1. Minimum—the lowest value
2. Maximum—the highest values
3. Range—(max.—min.)
4. Variance—the mean of the squared difference. The larger the variance, the greater the dispersion around the mean.
5. Standard deviation—a measure of the dispersion of scores around the arithmetic mean in the original score units. The larger the standard deviation, the greater the spread of scores around the mean.

Inferential Statistics

Inferential statistics attempt to infer from the samples about the population, draw conclusions, give explanations, or make predictions. In other words, they test the hypothesis.

I. Test of Association/Correlation

It tests how things change together: Positive or negative, high or low, statistically significant or not significant.

Tests: Chi Square, Spearman's Rho, Kendall's Tau, Pearson's r

II. Test of Differences

How significantly different?

Test: Chi Square, U test, Z test, t tests, F test, and ANOVA

Related Concepts

I. Hypothesis Testing

Research hypothesis, Null hypothesis: reject or fail to reject

II. Statistical Significance

Rejection levels
One-tailed or two-tailed
Statistically significant versus meaningful findings

Table 3.8 Choosing the Appropriate Type of Statistics

A. Descriptive Statistics

1. **Presentation of data:** Frequency distribution, percentage, graphs
2. **Measures of central tendency:** Mean, mode, median
3. **Measures of dispersion:** Minimum, maximum, range, variance, standard deviation

B. Inferential Statistics

Level of Measurement	Test for Significant Association/Correlation	Test for Significance of Differences
	➤ To what extent are the two variables correlated?	➤ Is the difference between groups at a significant level? ➤ Is the difference a result of chance or a result of the independent variable?
Nominal	**Mean, Mode, Median, Range, Percentage, Chi-Square** ➤ Two nominal variables ➤ The correlation between programs (nominal variable—BA or MA) and graduates' success in obtaining jobs (nominal variable—Yes or No) ➤ Is there a significant relationship between level of education (BA or MA) and graduates' success (successful or unsuccessful) in obtaining jobs?	**Chi Square, McNemar test** ➤ Two nominal variables ➤ The difference between BA and MA (independent variable) graduates' success (dependent variable) in obtaining jobs. ➤ Is there a significant difference between BA and MA graduates in their success in obtaining jobs following their completion of their studies?

(Continued)

Table 3.8 Choosing the Appropriate Type of Statistics   *(Continued)*

	Spearman's Rho, Kendall's Tau	**Mann–Whitney U, Wilcoxon, Sign test, Kolmogorov–Smirnov**
Ordinal	➤ Test for correlation (strength, direction) between two groups on an ordinal scale. ➤ Test for correlation between husbands and wives (nominal variable) on an ordinal scale (nonsupportive, supportive, very supportive) designed to measure spouse's attitudes toward each other regarding the fact that they are childless. ➤ Is there a statistically significant correlation between groups (husband or wife) and their attitudes toward their spouses regarding the fact that they are childless? ➤ Test for regression (prediction) between two ordinal scales. ➤ To what extent clients' level of satisfaction (low, moderate, high) has a correlation to clients' level of participation (low, moderate, high)? ➤ Will clients who have a high level of participation also have a high level of satisfaction and vice versa?	➤ Test for difference (significant or not significant) between two groups on an ordinal scale. ➤ Test for difference between husbands and wives (nominal variable) on an ordinal scale (nonsupportive, supportive, very supportive) designed to measure spouse's attitudes toward each other regarding the fact that they are childless. ➤ Is there a statistically significant difference between husbands and wives in their attitudes toward each other regarding the fact that they are childless?
	Pearson's *r*	**One-sample t-test, independent t-test, correlated t-test, Z test, F test**
Interval & Ratio	➤ Test for correlation (degree of linear relationship) between two interval/ratio variables. ➤ Is there a significant correlation between students' ages and their test scores for the course?	➤ Test for significant difference between two groups on an interval/ratio scale. ➤ Is the person really from this community—a true representative? ➤ A pre- and postcomparison postcomparison of students on their test scores. ➤ Is there a significant difference between the students' test scores and their ages? **ANOVA, ANCOVA** (Analysis of variance, "extended t-test") 1. Test for statistically significant difference between two or more groups on an interval/ratio variable. 2. Is there a significant difference among BA, MA, and PhD (nominal) on their IQ scores (interval/ratio)?

References

Atherton, C. R., & Klemmack, D. L. (1982). *Research methods in social work.* Lexington, MA: D.C. Heath.

Chafetz, J. (1978). *A primer on the construction and testing of theories in sociology.* New York: F. E. Peacock Publishers.

Grinnell, R. M., Jr., & Unrau, Y. A. (eds.). (2008). *Social work research and evaluation* (8th ed.). New York: Oxford University Press.

Moore, K. (1998). *Patterns of inductive reasoning: Developing critical thinking skills.* (4th ed.). Dubuque, IA: Kendall/Hunt Publishing.

Panik, M. J. (2005). *Advanced statistics from an elementary point of view.* Boston: Academic Press.

Pedroni, J. A., & Pimple, K. D. (2001). *A brief introduction to informed consent in research with human subjects.* Retrieved November 23, 2008, from http://poynter.indiana.edu/sas/res/ic.pdf.

Public Health Service Act 301(d), 42 U.S.C. §241(d), as amended by Public Law No. 100–607, Section 163 (November 4, 1988). Retrieved November 22, 2008, from www.irb.arizona.edu/investigator-information/certificate-confidentiality.

Royse, D. (2008). *Research methods in social work* (5th ed.). Belmont, CA: Brooks/Cole.

Stake, R. (n.d.). *Summative vs. formative evaluation.* Retrieved November 13, 2008, from http://jan.ucc.nau.edu/edtech/etc667/proposal/evaluation/summative_vs._formative.html.

Trochim, W. (2006). *Research methods knowledge base* (3rd ed.). Retrieved January 16, 2009, from www.socialresearchmethods.net/kb/qualdeb.php.

U.S. Department of Health and Human Services. (2005). *Code of federal regulations* [45 CFR 46.102(i)]. Retrieved November 23, 2008, from www.hhs.gov/ohrp/humansubjects/guidance/45cfr46.htm#46.102.

U.S. Department of Housing and Urban Development. *Federal definition of homelessness.* Retrieved December 9, 2008, from www.hud.gov/homeless/definition.cfm.

Yuen, F. (2006). Family health social work practice and change. In F. Yuen (ed.), *Social work practice with children and families: A family health approach* (pp. 1–20). Binghamton, NY: Haworth Press.

Yuen, F., Bein, A., & Lum, D. (2006). Inductive learning. In D. Lum, *Culturally competent practice: A framework for understanding diverse groups and justice issues* (3rd ed.). (pp. 166–167). Pacific Grove, CA: Brooks/Cole.

Yuen, F. K. O., & Terao, K. (2003). *Practical grant writing and program evaluation.* Pacific Grove, CA: Brooks/Cole–Thomson Learning.

4

Program Planning and Evaluation

What is the core purpose behind program evaluation? It is to determine the effectiveness of a program's response to the identified needs within the target community. Can the services offered by the program bring about some needed change for the target population? Responsible examination of the question of change attributable to the program's service requires that multiple processes, strategies, and structures are in place prior to the evaluation.

This chapter examines key elements in program planning and identifies tools that set the stage for the implementation of an evaluation.

> ➤ The *needs assessment* establishes and describes the compelling issues for a target population in the community and existing or new service plans for addressing those issues.

> ➤ The *program planning formula* outlines the key components of a program using a handy equation.

> ➤ The *theory of change* (also called program theory), a predecessor to the logic model, makes explicit the linkage between a valid conceptualization of the problem and an appropriate means of remedy provided by the program contribution. It answers the question of a program plan, "Does the response make sense?"

> ➤ By developing a *logic model*, a program obtains a snapshot of the alignment between the need, program services, and results. How are the intended improvements in the social conditions or lives of the beneficiaries to occur and under what circumstances (e.g., resources, activities)? It answers the question, "Does it or will it work?"

Program evaluation is built upon a framework, beginning with a careful description of the social problem the program is expected to address and using a particular service model attuned to the community factors. The theory of change and logic model further contribute to a strong evaluation process. This chapter reviews the necessary tasks and considerations preceding an evaluation that are essential to its successful launch and implementation.

Needs Assessment

What makes the assessment of the need for a program so fundamental, of course, is that a program cannot be effective at ameliorating a social problem if there is no problem to begin with or if the program services do not actually relate to the need. (Rossi, Freeman, and Lipsey, 1999, p. 119)

The La Vida Clinic has served the neighborhood Latino population in Fruitvale for more than 15 years, providing low-cost health care with a focus on prenatal care, infant/child health, and care for HIV/AIDS patients. In the last few years, staff have noticed changes in the neighborhood with the arrival of Hmong families, many of whom have begun to inquire about the clinic's services. La Vida struggles to support its current client base, Latino immigrants, but some program staff are advocating that La Vida develop and fund a new staff position in community health to serve the Hmong people. Others believe it is premature to plan a program expansion around a population that staff has little expertise in serving, not to mention limited knowledge about their health services use patterns. In the end, the board recommends a needs assessment.

Define Needs Assessment

The "[n]eeds assessment . . . is a systematic approach to identifying social problems, determining their extent, and accurately defining the target population to be served and the nature of their service needs" (Rossi et al., 1999, p. 119). As an evaluative study, the needs assessment responds to questions about the need for program services, whether it is to explore a new initiative or review an existing service to determine its priority and value among, within, and across service; or areas. This method of gathering and examining information is meant to determine the current status and service needs of a defined population or perhaps a geographic area.

In considering a needs assessment, there is an assumption of the existence of a need; the gap between "what is" and "what should be." This gap between the real and ideal is acknowledged by society as the social condition judged as substandard or unacceptable and deemed worthy of attention. Finally, the need is perceived as "potentially amenable to change," and social programs or interventions are identified as the vehicles to remediate the condition (Reviere, Berkowitz, Carter, & Gergusan 1996; Rossi et al., 1999; Witkin & Altschuld, 1995). Chapter 2 of this book, Community and Target Population, Service Providers, and Funding Sources, provides a more complete discussion of the need types.

Needs Assessment and Program Evaluation

Evaluations use various methods and approaches to address different categories of evaluation questions. The needs assessment tackles one of the most fundamental sets of program evaluation questions; that is, to develop an understanding of the characteristics of a social problem that a particular program is expected to remedy through the service or intervention with a targeted population.

Needs assessment and program evaluation share many of the same goals, strategies, and methodologies. Both are important to the decision-making process. Many of the methods, data collection processes and analysis, and reporting strategies are the same. Furthermore, each one informs the other; a strong needs assessment sets the framework for thoughtful activities (service, intervention) and structures the program evaluation questions. Likewise, the program evaluation, through the measurement of the impact of an intervention, serves as a catalyst for a needs assessment, specifying the questions that need to be addressed for program expansion and improvement, realignment of services, or the reexamination and update of the earlier defined social problem or condition.

The program evaluation responds to the question "Did the services address the need?" The evaluation measures the current or past service; that is, "What happened or changed as a result of the intervention?" The needs assessment informs the future, "What should happen or exist in the target community?" (Titcomb, 2000). The goal of the needs assessment is to ascertain, "What is the need in the community?" The interplay of the needs assessment and evaluation are apparent in the following example. A needs assessment uncovers high rates of infant illness among recent East Asian immigrants because of limited access to early child health care. The need will inform the evaluation. Even before the intervention is up and running, in this case, an Infant Health and Vaccination program, the evaluation questions are formulated to respond to the identified need, "Did the vaccination program reduce infant illness among recent immigrants?"

Purpose of the Needs Assessment

The needs assessment is used by human service providers for program planning and advocacy of program direction, for proposals for funding, and to set the course of the program evaluation of services. Program services require financial decisions and community commitments in the context of limited or diminishing resources. Ever increased levels of program accountability to stakeholder groups require prudent expenditures, and interventions, especially during economic downturns. The needs assessment can be a powerful tool in the decision-making milieu.

The needs assessment can produce information that is used to prioritize who gets assistance or service, how much assistance to provide, and what service model or strategy is used. It assists in determining the appropriate service approach for the target population. The needs assessment serves human service organizations that are interested in planning a new service, expanding existing services, or reducing or eliminating services. Furthermore, it can shed light on how an organization's mission is aligned with the needs of the community it currently serves or hopes to serve in the future. By uncovering community conditions, the needs assessment can identify gaps in service; what does not exist but is needed. The needs assessment also renders an inventory of resources, complementary services, or competition to providing services.

The needs assessment is critical to the effective design of new programs. The inquiry will inform the program components, including the program's theory of change, mission, and practice. It is equally important for an existing program, such as La Vida Clinic. The needs assessment is the means by which an evaluator or staff determines if there is an actual need for program expansion, and if so, what program services are most appropriate to fulfill that need for the target population. In many circumstances, whether in response to community accountability or funding, an established program mission and implementation may be called into question. It cannot merely assume that a proposed set of services is needed or that the services it provides are well suited to the nature of the need. Rossi, Freeman, and Lipsey (1999) note the opportunity to scrutinize assumptions in detail and review social conditions of the target population and the appropriateness of service.

Key Steps in Designing a Needs Assessment

Let's look at the steps of inquiry commonly employed in a needs assessment (modified from the work of McKillip, 1998). The steps include the following:

1. Determine the purpose and target population.
2. Describe the target population and service environment.
3. Determine the scope of the problem/social condition.
4. Describe the nature of the need.
5. Report findings.
6. Make decisions based on the assessment.

1. *Determine the purpose and target population.* (McKillip uses the terms *uses* and *users*.) Why is the needs assessment necessary? What do you want to know? How will the information be used, by whom and for whom?

La Vida Clinic wants to know if it should expand its service and target a new population. First, it must clearly describe the explicit concern driving the inquiry. The overall purpose of the needs assessment—to be able to make a decision—requires early consideration of communicating the needs assessment results to the key stakeholders and decision makers; that is, those who will act on the results of the needs assessment and those who will be affected by it.

Define the target population of the needs assessment. The involvement of multiple stakeholder groups will facilitate the process and influence the implementation of its recommendations. The needs assessment will be most successful when the content and scope of inquiry is well defined. Clarifying the uses of the needs assessment allows for a more focused investigation of the problems and solutions that can be entertained. On the flip side, such specificity may limit the problems and solutions identified in Step 4.

Check the fit with the theory of change, resources, and barriers. Before moving forward, address other relevant questions which, if left unanswered, will compromise the utility of the needs assessment. For instance, is the perceived need in line with the organization's mission? Does the organization have the capacity to meet the need? Is there another organization better suited for this service and partnering with them would be more appropriate? If the need is as one expects, will funding and staff be available to implement the intended program? Does the organization have the ability to access the population? In the case of the earlier example, La Vida Clinic currently focuses on serving the Latino population. They will need to review the organizational mission, capacity, and values before conducting a needs assessment targeting the Hmong population.

Establish a working group and determine roles. What human resources are needed? Who can help find out? Depending on the scope of the needs assessment and the external resources available, establishing a working group ensures accountability and shares the workload. A needs assessment working group might include stakeholders representing the organization's interest from varied perspectives:

➤ Decision makers (board members, staff members, community representatives)

➤ Partners (formal and informal community leaders—church, school)

➤ Existing nonprofits (health services and professionals) working in the content and geographic area and with the intended recipients of service

➤ Internal or external evaluator

2. *Describe the target population and service environment.* Develop a full account of the target population and service environment.

First, define the target population. Rossi, et al. (1999) note that a target population may be defined as the individual (e.g., pregnant teenagers, AIDS patients), group (e.g., families, institutions) "geographically and politically related areas" (e.g., towns), or physical entities (e.g., stores, houses).

Furthermore, targets can be understood as direct and indirect; the group that immediately receives services (direct) and the group that eventually receives services or service effects (indirect). If indirect targets are the focus, effective pathways leading from immediate to ultimate targets need to be clearly articulated. A health program whose goal is to train community health workers (direct) to provide health outreach services to homebound elders (indirect) will want to ensure that the health workers have access to those elders (Rossi et al., 1999).

Once defined, describe the target population. What are the characteristics of the target population? The target population can be identified by social and demographic characteristics (e.g., socioeconomic, linguistic, and cultural), location and dispersion, the problem, level of difficulty, and conditions.

Other target population components to consider:

➤ *Specify Target.* Politicians, professionals, funding agencies, and other key stakeholders may hold different and even conflicting opinions of the target specifications. The needs assessment can help eliminate conflict that might arise from groups talking past each other by investigating the perspective of all the significant stakeholders on target definitions and ensuring that none is left out.

➤ *Establish target boundaries.* This determines who or what is included and excluded when the specification is applied. Generally, the more criteria a target population has, the smaller the possible population. The target specification,

"Latina women in Los Angeles," would yield a very large population whereas "Guatemalan women who have children in public schools in South Central Los Angeles" would specify a much smaller target population.

➤ *Determine need and demand.* The in-need population (population who currently manifests the condition) may not want the program. The needs assessment determines the in-need population who want and will use services.

➤ *Investigate target rates.* The occurrence or existence of a particular condition expressed as a proportion of units in the relevant population further defines the population. For instance, knowing that two out of three smokers will die of smoking-related illness (e.g., respiratory disease, mouth or lung cancer) is crucial to understanding the target and designing effective program services.

Correctly defining and identifying the targets for intervention is critical to success of the service. Correct target identification shapes the approach and sets the parameters both at the beginning of the policy, planning, and proposal phase and later during implementation and evaluation. Target identification is not an easy process to accomplish, because definitions and estimates of target populations are often in flux and the target population definitions may be altered or even abandoned. Even so, one must attempt an accurate understanding of the target population if one hopes to design useful policy and effective programs.

➤ *Review use and appropriateness of current services.* What service models have worked well with this population? Understanding the cultural and social context informs the service strategy and approach. Ascertain how the target population defines success, what they value, if they are receiving services, and how the population you hope to serve is currently receiving services. How do clients (beneficiaries) access services now? Compare those who currently use services with the target population to reveal unmet needs or barriers to implementation. Consider the modifications needed to handle the target population or unique social conditions.

Describe eligibility requirements (What does it take to get the service?), service capacity (How much service is available?), and accessibility (Is the service being delivered in a culturally appropriate fashion?—i.e., does the population have access to speakers of their language and culturally competent staff?). Resource inventories detailing services available can identify gaps in service, programs already providing the services, and potential competing programs.

3. *Determine the scope of the problem/social condition.* At this juncture, the needs assessment focuses on determining the scope of the target population's problem (How big is the population problem and how pervasive?) and possible solutions.

Ultimately, the description of those solutions become the design and funding requirements of an intervention geared to the size, distribution, and density of the problem. How can the information be collected? How will you find out what you need to know? Specifying the size of the problem and where it is located geographically (e.g., rural, inner city) and socially (e.g. low income, migrant labor) requires detailed knowledge about the population.

For example, a program considering how to best serve the homeless population (defined as those living in cars, shelters, or on streets without family ties) might investigate neighborhoods where the population is found and also identify other social problems associated with the homeless individuals (e.g., drug addiction, alcoholism, mental illness).

There are several needs assessment approaches. The questions and scope of the assessment inform the type of methods and how many methods to employ. Multiple sources for the assessment strengthen the identification of the need. Rubin and Babbie (2008) list several major needs assessment approaches for a community. They include both existing and original data such as key informants, community forum, rates-under-treatment, social indicators, survey of communities or target groups, and focus groups.

Existing data sources can provide information to identify the need:

> *Current population survey.* The U.S. Census is the primary population survey and can be disaggregated to state and local levels. Like all instruments, it has limitations, such as it undercounts several population groups, including African Americans, Hispanics, and the homeless.

> *Social indicators.* Social indicators are often used to describe or project population trends and report statistics on relevant variables and estimate the needs. These regularly occurring measures are used to estimate the size and distribution of a problem and the status of social conditions. Social indicators are limited in coverage, mainly providing data in the areas of poverty and employment, criminal victimization, and national program participation. The poverty rate, school dropout rate, child abuse reports, and drug use statistics are the common indicators. Existing data sources, often federal agencies, are charged with tracking trends (e.g., Bureau of Justice Statistics in Department of Justice, Survey of Income and Program participants tracking participation in various social programs such as food stamps).

> *Agency records.* Agency records tend to be excellent for describing the characteristics of the population. However, they are typically limited with respect to the rate of incidence in the community. For instance, an organization that works with AIDS clients will certainly be able to provide rich detail about the AIDS cases that come through their door, but will have only partial information about the incidence of AIDS.

Existing data may not be available or may not be specific enough to the particular locale or target population in question. In this case, *original data* will need to be collected. The degree of accuracy needed of the estimates will reflect the method used. Expert testimony or knowledgeable informants may be able to provide the level of accuracy needed. If not, a more comprehensive or large-scale sample may be needed. For instance, in the case of identifying the number of AIDS cases in a community to determine appropriate services, accurate measures may well be required. The following are common methods used to collect original data for needs assessment:

➤ *Key informants (interviews or surveys)* prove to be one of the easiest approaches to obtaining estimates. Key informants are those persons whose position or experience provide them with unique knowledge of the community and perspective on the magnitude and distribution of the problem. Included among key informants are community leaders and professionals, current clientele, or, in the case of a new program, representatives of those who are being affected. Grassroots individuals often provide as much, if not more, important information as elected officials, formal leaders, or professionals. There are limitations to being able to extrapolate to a larger or different population set, and service providers themselves are prone to overestimate the incidence in the general population. However, they provide useful information about characteristics of certain populations and the nature of service needs. (Hamilton, Rabinowitz, and Alschuler, Inc., 1987)

➤ *Surveys of communities or target groups* are methods that directly gather information from a large number of respondents in the community. Using appropriate sampling methods and appropriate research designs improves the quality of the information when these surveys are used. See Chapter 7, Learning by Doing, for a sample of a needs assessment survey.

➤ *Focus groups and community forums* bring together selected knowledgeable people for a discussion of a particular topic, supervised by a facilitator. The group selection may be based on the experience or possible use of service by individuals in the group.

Focus groups provide immediate, interactive, and collective information to the service providers. There are many ways to use a focus group for data collection. Chapter 7, Learning by Doing, presents a focus group protocol. However, because focus group results are highly dependent on the selection of participants, personal bias, and other factors, using focus groups has many disadvantages. Community forums, such as town hall meetings and open forums, provide an opportunity for people to come together to express their concerns, seek common ground, and identify solutions. Similar to a focus group, existing community forums or those called together on behalf of the evaluator, can provide collective insights.

➤ *On-site observations* allow an eyewitness account of the condition and/or target population, although this is not always easy. Visiting complementary or competing agencies can render rich descriptive information about the nature of the population.

➤ *Forecasting needs* requires a critical review of the forecast techniques and the expertise and specialized skills necessary to do credible forecasting. Forecasting works on assumptions and judgment for an unknowable future. The validity of forecasting is always open to challenge and thus, it is imperative that there is an explicit rendering of the assumptions and techniques.

➤ *Rates-under-treatment* is a documentary study or secondary data analysis on service utilization. It demonstrates the gap between demand and supply of services. Utilizing a waiting list is one of the common methods that could provide such information. This is used to predict and plan for future service usage.

➤ Depending on the level of effort appropriate for the context of the needs assessment, one or several methods of inquiry may be employed.

4. *Describe the nature of the need.* At this point in the process, the analyses of the data collected contribute to a fuller understanding of the problem and appropriate and, hopefully, creative solutions. The quantitative data of the needs assessment yield estimate the extent of the condition and distribution of the problem. The qualitative data produce useful descriptive information about the specific characteristics of the need within that population. Together the data portray the detailed, structured knowledge of a specific need including its nature, the nuance of the problem or condition, and potential service opportunities.

As it is not sufficient for an organization to offer a program in some standard fashion, unresponsive to the appropriateness to the target population, the needs assessment reveals how the target population experiences the problem, their perceptions about relevant services, and barriers and difficulties they encounter in attempting to access services. In short, understanding the target population and its popular beliefs and perceptions reveals how the problems manifests themselves in the context of the target population. The needs assessment should also expose service gaps and suggest potential solutions. With the identification of the need, the problems, and possible solutions, the gathered information can be integrated to produce recommendations for action.

5. *Report findings.* Thoughtful communication to stakeholders must not be underestimated. Who needs to know what and how? What reporting vehicle is suitable to the stakeholder groups? Which stakeholders will you need to consult as you make decisions about what you found out? How will they want to see the data analyzed? These are important questions to frame early in the planning stage. Consider reporting format and timelines for key audiences. The form of communication

necessarily will vary by stakeholder group. Whereas a short oral presentation at the local library may be effective for interested community members and potential clients, a comprehensive written report submitted in a particular format may be the requirement of a potential funder or partner agency. As part of needs assessment reporting, the program will need to identify met and unmet needs, including a gap analysis that provides enough specificity so decisions can be made. Results of the analysis must be communicated clearly to decision makers, users, and other stakeholder groups.

6. *Make decisions based on the assessment.* Ultimately, the goal of the needs assessment is to be able to provide information necessary for decision making. The more explicit and open the needs assessment is throughout the process, the greater the likelihood that results will be accepted and implemented. What does the information gathered say about the proposed program expansion or new interventions? Are there other essential questions that must be addressed before moving on? The needs assessment aids decision makers in the process by providing the evidence and justification on whether to implement a new program, expand existing services, or reduce/eliminate services.

See Chapter 7, Learning by Doing, for a complete needs assessment scenario and samples of instruments.

Program Planning Formula

With a needs assessment in hand, program planning moves to the next stage. Program planning is both a process and a product. As a process, it is a dynamic and evolving course of development. As a product, using a Systems Theory expression, it represents a whole that is greater than the sum of it parts. A program plan is the result of the active interplay of its many key elements. The key elements and their relationships are summarized in a simple, nonmathematical, Program Planning Formula (Yuen and Terao, 2003):

$$P^2 = W^5 \times H^2 \times E$$

- ➢ P^2 = Program Planning
- ➢ W^5 = Why, Who/Whom, What, Where, When
- ➢ H^2 = How, How much
- ➢ E = Evaluation

Let's look more closely at each of these factors.

Why, Who/Whom, What, Where, When

The most important W is the "Why," the reason and purpose of any plan. As a reason, it could be the motivation and the need for the program. It is the rationale for the plan and the action. As a purpose, it represents the aim of the program. Program planning is a goal-oriented activity. Program planning without the "Why" could easily lose its function of being an agent of change and become merely work. Although the "Why" is the anchor of the program, it is not static. It should be dynamic and reflective of the changing demands and evolving conditions. A program that lacks rationale could become confusing and without a goal could cause the people involved to become lost. "Beginning with the end in mind" is one of the mottos for this book.

"Who" and "Whom" are the target population and the people who carry out the program. A Chinese proverb says, "Know others and know yourself, one hundred battles with one hundred wins." The question of "who the clients (or customers) are" may seem basic but is a vitally important one that guides the program to meet the unique needs of the population. Understanding the population may include its demographics, strengths and challenges, history and social backgrounds, as well as its unique connection to the proposed program. The "Whom" includes the program staff, the volunteers, community resources, and other providers. The needs assessment ensures that a program plan matches the needs of the population and the resources required: staff, volunteers, and providers of appropriate qualities and qualifications. Cultural competency is inherent in this consideration. Program activities cannot be effective until they have meaning and value to the service recipients within their cultural context.

"When" is about the schedule and timing; "What" is about the resources and inputs (e.g., equipment and supplies); and "Where" is about the location, facilities, and accessibility. These are basic logistics for the implementation of the program and the attainment of the program goals.

"When" includes the life span of the program. Many programs are time-limited programs in which services are provided within a certain time frame to achieve the objectives. A clearly delineated timeline for the whole project and each of the activities provides the tempo and time table for the program. "What" concerns having the right tools for the right jobs. It would be difficult to teach a computer class on a blackboard without the actual computers and the appropriate software programs.

"Location, location, location," a familiar motto for success in real estate, also applies to human services. Whether the program is appropriately and conveniently located affects its visibility and degree of utilization. Varied and convenient transportation including public transit is often a key concern, particularly for low-income participants. To be more client-centered and less agency-focused, an agency may consider bringing the service to the clients instead of bringing the clients to the agency. The facility used needs to be suitable for the program activities. A cooking class would need a kitchen, and a basketball team needs a basketball court.

In addition to facilities within the agency, program staff needs to be knowledgeable and resourceful in utilizing other facilities in the community. In addition to physical location (i.e., accessibility of the facility), there is also the cultural aspect and other accessibility. A culturally competent agency could provide a sense of cultural connection and accessibility to its clients. Hiring staff who represent the gender or ethnic background of the target population is one of the many strategies, but ethnic and background match is no guarantee for a desired cultural match.

The following is an example that demonstrates the effect of location and cultural competence on successful program implementation. In the 1990s, one of the authors developed a reproductive health education program for newly arrived refugee Cambodian women. The program had a difficult time recruiting participants. All of the targeted women relied on their husbands to drive them to the agency for the two-hour class. The husbands called it a "female's problems" class. It was a dreaded task for these Cambodian men. Using a well-trained Cambodian female staff instead of a non-Asian medical professional, and having the program at the clubhouse of the apartment complex where many of the women lived, and later on in participants' own homes, changed the dynamics of the program. Naming it "Sister to Sister Tea Time" also turned it into something more like a psychosocial group than a class.

With those changes, the clients no longer relied on their husbands to access the program. They could simply drop in, bring a friend, and show off their culinary skills by bringing in the goodies for the gathering. They ate, chatted, exchanged tips, and provided support to each other. They also turned to the agency staff for information and assistance. In the end, the class went beyond the topic of reproductive health. It had become a self-help support group for the participants and a gateway for the agency to engage the underserved population. It all started when the program went to the participants and met them where they were.

How and How Much

"How" is about the program activities. What program activities or interventions are used to achieve the program objectives? Through what steps will the program objectives be achieved? It concerns the program procedures guided by the program objectives and goals. "How" is the operationalization of the program ideas and beliefs. It plays out what should take place when the program puts its idea to work. It is not about what should be done but what *will* be done. "How" could be further broken down into strategies, activities, and tasks.

"How Much" is the fiscal consideration for the program: costs, revenues, and expenses. It is the budget of the program and is a program plan in dollars and cents. There are many ways to develop a budget, which will be discussed in Chapter 5, Grant Proposal Writing. Budgeting provides the program planner a means by which to estimate the cost and benefit of the program and set the parameters for fundraising and expenses. Ideally, program activities drive the budget; in reality, program budget often drives the program activities.

Evaluation

Evaluation helps the program tell its stories: both challenges and successes. It measures the attainment of the program objectives. It provides ongoing feedback as well as an end-of-program report for program improvement. Evaluation asks key questions regarding what was accomplished, what changed, and what the impacts were.

Logic Model as a Tool for Planning and Evaluation and Theory of Change

Successful grant writing and program planning require an understanding of the big picture of the service as well as a thorough articulation of program components. The logic model is a tool that can capture the big-picture concept in a simple and visually helpful format. This section presents the nature of the logic model, its benefits, and how to go about creating a logic model as a program planning tool and in preparation for program evaluation.

Wyatt Knowlton and Philips (2009) classify logic models into two types: theory of change and program logic model. Both are representatives of the same logic but differ in the appearance, detail, and use. The theory of change is conceptual and tests plausibility, "Does it make sense?" whereas the program logic model is operational and tests feasibility, "Will it work?" "A *theory of change* model is simply a general representation of how you believe change will occur. A *program logic* model details resources, planned activities, and their outputs and outcomes over time that reflect intended results" (Wyatt Knowlton and Philips, 2009, p. 5).

What the logic model and theory of change share are a common theory, research practice, and literature. Where they diverge is their point of view and the utility of that viewpoint.

Theory of Change

Theory of change uses limited information to present an idea or program that links to strategies and results. For instance, a program that teaches youth conflict management identifies some strategies, curriculum, and role-play experiences in small groups that will result in positive youth relationships at school. The theory of change presents the core rationale for the expanded program logic model, whether explicit or implicit (part and parcel of program's service and practices but not articulated or recorded as such). Programs are typically very good at knowing what they are doing, but weaker in articulating why they chose to conduct the activities.

The theory of change is a set of assumptions on which the service model is based—why we think the program will work. It embodies expectations, beliefs, experiences, and conventional wisdom, the concept that underlies the activities and structure of service. It influences ideas about the nature of the problems, the resources needed, the expectations for impact, and how the participants work—their behavior motivations and learning styles. These underlying beliefs are validated with research and experience.

Logic Model

Definition and Purpose of the Logic Model   The logic model is a linear approach to program planning and thinking through what should be evaluated. A logic model is a planning tool that diagrams how project goals should be achieved. It combines resources (inputs) and service activities to produce specific results (outputs or outcomes) that address the community need identified by the project. Logic models were introduced in the 1970s, although they did not become part of the commonly used tools available to programs until after the United Way of America published *Measuring Program Outcomes* in 1996 (Wyatt Knowlton and Phillips, 2009).

The program logic model provides a concise visual representation of activities that are the core services of a program. A logic model can assist a program in thinking about the big picture. Logic models can be very helpful in multiyear planning. Logic modeling can be used during the planning and development of the program design, including identifying the results the program intends to achieve. The logic model is particularly valuable for developing results that will be aligned with the activity (i.e., the activity produces the output; the activity and the output produce the outcomes). The "if-then" logic displays how each element is related to one another.

For example, if a children's immunization program is implemented, then children ages 2 through 6 will be immunized; if children ages 2 through 6 are immunized, then fewer children will catch a communicable disease; if fewer children catch a communicable disease, then the schools and neighborhood will be healthier places to live. The logic model can also illustrate how the results from one year may support the anticipated results for the subsequent year. Ultimately, the logic model can help guide the program in selecting important outputs and outcomes related to its project efforts.

Taylor-Powell, Jones, and Henert (2002) note that the logic model is a tool that illuminates and, therefore, strengthens program elements during the planning, management, evaluation, and communication phases.

Planning   In particular, during the planning phase, the logic model makes clear program premises and makes visible (unpacks) stakeholder assumptions. The logic model process uncovers shared understandings about program theory of change, hopefully revealing what is really happening at the ground level. "A logic model serves as a framework and a process for planning to bridge the gap between where you are and where you want to be. . . . Planning a course of action, such as managing a program or charting a course of policy, generally implies some sort of logic model" (Millar, Simeone, and Carnevale, 2001, p. 73).

Program Management   Although the logic model is not a work plan, it can display the connections between inputs or resources, activities, and outcomes. It serves as the basis for more detailed work or management plan. During the course of program implementation, it provides a quick check-in to explain why the intervention is needed and to track program functions and processes. "It serves as a management tool as well as a framework to monitor fidelity to the plan" (Taylor-Powell, Jones, and Henert, 2002, Module 1: Section 1, slide 3). It can improve program planning and performance by identifying how to measure program success and identify areas for program improvement.

Evaluation   A logic model is the first step in planning for an evaluation. The logic model allows program stakeholder groups the opportunity to identify what they understand to be the program successes and to set up their own accountability system. It helps determine the key program elements that must be tracked to assess program effectiveness, the results the program is expected to achieve. "Through evaluation, we test and verify the reality of the program theory—how we believe the program will work. A logic model helps us focus on appropriate process and outcome measures" (Taylor-Powell, Jones, and Henert, 2002, Module 1: Section 1, slide 3).

Communication   Through a visual diagram, the logic model communicates to others, and to ourselves, the core of the program service or initiative. The logic model approach does not attempt to catch the program details; its value is in its ability to convey programmatic concepts using a simple, concise graphic presentation. At its core, the goal is to create shared understandings. Communicating to all stakeholders—program staff, funders, clients—is essential for program success and sustainability; the logic model is a powerful tool in this endeavor.

Components of a Logic Model   There are a variety of ways to construct a logic model. The visual displays commonly move left to right. A basic logic model consisting of six components is illustrated in Figure 4.1. The continuum of elements begins with the community need and finishes with the end outcome.

Figure 4.2 shows how the logic model progresses from project planning to intended results, employing an "if *A*, then *B*" sequence. Reading this logic model from left to right, you can see how the anticipated changes move in a *logical* continuum through inputs, activities, and culminating with the end outcome.

Multiple Chains and Varied Directional Flows   Programs are rarely as simple as the single chain of "if *A*, then *B*" relationships described in Figure 4.1. More likely, there may be multiple activities that address one community need with multiple outputs and outcomes. Visual displays of multiple chains and directions may include circular

Figure 4.1   Logic Model Components

Figure 4.2   The "If–Then" Sequence of the Logic Model

Community Need	Inputs	Activities	Outputs	Intermediate Outcomes	End Outcomes
There is a problem in your community that your program would like to address.	Certain resources are needed to operate your program.	If you have access to resources, then you can use them to carry out your planned activities.	If you carry out your planned activities, then you will deliver the amount of product and/or service you intended.	If you carry out your planned activities to the extent you intended, then this will lead to the intermediate steps necessary for your desired end outcomes.	If you carry out your planned activities to the extent you intended, then this will lead to your desired end outcomes.

flows of action or models that move from top to bottom or bottom to top, or an image that may look like a spiral involving various feedback loops. This spiral effect can also occur when knowledge gained during program implementation is utilized to improve the program, which then informs next year's planning.

Considerations in Developing a Logic Model   Logic models "support design, planning, communication, evaluation, and learning. They are often used when exploring an idea, resolving a challenge or assessing progress. They can untangle and clarify complex relationships among elements or parts" (Wyatt Knowlton and Phillips, 2009, p. 4). The logic model is a tool used to clarify key program components, particularly the results, by employing a visual representation. Developing a logic model uncovers assumptions and expectations. The logic model is particularly valuable for developing a set of aligned performance measures for your primary activity (i.e., the activity produces the output; the activity and the output produce the outcomes).

Developing a logic model often works best as a group exercise for staff and other key stakeholders, rather than as an "armchair exercise" for one individual. When putting together your logic model, consider the following steps:

Step 1: Involve appropriate stakeholders in the process.

Step 2: Start with the end in mind—anticipated results.

Step 3: Visualize how each component supports the next.

Step 4: Look at what will actually occur.

Step 5: Keep it simple, brief (one to two pages), and be creative.

Step 6: Consider developing a multiyear logic model.

Step 1: Involve Appropriate Stakeholders in the Process   Developing a logic model as a group builds consensus by focusing on the values and beliefs influencing what your organization wants to accomplish and why. This is an opportunity to explicitly uncover your program theory of change. Table 4.1 provides strategies in working with stakeholders when developing a logic model.

Table 4.1 Strategies for Working with Stakeholders in Developing a Logic Model

The logic model process works best with a small group of stakeholders, those interested in or benefiting from the services or interventions of a program. An experienced facilitator is ideal, but not essential. The group can reap the benefits of creating a shared meaning and uncovering assumptions through the following:

1. **Diversity of points of view**. Those on the board and those receiving the service (beneficiaries) each have unique views of the existing or proposed service. Each holds part of the whole.

2. **Agreement to learn**. To ensure success, the group agrees to be a part of the learning community and all that implies: asking the question everyone assumes is already answered, willingness to change one's mind, etc.

3. **Transparency in differences**. Each one has a unique perspective that the creation of a logic model can tap. By making those differences apparent, the process will provide a fuller and more accurate picture of the program.

4. **Mistakes welcome, tinkering mandatory**. When creating your logic model, work back and forth between the elements of the logic model to ensure there are clear links between the components and the inputs support the program service, which will bring about the interventions intended. Don't expect to get it right the first time. Revise and tinker!

Table 4.2 Strategies for Identifying Key Outcomes and Impacts

There are a variety of ways to identify meaningful results for your logic model:

Conduct focus groups with clients to identify what they want and expect from the services. With an ongoing program, find out what happens to them as a result of the service.

Investigate what similar programs elsewhere have identified as outputs and outcomes and tailor those to your own program context and needs.

Draw from your theory of change and the research and experience that supports the program model.

Step 2: Start with the End in Mind—Anticipated Results   Consider starting with the desired outcomes, the outcome you hope to achieve by the end of the project or a particular year, and then develop the best activities to meet those outcomes. Table 4.2 provides strategies to identify key outcomes and impacts.

Step 3: Visualize How Each Component Supports the Next   Whether beginning at the end, the middle, or at the front end, understanding how the logic model components are linked together will be important for both project planning and determining what is to be accomplished. Even though the logic model is read from left to right, moving back and forth between the various components when developing the logic model may be necessary to ensure the components are aligned. Tinkering with the logic model and going through various drafts is part of the process. It is likely that more than one output, intermediate outcome, and/or end outcome will be identified, but try to select only the core results. Likewise, listing only the key activities—not all possible activities—will help maintain the focus with other logic model components. Keep in mind there is no one right way to create a logic model.

Step 4: Look at What Will Actually Occur   Look realistically at what the program can accomplish and how the program can be implemented. Identify the primary service activities of the project, and choose those anticipated outputs, intermediate outcomes, and end outcomes that will best describe the purpose of your program.

Step 5: Keep it Simple, Brief (One to Two Pages), and Be Creative The simplicity and visual portrayal of the logic model makes it helpful. The logic model does not include all program information; it describes the core program components and the anticipated changes after services are delivered. Include only those inputs and activities directly applicable to the intended changes. Separate logic models may be needed for each major program activity.

Step 6: Consider Developing a Multiyear Logic Model A multiyear logic model is often useful when developing a new program and components of the program are identified for several years. For instance, the program infrastructure may be the focus of anticipated results for the first year. The second year may be a start-up year, and the anticipated results may demonstrate that all service areas are functioning. Subsequent years would examine the results on those served by the new program. A multiyear logic model allows programs to:

> Identify different results each year covering the anticipated life span of a project *and* identifying anticipated results for the program year.

> Incorporate activities and anticipated results that relate to the development of organizational capacity (e.g., creating or expanding new services), as well as activities and anticipated results for clients when the program is up and running.

Completing the Logic Model Components

By developing a complete logic model, you will have several of the basic components for an evaluation plan. For each logic model component that follows, questions are suggested that can help you think through the development of complete components and assist in uncovering key assumptions and factors that could potentially influence project results. Try tackling the components in the order suggested, but feel free to order them according to what makes the most sense to you. Expect to work back and forth between components.

1. Identify the Community Need The community need is the problem or issue in the community the project will address (see Figure 4.3a). This component is the foundation of the logic model. As Taylor-Powell, Jones, and Henert (2002) note, "The problem or issue that the program is to address sits within a setting or situation—a complex of sociopolitical, environmental, and economic conditions. If you incorrectly understand the situation and misdiagnose the problem, everything that follows is likely to be wrong" (Module 1: Section 1, slide 10). Consider the following questions in developing the community need.

> What is the problem? What is the issue in the community that needs to be changed or improved?

> What are the key factors that contribute to or cause these problems?

> Who is most affected by these problems (individuals, families, ethnic group)?

Figure 4.3a   Logic Model A

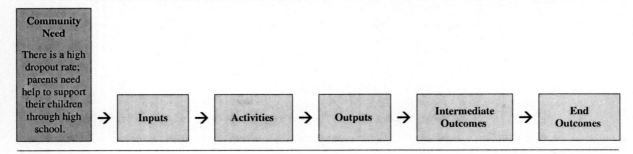

> Which community assets are currently being underutilized?

> What are the barriers to fully utilizing these community assets?

> What opportunities exist to address these contributing factors?

> Which of these opportunities can be addressed with the existing resources?

> What research or study is available that provides evidence of this need in the community?

> What does existing research/experience say about this problem/issue?

In summary, the community need statement should be backed up by a reliable source to establish the compelling nature of the need.

2. Determine the Anticipated Results   After identifying the community need, move to the end of the logic model and focus on the results, the output, intermediate outcome, and end outcome (see Figure 4.3b). As a group (of stakeholders), brainstorm what the community would like to see changed as per the stated community need. The group then needs to select possible results it feels can be accomplished if additional service activities are provided. Start by asking the group, "Ultimately, what do we want to change? During this program year? After 3 years what do we expect will change?"

Start with the end outcome (definition follows), the big change. As the results are identified, use the logic model's "if *A*, then *B*" sequence to determine the type of results.

Results are the accomplishments or changes that occur after the program's services are provided. Results are evidence of the accomplishment of service and change in attitudes, skills, knowledge, and behaviors of the beneficiaries receiving service. The results are categorized as outputs, intermediate outcomes, and end outcomes. Following are definitions of each type of result and then questions to help identify the type of result.

> *Outputs*. Outputs refer to the amount of work or products completed and services delivered by the program. These are the counts, often identified as "bean counting." This is what staff or volunteers have accomplished or the number of community beneficiaries the program has served. These are often identified as process results. Examples include service hours completed by staff and volunteers, vaccines administered, neighborhood cleanup projects completed, and community health workers recruited. Outputs answer the question, "How much work did we do?" but do not answer the question, "What changed as a result of our work?"

➤ *Intermediate outcomes.* Intermediate outcomes are changes or benefits experienced by service recipients that are milestones or indicators of more significant future change. However, intermediate outcomes do not represent the final result the program hopes to achieve. Intermediate outcomes are expected to lead to or support the achievement of end outcomes. They may include quality indicators such as timeliness and client satisfaction: "What change? How well did you do?"

For example, if the final result is to improve parenting skills for at-risk parents, then intermediate outcomes might be improved knowledge or attitudes toward parenting and child development. These are likely preconditions for improved parenting skills. Positive results for intermediate outcomes are usually a sign that the program is on track to achieving the related end outcomes.

➤ *End outcomes.* End outcomes are the positive changes the program ultimately hopes to achieve for its beneficiaries. End outcomes address community conditions or needed changes in the condition, behavior, skills or attitudes of beneficiaries. These are the changes hoped for in the lives of beneficiaries that constitute the most important or significant benefits to them: "So what? What impact?"

Intermediate and end outcomes are the consequences of what a program does. They depict the program theory of change. Many outcomes can occur over the course of the program. A set of outcomes linked together are aligned—that is, they are related. Keep in mind, there may be several "outcome chains" (United Way, 1996).

These questions can help clarify results:

➤ What long-term impacts or changes do you hope to institute within the community you serve? (End outcomes)

➤ What other changes (benchmarks) can you look at along the way to help assess if you are on track to achieve these longer-term impacts? (Intermediate outcomes)

➤ What do you hope to complete or accomplish? (Outputs)

➤ Are your intended results SMART (**S**pecific, **M**easurable, **A**chievable, **R**ealistic, and **T**ime-sensitive)?

➤ How will you assess your work along the way to ensure you are achieving what you set out to do?

Figure 4.3b   Logic Model B

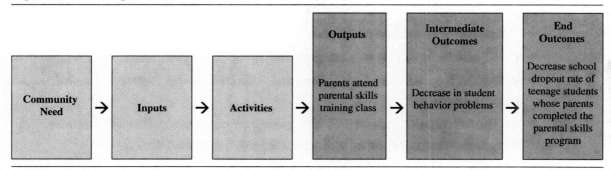

Figure 4.3c   Logic Model C

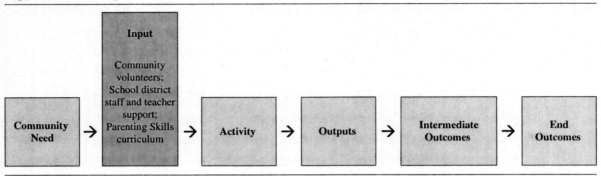

In summary, the results should reflect the main accomplishments (outputs or outcomes) the program hopes to achieve over the specific period of time. For most human service programs, annual measures are the time frame used for internal measurement. However, if the program works with the same clients over several years, the intermediate outcomes may be measured after one year, whereas the end outcomes are measured after multiple years of service. Keep the alignment of the goals, activities, and results in the forefront when determining the anticipated results.

3. Highlight Key Inputs   The inputs are the resources needed to implement the service activities (see Figure 4.3c). These are the key resources, or big-picture resources needed before a program can begin. Examples of key resources include number of staff, facilities or buildings, equipment, partnerships with other organizations, as well as funding to operate the program. The following questions clarify inputs:

➤ What resources, human and financial, are necessary before your program can begin?

➤ What resources are currently available to assist in the implementation of your program?

4. Describe your Service Activities   Service activities are what will be offered to the community to effect change (see Figure 4.3d). Service activities address the community need and hopefully achieve the anticipated results, the outputs, intermediate outcomes, and end outcomes. The activity statement should describe who does what, when, where, how, and with whom for how long. The additional questions that follow will assist in the development of a strong service activity statement:

➤ What activities will be implemented to address your strategies?

➤ What research, theory, or past experience supports your choice of strategies?

➤ What kind of skills and qualifications will staff/volunteers need to implement these activities?

➤ Do the activities consider FIT (Frequency of occurrence, Intensity or strength of the given efforts, Targeted at a specified market of audience)?

Figure 4.3d   Logic Model D

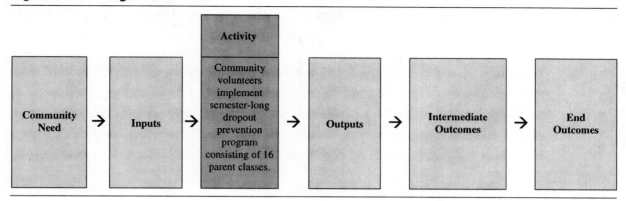

Figure 4.3e shows the complete abbreviated logic model (see elaborated logic model in Chapter 7, Learning by Doing).

Checking the Logic Model   No logic model fully articulates a program effort, and all logic models need continual refinement. Furthermore, organizations each have their own particular blind spots and cultural beliefs that color their program description. The following areas should be considered when developing and reviewing a logic model.

Scale of Effort   "Scale is about the relative size of a given effort. In particular, we meant the relationship between the result sought and the quality, volume frequency, and other characteristics of the intervention . . . " (Wyatt Knowlton and Philips, 2009, p. 51). Can 10 community volunteers mentor 100 children who were neglected or abused and form a strong positive relationship in one program year? Are activities that focus on conflict resolution once a week at a middle school so small that they will have little influence on reducing conflict at the school, much less lowering violence in the entire community? Verify that the resources available can support the service activities proposed and identify anticipated results.

Figure 4.3e   Logic Model E

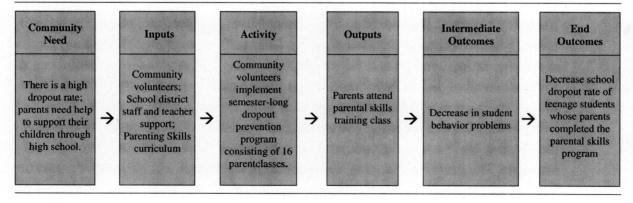

Specificity   Programs are reminded that the more specific they are in identifying the community need and results (outputs and outcomes), the more likely they will be able to demonstrate how the activities provide strong links between the two.

Feasibility   Use the logic model to test how realistic or feasible the proposed program services are given the available resources (e.g., staff, time, money, facilities, and materials). Test whether the proposed service activities will address the community need by utilizing the logic model. Test, via the logic model, whether the service activities will actually accomplish what they set out to do; address the anticipated results.

Plausibility   Check the model for plausibility. Can you really do it? Wyatt Knowlton and Phillips (2009) note that, by creating a logic model, you have a means to demonstrate where you are going, make appropriate decisions to get there, and the awareness of doing "the right work."

The logic model is a simple working document; it is a snapshot of the program activities at one point in time. It allows programs to review program services and anticipated results annually or more often, throughout the life of the program to adjust to the changing needs of the community. Not only is it prudent to anticipate writing several drafts before coming up with a final version, but you should also be ready to modify the logic model annually. Revisit the logic model at least annually to see if the assumptions have withstood the test of time and actual project experience. Program activities are not static; resources, partners, and the influence of expected and unexpected outcomes are but a few of the variables that change program activities. The logic model requires continuous refinement and tinkering to serve programs. When revisiting your logic model, consider the following questions as you contemplate refining your logic model:

➢ Has your original service activity and result(s) proven realistic?

➢ How does your actual progress compare to your anticipated timeline for achieving result(s)?

➢ Do the actual results reflect change related to the identified community need?

The Logic Model: Moving into the Program Planning and Evaluation Worksheet   An elaborated logic model serves as the basis for key evaluation questions. In turn, the evaluation questions form the cornerstone of the program planning and evaluation worksheet and evaluation plan. See Chapter 5, Grant Proposal Writing, for the discussion of logic model and the program planning and evaluation plan. Chapter 6, Program Evaluation, further elaborates on the evaluation process. By creating a logic model, the hard work is done upfront or at least a good portion of the work needed to build the program planning and evaluation worksheet. This is especially true when developing key results—outputs, intermediate outcomes, and end outcomes—for core activities. The program planning and evaluation worksheet will elaborate the concise logic model and add further detail necessary for clarity and implementation.

References

Hamiliton, Rabinowitz and Alschuler, Inc. (July 1987). *The changing face of misery: Los Angeles' skid row area in transition-housing and social service needs of Central City East Lost Angeles.* Los Angeles, CA: Community Redevelopment Agency

Kellogg Foundation. (2001). *Logic model development guide: Logic models to bring together planning, evaluation and action.* Battle Creek, MI: W. K. Kellogg Foundation.

McKillip, J. (1998). Need analysis. In Bickman, L., and Rog, D. J. (eds.), *Handbook of applied social research methods.* Thousand Oaks, CA: Sage Publications.

McNamara, C. *Basic guide to program evaluation.* Retrieved February 17, 2009, from www.managementhelp. org/evaluatn/fnl_eval.htm#anchor1586742.

Millar, A., Simeone, R. S., & Carnevale, J. T. (2001). Logic models: A systems tool for performance management. *Evaluation and Program Planning, 24*(1), 73–81.

Reviere, R., Berkowitz, S., Carter, C. C., & Gergusan, C. G. (eds.). (1996). *Needs assessment: A creative and practical guide for social scientists.* Washington, DC: Taylor & Francis.

Rossi, P., Freeman, H., & Lipsey, M. (1999). *Evaluation: A systematic approach* (6th ed.). Thousand Oaks, CA: Sage Publications.

Rubin, A., & Babbie, E. (2008). *Research methods for social work* (6th ed.). Belmont, CA: Brooks/Cole–Thomson Learning.

Taylor-Powell, E., Jones, L., & Henert, E. (2002). *Enhancing program performance with logic models.* Retrieved February 24, 2009, from the University of Wisconsin-Extension web site: www1.uwex.edu/ ces/lmcourse.

Titcomb, A. (2000). *Need analysis.* Retrieved February 17, 2009. from http://cals-cf.calsnet.arizona.edu/ icyf/docs/needs.pdf.

United Way of America. (1996). *Measuring program outcomes: A practical approach.* Arlington, VA: United Way of America. www.unitedway.org/outcomes.

Weiss, C. (1993). Where politics and evaluation research meet. *American Journal of Evaluation 14* (1), 93–106.

Witkin, R. & Altschuld, J. (1995). *Planning and conducting needs assessments.* Thousand Oaks, CA: Sage.

Wyatt Knowlton, L., & Phillips, C. (2009). *The logic model guidebook: better strategies for great results.* Thousand Oaks, CA: Sage Publications.

Yuen, F. K. O., & Terao, K. (2003). *Practical grant writing and program evaluation.* Pacific Grove, CA: Brooks/ Cole–Thomson Learning.

5
Grant Proposal Writing: Beginning with the End in Mind

Grant and Contract

Request for Proposal, Request for Application, and Program Announcement

Letter of Intent/Letter of Inquiry

Getting Ready, Logic Model, and Program Planning and Evaluation Worksheet

Key Components of a Grant Proposal

Abstract: Write Last, Read First, Most Frequently Used

Table of Contents: A Roadmap for Your Proposal

Specific Aims: A Summary of Purpose and Results

Target Population: To Whom It May Concern

Approaches and Methods: What, Why, When, Where, Who, and How

Agency Capacities and Project Management: The Service Providers and Program Management

Budget and Budget Justifications: Program Plan in Dollars and Cents

Evaluation Plan: Tell the Stories—Successes and Challenges

Proposal Reviews

List of Tables

In human services, a program proposal is a detailed written plan of action that aims to address an identified social issue or meet the needs of a target population. It is often used to solicit funding support to implement the proposed activities. When the proposal is used to gain support from a grant fund, it becomes a grant proposal.

Grant and Contract

Funding support for human services comes in two main forms: contract and grant. A *contract* is an agreement between the funding source and the recipient in providing the prescribed services or goods with the designated resources. It is an agreement to purchase services or goods. A local mental health agency may have a contract with the county mental health department to provide certain units of therapeutic sessions for a minimum number of eligible clients annually. The agency needs to demonstrate its capacity to provide the service and to fulfill the terms of the agreement. It needs to present the information and data through proposals, reports, and other documentation. Most importantly, the contract concerns whether the deliverables (i.e., numbers of therapeutic sessions and clients served) are achieved. Usually, this contract is renewed annually pending a favorable performance review. Modifications of the terms take place during the negotiation of the contract. On the other hand, repercussions such as loss of contract or legal and financial consequences are likely if the contract is not fulfilled. The mental health department may have many such contracts in the community to serve various needy populations.

A *grant* is funding support provided to the recipients to explore or test specific programs or activities that may generate outcomes of interest to the recipients and the grant maker. A grant could be used to initiate new and innovative services or to support ongoing efforts of desirable programs. For instance, a local service agency designs a street-level HIV prevention and intervention program, and believes it will help address the recent increase of HIV cases among the target population. It is not only an innovative and creative program, but it also coincides with the grant maker's funding and service priority. The grant maker awards a three-year grant to the agency to implement the proposed program. Both of them are interested in learning from this program and further advancing effective services to the target population.

At the end of the grant award period, the project may or may not deliver all of the planned activities or achieve all of the goals. It is through these explorations and experimentations that new knowledge and innovative service modalities will be achieved. In this process, the service agency needs to submit a grant proposal to solicit the funding support, carry out the proposed activities, submit proper documentation and reports, and implement a suitable evaluation to monitor progress and assess outcomes.Renewal of grant support for the same project is not automatic or expected. A new grant proposal application will need to be submitted to continue the funding for the established project.

The differences between a service contract and grant are also similar to those between a salary (or a service payment) and a scholarship (or a stipend). A contract is a purchase, whereas a grant is a type of assistance. In an employment situation, an employee is expected to fulfill specific tasks and responsibilities that come with the job. When a contractor is hired to remodel a kitchen, the contractor is expected to complete all of the tasks specified in the service contract to the homeowner's specifications. Unfulfilled tasks and responsibilities may result in termination and legal consequences.

A university professor receives a research grant to investigate the use of green (eco-friendly) chemistry methods. She wants to discover the extent to which a certain chemical compound could be produced using a laboratory-grade microwave oven instead of the conventional laboratory methods. Her grant-supported study may or may not be successful in producing such a compound with the green technology. However, her study findings contribute to the body of knowledge on the subject matter.

A gang intervention grant project may be successful in curtailing gang involvement among its male target population. It even has the potential to be replicated in other locations. At the same time, the project may be found ineffectual in reaching its female target population. The project director may decide to propose a new service model that targets the female population.

At this point, we need to clarify that the term *contract* in contract and grant discussed here is not exactly the same as the term *contract* in a legal contract. It does not matter whether the agency receives a contract or a grant; both are types of legal agreements between parties and, therefore, contracts in a legal sense. In this discussion, what distinguishes the contract from the grant is the funding mechanisms. An agency could have a contract from the county social service department to provide services to the homeless population. It also receives a grant to implement special activities to help the homeless families with young children. Both the contract and the grant have legal contractual relationships between the agency and the funding sources.

This book focuses on the development of a grant proposal. The format and contents of a proposal for a grant and for a contract, however, are rather similar. Mastery of the craft of writing a quality proposal could be applied to a grant, a contract, and other funding mechanisms.

Request for Proposal, Request for Application, and Program Announcement

Funding sources solicit bids or proposals through the announcement of a request for proposal (RFP), request for application (RFA), program announcement (PA), and other notices. Human service agencies need to know the differences between these different types of announcements.

A *request for proposal* (RFP) is the announcement of the availability of funding to support programs. It is often used as a procurement process to solicit bids from vendors, including service agencies, for services and products. An RFP provides detailed descriptions of terms for a contract, and procedures for preparing and submitting the proposals. For example, the Substance Abuse and Mental Health Services Administration's (SAMHSA) Division of Contract Management would issue an RFP for its Coordinated Technical Assistance Project on Emergencies and Disasters program.

A *request for application* (RFA) is the funding source's call for submission of applications for specific grant projects. An RFP indicates the availability of funding for program contracts and, therefore, proposals; an RFA calls for applications for particular grant projects. A single particular deadline is set for the receipt of applications. For example, SAMHSA's Center for Substance Abuse Prevention (CSAP) issues an RFA for its Drug-Free Communities Mentoring Program. It has one deadline for proposal submission.

A *program announcement* (PA) is the notice regarding the availability of funding support, and the funding source's priorities and interests. A PA has several different deadlines for proposal submission. A PA also employs the RFA process. SAMHSA's Center for Mental Health funds the Knowledge Dissemination Conference Grants. Its RFA has recurring receipt dates for March and September of each year.

The National Institute of Health (NIH) provides the following descriptions on the difference between these funding mechanisms for its research projects:

> An RFP is the Government's official solicitation document that communicates to prospective offerors, what it is the Government needs to buy/acquire, and formally invites the submission of proposals. The purpose of the RFP is to convey all information that prospective offerors need to prepare a proposal. In addition to a description of what it is the Government needs to buy, the RFP also contains various representations and certifications that are required of prospective offerors, proposed terms and conditions that would be applicable to any resultant contract, instructions on how to prepare proposals, and information as to how the Government will evaluate proposals and determine who is selected for an award.
>
> Requests for Applications (RFAs) are typically one-time solicitations for grant applications addressing a defined research topic. Each RFA specifies the scope and objectives of the research to be proposed; application requirements and procedures; and the review criteria to be applied in the evaluation of applications submitted in response to the RFA. Although there are exceptions, these types of solicitations offer only one Application Receipt Date.
>
> A Program Announcement (PA) is used by the institute to announce its interest in building or enhancing its research program in a particular area.

The PA is typically an ongoing solicitation, accepting applications for multiple receipt dates, for up to three years. The PA specifies the scope and objectives of the research of interest, application requirements and procedures, and review criteria to be applied. (www.ninds.nih.gov/funding/differences.htm)

One of the important considerations for proposal writing is to avoid focusing on what the service agency can offer to please the funding sources. The focus should be on what the agency can do to achieve the agency's mission and to meet the funding source's expectations and standards of success. The agency that has a clear understanding of its mission, functions, and capacities has a better chance of gauging how best to pursue suitable funding opportunities. The agency will remain a mission-driven agency instead of a funding-driven agency. Such an agency conducts programs that actualize its mission and, thereby, serve targeted community members appropriate to its expertise and capacity. It does not become an agency that goes after any available funding and loses sight of the mission and charter of the agency.

A funding source lays out its expectations and terms in details in the RFA. It is, therefore, vitally important for the agency and grant writer to dissect—let us say it again—dissect the RFA to see if this is the right funding source and, if so, how to go about acquiring it. Depending on the funding source and the size and scope of the funding, the RFA could be as thick as a book or as simple as a one-page announcement.

Although application information and eligibility screening are being offered online, some major funding sources set up technical assistance workshops or bidder's conferences that take place immediately after the release of the RFA. The funding source provides detailed information regarding the RFA, provides updates, and clarifies and answers questions in these workshops. Additional unspoken benefits of workshop attendance are to see which competing agencies are attending the workshops and to make connections with the program officers. That personal contact allows the agency not only to give a sales pitch to the program officer, but also to identify a contact person within the funding organization for follow-up questions.

Funding sources may want to gauge how many people will be coming to the technical assistance workshops or submitting proposals. They may request that all interested agencies submit a letter of intent to register for the workshop or submit proposals. This letter would assist the funding source to screen out potential applications that are not appropriate to the RFA.

Different funding sources construct their RFAs based on the nature and the purpose of the funding. Although there is no uniform format for RFAs, they usually include some common elements. Table 5.1 is a sample of a simplified one-page RFA from a government agency. Following are additional notes have been added to this sample RFA that call attention to key elements of the RFA.

Table 5.1 Sample Request for Application

DHHS Grant Announcement #711

Request for Application (RFA)

The Department of Health and Human Services (DHHS) announces the availability of support for new service projects that address the critical needs of the low-income, underserved, or at-risk populations in the United States. The funding is authorized under Section 123 of the 2010 Public Well-Being Act. A total of $2 million ($2,000,000.00) is earmarked for this program during this fiscal year.

The DHHS is interested in receiving applications for projects that are innovative and well developed in addressing the critical needs of the targeted communities. All funded projects should begin no earlier than January 1, 2016 and be completed no later than December 30, 2018. Local government and private nonprofit human service or educational organizations are eligible to apply for funding support. Applications under this announcement must be received at the DHHS Grant Management Office no later than **5:00 p.m. on April 1, 2015.** Absolutely no late applications will be accepted after the deadline.
All applications should include the following sections:

1. Abstract—*45 lines max.*
2. Table of Contents—*2 pages max.*
3. Specific Aims (Needs/Problems, Background and Significance, Working Hypothesis, Literature Review, General Program Plan, etc.)—*3 pages max.*
4. Target Populations—*2 pages max.*
5. Approaches and Methods (Project Goals and Objectives, Activities and Time Lines, etc.)—*6 pages max.*
6. Evaluation Plan—*3 pages max.*
7. Agency Capacity and Project Management—*3 pages max.*
8. Budget and Budget Justification—*3 pages max.*
9. Community Support—*no page limit*
10. References and Appendices—*no page limit*

Agencies interested in applying for the funding support must submit a **letter of intent** to DHHS **no later than February 5, 2015.** The letter should briefly describe the proposed project including project goals, target population(s), activities and location(s), budget, and the name of a contact person. Applicants who have submitted a letter of intent are invited to attend the **technical assistance workshop** held in Washington, D.C. on March 1, 2015. Alternatively, applicants can participate in one of the two on-line web conferences scheduled for March 2 and March 3, 2015.

The agency administrationor the grant writer who receive this RFA should dissect it and call attention to the following key points:

1. The Public Well-being Act has specific mandates and limitations. Find out what they are.

2. The earmarked funding amount and the total grant awards would give a sense of how big the grant would be, if not clearly specified elsewhere in the RFA.

3. The intended targets of the grant are "the critical needs of the low-income, underserved or at-risk populations." Make sure the proposed program targets the identified population(s).

4. The grant is intended to fund "service" projects. Construction, remodeling, or other type of nonservice projects are not eligible.

5. The proposed programs and the applications have to be "innovative and well developed." A program with standard or patchwork approaches will likely not work for this application.

6. All of the important dates are listed, and the funding period is up to three years.

7. Who is eligible to apply? "Local government and private nonprofit human service or educational organizations." Churches and temples or for-profit organizations may want to save their efforts and not apply.

8. The deadline for receiving the proposal is April 1, 2015, at 5 p.m. The keyword here is "received," not "postmarked." The proposal has to be physically in the office at that time, not "in the mail." Special delivery with signature upon receipt or tracking of delivery would be a good idea.

9. The contents and sections of the proposal are listed. In this example, to provide a guide and highlight the uniqueness of each section, focuses, contents, and page limits are clearly indicated. Page limits are one of the essential technical compliances for the proposal. In many RFAs, although the page limits may not be clearly indicated or are buried in the text, they should be strictly adhered to in order to avoid disqualification on a technicality.

10. The requirement for a letter of intent and the technical assistance workshop and web conference dates are listed.

Letter of Intent/Letter of Inquiry

A *letter of intent* or *letter of inquiry* is often requested by the funding sources and has many purposes. It can also be initiated by the agency seeking support. An agency wants to explore whether certain program ideas are of interest to a funding source that, like foundations, will use the letter of intent to start the conversation. A funding source will ask the prospective applicant to submit a two-page letter of inquiry to help assess the program's potential. This letter of inquiry can be viewed as a concept paper. If the funding source is interested in the proposed program, it will invite the agency to submit a full proposal. It also helps the agency by not requiring a commitment of resources to put together an unneeded full proposal.

A letter of intent can be used to assess the extent of demand or degree of interest regarding a particular RFA (e.g., as requested in Figure 5.1). It is used to sort out appropriate and inappropriate applications. The letter of intent is not supposed to be lengthy; it is similar to a theatre's upcoming attractions announcement. It gives enough information to generate interest, but does not detail the whole story at length. Table 5.2 is an example guideline for such a letter.

Getting Ready, Logic Model, and Program Planning and Evaluation Worksheet

Now, after much preparation, the RFA is in hand, and the proposal writing is ready to begin. Writing a grant proposal for the first time could be intimidating. Like everything else, lack of experience and unfamiliarity make the task feel even

Table 5.2 Sample Format for a Letter of Intent

No more than two pages in length, shorter is better. On letterhead stationery. Designed to see if your project would be of interest to a funding source.

➤ Quote "ringer," attention grabber. Touch the heart! (Optional) (Don't get too sappy!)

➤ 2 sentences telling what the community *need(s)* is (are) and what you are proposing (include the title of your proposed program).

➤ 3 sentences giving your agency's background/mission, history, budget, sources of funds, staff, capacities, eligibility, and qualifications.

➤ 2 sentences describing your current services and clients—types and numbers.

➤ 3 sentences explaining what services the proposed program will provide; also, how many will be served and by whom.

➤ 2 sentences suggesting what results/products will be achieved.

➤ 2 sentences telling why you and your proposed program are *unique*.

➤ 1 sentence telling the approximate funding amount requested.

➤ 2 sentences on why they should care; possible benefits to the funding source, the community, or the world.

➤ 2 sentences on when you'll follow up (if appropriate), who the contact person is. (Do not rely on "feel free to call me"; the follow-up is the responsibility of the applicant.)

➤ *Thank You.*

➤ Signed: Board Member or Agency Director

➤ Attachment: a brochure or one interesting thing about your services

more difficult. It is often true that a new grant writer needs to start everything from scratch and finish the proposal within the same short time frame. Usually, there are about six weeks between the release of the RFA and the due date for submission. There are many things the grant writer could do beforehand to facilitate a successful proposal development process:

➤ Collect and organize all relevant literature and information.

➤ Identify needs through proper assessments.

➤ Articulate the proposed service program activities.

➤ Sketch out the basic program plans.

➤ Identify stakeholders including service recipients, and seek their input and support.

➤ Get all the basic required certifications, appendices, and documents ready.

➤ If possible, find an experienced proposal writer to be your coach.

➤ If an outsider grant writer is used, prepare the writer to truly understand and reflect the agency's perspectives and intention.

To facilitate a systematic way to construct a quality proposal, a logic model (see Chapter 4) is used. A well-planned logic model could help develop a proposal that has the following desirable characteristics:

1. Service-recipient–centered

2. Needs-based

3. Purposeful activities

4. Clear indicators and level of success

5. Results-oriented

6. Program-driven evaluation

A Program Planning and Evaluation Worksheet (Table 5.3) is a tool that applies the logic model to planning programs and their associated evaluation approaches. It helps organize the program strategies and evaluation approaches. It could be used for some grant proposals as the Approaches and Methods section and the Evaluation Plan. If the proposal has detailed or separate narratives or explanations of Approaches and Methods and Evaluation, the worksheet could be used as a summary sheet that integrates both sections. It could then be included as an appendix.

A logic model starts with the identified needs and concerns, and with the end in mind—that is, the results and ultimate impact of the program. The first step for a logic model is the identified needs. The expected result is the next step in developing the model. Based on the anticipated results and the available resources (inputs), activities or interventions that would produce the results are developed. At the same time, evaluation instruments are designed, and other evaluation considerations, such as data sources, are assessed. Table 5.3 provides an example of how a logic model is connected to the use of a Program Planning and Evaluation Worksheet for a School-based Youth Development Project—Parental Skills Training program. A blank worksheet is also provided. Modify the worksheet as desired to meet the program needs.

Key Components of a Grant Proposal

A grant proposal could be as short as a page or two or as long as hundreds of pages. Their formats also range from filling out blank spaces on a form to a complex set of narrative, documents, charts, and tables. In general, most proposals require the following information:

➤ Abstract: Write last, read first, most frequently used

➤ Table of Contents: A roadmap for your proposal

➤ Specific Aims: A summary of purpose, results, interventions, and structure of the proposed program—it may include Background and Significance, Needs and Problems Statement, such as "Why is the proposed program important and needed?"

➤ Literature Review: What do we know? Present knowledge that informs our proposal.

➤ Target Population: Who are the beneficiaries?

➤ Approaches and Methods: Detailed plans of what the proposed activities are and how they will be achieved

Table 5.3 From Logic Model to Program Planning and Evaluation Worksheet

Logic Model: School–based Youth Development Project—Parental Skills Training

Needs (Step 1)	Inputs (Step 3)	Activities (Step 4)	Results (Step 2)		
			Outputs	Intermediate Outcomes	End Outcomes
High dropout rate; severe parent–child conflicts, parents want additional support for their children and themselves.	Program staff School district staff and teacher support Parenting skills curriculum	Program Staff will implement a coordinated dropout prevention program for students including an 8 weeks positive parenting class.	Parental skills taught Hours of training Parent participants Instrument: Class rosters and attendance	Parents demonstrate positive parenting skills Instrument: Parent Skills Assessment	Decrease in student behavior problems in school Data Source: School records	Decrease school drop-out rate of teenage students whose parents completed parental skills program Data Source: School records, & Parent survey

Program Planning and Evaluation Worksheet

Program Name: School-based Youth Development Project			
Objective Title: A short easy to remember name for the Objective	Parenting Program	Activity	Parental Skills Training
Activity Start and End Dates: 09/01/2015	05/31/2016	Staff	Ed Jucate, MSW, Dee Valarman, BA

1. Identified Needs Describe what identified needs are to be addressed. (The Why)	One in five students in this school dropped out last year (*Ridgeway School District Annual Report*) and many are involved with the criminal justice or child welfare system. Parents have indicated they need help to support their children through high school (*Survey of Ridgeway Parents*, conducted by the School District and the Successful Parenting Project).
2. Target populations/ Service Recipients Briefly describe the target groups (and the estimated number) your activity will serve. (The Whom)	50 current students and their parents who are referred by the child welfare judge, teachers, social workers, or self-referred
3. Activities/Interventions Describe the service or interventions. (The What) (Also include who, what, when, and where that are involved.)	Program staff will implement a dropout prevention program including an 8 weeks class sessions for parents. The class activities will prepare parents with the skills they need to support their children and keep them in school and out of trouble.
4. Desired Results (Outputs, Outcomes) Explain what results will be achieved because of the described activity. (The Products and Effects) (Number and type of results vary, e.g., Output only, Output and Intermediate outcomes, two Intermediate outcomes and one End outcome, etc.)	***Output:*** 20 parents enrolled and 75% completed the training. ***Intermediate Outcome:*** Among the parents completed the course, at least 60% of them will demonstrate effective parenting skills as measured by the assessment form. Their children will also be at least 10 percent lower in reported behavioral problems according to the school records. ***End Outcome:*** 12% lower dropout rate compared to students of parents who are on a waiting list (if available) for the program or previous dropout rate according to school record and parent survey.
5. Method of Measurement Describe the method and the instrument used to assess results	Roster, Attendance Record, School records, Parenting Skills Assessment Form, Survey Questionnaire
6. Indicators/Benchmarks Describe the concrete and observable evidences.	Dropout statistics, attendance, student behaviors report, and responses on the survey questionnaire.
7. Targets/Standards of Success Define a level of success expected. (How good is good enough? At least *X*% show improvement.)	20 enrolled, 75% completed, 60% demonstrate skills, and 12% lower dropout.
8. Resources and Inputs Briefly describe the resources/input needed.	Program staff, school district staff and teacher support, parent support, parenting skills curriculum
9. Data Collection, Analysis, and Reporting Describe when and who will be doing these.	Program staff and teacher, before and after training.
Objective Statement: Combine 1–7 into a single statement of objective.	***Example:*** Among the parents of the 50 identified students, 20 of them will enroll in the parenting program and 75% will complete the program. It will lead to the increase of parenting skills and the decrease in student behavioral problems and dropout rate.

Program Planning

Program Evaluation

Program Planning and Evaluation Worksheet

Program Name:				
Objective Title:		Activity		
Activity Start and End Dates:			**Staff:**	
1. **Identified Needs**				
2. **Target Populations/Service Recipients**				
3. **Activities/Interventions**				
4. **Desired Results (Outputs and Outcomes)**	*Output:*			
	Intermediate Outcome:			
	End Outcome:			
5. **Method of Measurement**				
6. **Indicators/Benchmarks**				
7. **Targets/Standards of Success**				
8. **Resources and Inputs**				
9. **Data Collection, Aggregation, Analysis, and Reporting**				
Objective Statement:				

➤ Agency Capacities and Project Management: List the service providers and program management.

➤ Budget and Budget Justifications: Provide the program plan in dollars and cents.

➤ Evaluation Plan: Tell the stories—successes and challenges.

Abstract: Write Last, Read First, Most Frequently Used

An abstract is a synopsis of the proposal. Although the abstract is the shortest section of the proposal, it is one of the most important. For many of the busy reviewers and funding committee members, this will be the first, and could be the only, section they read. It is, therefore, important to write it in a clear, succinct, and comprehensive manner. An abstract is always the first portion of the proposal reviewed by the reviewers, but it is the last section written by the proposal writer.

An abstract is usually short and has limited length. Depending on the funding program, it may have a limit of 45 lines, 250 to 500 words, or one to two pages. An abstract summarizes the major components of the proposal. It may include the following:

➤ Name of the applicant agency

➤ Type of organization (e.g., 501(c)3 nonprofit organization)

➤ Title and purpose of the proposed program

➤ Identified needs to be addressed

➤ Target populations

➤ Locations and settings of the program

> ➤ Major interventions or activities and their objectives or expected outcomes
> ➤ Program evaluation approaches
> ➤ Program cost or amount of funding support requested
> ➤ Relevance of the program to the funding source's funding priority or intention

To put all of this information into a short essay is not a simple task. It is, however, a very important piece of the proposal. It gives the reviewers the first, and often the last, impression of one's proposal. Potentially, it could make reviewing and reporting an easier job for the reviewers and the program officer. A well-written and well-presented abstract provides key information for the reviewers. It starts the proposal off on a positive step and in an advantageous direction. A good first impression is always a good start.

Table of Contents: A Roadmap for Your Proposal

Imagine that you are the reviewers who have to read through a large number of proposals. The last thing you want is a proposal that is scattered and unstructured. You want to be fair and objective in your review of the proposal, but it is extremely frustrating if the information is not located in the right place or it has to be sorted or restructured to know what is being presented. The process of sifting through the proposal to find one piece of information may lead the reviewers to find more issues or problems with the proposal. This situation certainly is related to the overall clarity and quality of the writing and the proposal, but it could be managed by a well-constructed table of contents.

A table of contents is a roadmap of the proposal. It has to be simple to use, clear, and uncomplicated. It points the readers to the right place without excessive details or insufficient information. Some funding sources have a preset table of contents that applicants must follow. If not, the applicant may wish to construct one by carefully reading the RFA and developing a very detailed list of required contents. This list could then be used as a checklist for the grant-writing process to make sure all required information is provided. When the writing is done and corresponding page numbers have been added, the applicant should simplify and organize the list into the table of contents. Along with the abstract, a table of contents is one of the last portions of the proposal to be completed.

Table 5.4 is an example of a table of contents for a federal Substance Abuse and Mental Health Service Administration (SAMHSA) demonstration grant proposal. It is a more comprehensive table of contents than most grant proposals would require. Different funding agencies have different application requirements and, therefore, require different tables of contents. With the ever-changing local and federal requirements, the list of required assurances and certifications are different from one funding source to another. Because many of these documents are common requirements and are applicable to most funding applications, agencies

Table 5.4 Sample Table of Contents

1. Application for Federal Assistance (Form 424)
2. Budget: Nonconstruction Program (Form 424A) and Letter of Intent for Indirect Cost
3. Abstract
4. Table of Contents
5. Narrative
    A. Specific Aims
    B. Specific Outcome Objectives
    C. Target Populations
    D. Approaches and Methods
    E. Evaluation Plan
    F. Project Management/Implementation Plan
    G. Project Staff and Organization
    H. Budget Justification and Existing Resources
    I. Confidentiality/Participant Protection
6. Checklist
7. Certifications and Assurances
    A. Assurances: Nonconstruction Program (Form 424B)
    B. Civil Rights Assurance (45CFR80)
    C. Assurance Concerning the Handicapped (45CFR84)
    D. Assurance Concerning Sex Discrimination (45CFR86)
    E. Assurance Concerning Age Discrimination (45CFR90&91)
    F. Certification Concerning Supplantation of Funds
    G. Letter from IRS and State Franchise Tax Board
8. Appendices
    A. Appendix 1: Activities Gantt Chart
    B. Appendix 2: Program Curricular Outlines
    C. Appendix 3: Resumes/Job Description
    D. Appendix 4: Project Structure
    E. Appendix 5: Applicant Agency's Organizational Chart
    F. Appendix 6: Board of Directors List
    G. Appendix 7: Program Evaluation Plan
    H. Appendix 8: Data Collection Instruments
    I. Appendix 9: Sample Consent Forms
    J. Appendix 10: Letter To/From Single State Agency
    K. Appendix 11: Letters of Commitment from Collaborating Organizations
    L. Appendix 12: Letter of Support
    M. Appendix 13: Reference

should have these documents updated and readily available at all times to be included in a complete proposal package.

Specific Aims: A Summary of Purpose and Results

The Specific Aims segment sets the stage for the grant proposal. It identifies the impetus that drives the development of the proposal. It justifies the needs for the proposed project, the problems to be addressed, and the importance for having such a project. This section also describes the current state of knowledge on the subject matter and demonstrates that the proposed project is needs-driven and knowledge-based. To those ends, the logic model for the project is articulated and the expected outcomes of the project are estimated.

This section of the proposal is intended to show the funding source that the applicant agency knows the needs and problems to be addressed. This knowledge is uniquely gained through community input, practice wisdom and expertise, evidence collected through research and literature, and the unique understanding of the target problem and the target populations. Therefore, it is with this unique expertise and insight that promising interventions or activities are proposed to address the problems or meet the needs.

"Specific aims" could be referred to as any one of several narrative sections of a proposal, such as Needs and Problems Statement, Working Hypothesis, Literature Review, or General Program Plan. Some funding sources have treated these various sections as independent sections, whereas others use them as subtopics of the Specific Aims section. Connecting these various components together would in effect construct the logics of the proposed program and show the thinking or theories behind the proposal (see Table 5.5).

Table 5.5 Sample Outline for Specific Aims

1. Statement of Problems or Needs
   - ➤ Define the problems or needs to be addressed specifically by the proposal. There are many problems and needs, and they are all interconnected. This proposed project, however, is going to focus on the selected ones.
   - ➤ Describe how these problems and needs are identified. They may include agency service records (e.g., waiting list) and experience, current literature, or community input through formal needs assessment approaches (e.g., a survey, expert interview, or town hall meeting).
   - ➤ Explain why these problems and needs are addressed, but not others. Possible reasons may be the intensity, frequency, and duration of the problems or needs in the target community; local input and desire; agency mission and capacity; etc.

2. Literature Review
   - ➤ From general discussion on the subject matter to the detailed understanding and appreciation of the unique condition of the identified problems and needs within the context of the local community and service recipients

3. Working Hypothesis
   - ➤ What is the educated hunch behind the logic and design of the proposed program and its interventions?
   - ➤ What are the philosophies or beliefs that bind all the approaches proposed?
     - ➤ E.g., Active social connections will increase older adults' mental and social well-being.
     - ➤ E.g., Active learning will increase students' interest in school and their academic achievements.

4. Briefly describe the proposed interventions/activities and expected outcomes.
   - ➤ Describe the type of interventions proposed, including the rationale and efficacy.
   - ➤ Explain why the proposed interventions are uniquely appropriate for the problem/need to be addressed.
   - ➤ Describe the expected results of the intervention.
     - ➤ E.g., To improve foster care youth's chances of success in achieving independence through a six-week home-based life skills coaching program.

Needs and Problems Statement, Background and Significance

In Chapter 2, the concept of need was defined, and the four types of needs were discussed. It is important for a grant proposal to have a convincing need and problem statement. After all, this is the reason the program is proposed. Coley and Scheinberg (2008) state that "the need statement or problem statement provides the rationale for the request for funding and uses data and other objective resources that substantiate the need for finding a solution to the concern" (p. 39). They further explain that "need statement is generally used in seeking funding for programs or services, while problem statement usually applies to social or community concerns or research-orientated proposals. Oftentimes, the terms are used interchangeably" (p. 39). In many cases, they are used together as a needs and problems statement (see Table 5.6).

A needs and problems statement should not be a lengthy social problem paper. It is instead a set of well-developed descriptions of what has been happening, what has been done, and what will happen if no action is taken. The proposal writer need not spend too much time convincing the funding source that the target problem is a concern. The funding source knows it is a problem; otherwise, it would not have issued an RFA addressing that topic. A proposal writer, however, needs to show that the applicant knows the problem well and is familiar with the current efforts addressing the problem. What the funding source does not know is how the target problem has affected the local community and the people the proposed project will serve.

For example, everyone knows that substance abuse negatively affects individuals and families. However, not too many people are aware of the effects it has on foster care youth who live in this rural county with little economic and social opportunities for young people. The applicant's expertise and genuine understanding of the problem and the target population(s) afford a unique position to effectively address the problem. In turn, it will assist the funding source in achieving its own goals. Yuen and Terao (2003) state that the applicants should "use this section to highlight the uniqueness of their situation, their unique insight of the situation, and their innovative approaches that address the problem" (p. 24).

A proposal writer should avoid the mistake of circular reasoning. This is a fallacy that uses a premise to support another premise. In addressing a need for a service, it is easy to say, "We need this service because we don't have this service." This is similar to the situation of a kid whining for candy at the checkout counter. The parent asks, "Why do you need candy?" The kid would say, "I need candy, because we don't have any candy!" or "We don't have any candy; therefore, we need candy." An analogy for circular reasoning could be a dog chasing its own tail. It goes around and around and does not end. "We need this service, because we don't have this service." "Since we don't have this service, therefore, we need this service."

Table 5.6 Sample Needs and Problems Statement

The 150 single teen mothers aged 14 to 18 are students in the Central Continuation High School. The majority of them are coming from the working-class neighborhoods in the City of Springville. About 35 percent of them have dropped out of school in the last year. Their academic performances in Math and English have been lower than the statewide standardized scores and are ranked in the lower 40th percentile. Truancy, substance abuse, violent relationships with partners and families, and gang involvement are common issues among these teens. Many of their parents have approached the school district and our school-based intervention social workers about their concerns. Their situations have attracted the attention of teachers, local law enforcement, and child welfare professionals.

A schoolwide questionnaire survey of teachers and several town hall meetings with parents and students last semester find many of these students have strong desires to be successful in life. They are, however, academically underprepared and are overwhelmed by childcare responsibilities and relational conflicts. Many suggest having an on-campus, low-cost childcare program, along with family counseling and support services in parenting, nutrition, and academic tutoring. Currently, these services are available in the city. However, they are very small operations and not easily accessible by these students through public transportation. A similar on-site childcare and wraparound service operation was established two years ago with a federal grant in the City of Summerville, which is about 30 miles away. Its recent program evaluation report indicates some very positive program outcomes.

These students continuing to drop or fail out of school would not only affect the future and well-being of these students, but also their children and the community as a whole. Due to the recent economic downturn, a 50-year-old jean manufacturing factory, the major employer in Springville, has shut down. Several grocery stores and banks have also been closed. With the economic hardship, tight city budget, and cutbacks of various services, city officials and residents are expecting an increase in unemployment and gang activity.

The applicant, Youth Service Agency, is in cooperation with the Springville School District proposing a wraparound intervention program titled Destination Success.

To break away from this endless circling, the writer must provide a conclusion, instead of a second premise, to the first premise. An example statement could be: "This foster youth mentoring program could facilitate more youth achieving successful independent living. Not providing this vital service could mean the continuation of a significant number of foster care youth becoming homeless and involved in a criminal justice system soon after they are emancipated."

Cultural competency is an important area of concern in describing the needs and problems. Yuen and Terao (2003) propose to assess the "five As: accessibility, availability, awareness, appropriateness, and acculturation" (p. 25). Cultural factors could block as well as facilitate services. Yuen (1999) states that "accessibility refers to both geographical and cultural relevance as well as difficulties in service delivery. . . . Availability refers to the existence, recruitment, and retention of services, clients, and a qualified service provider" (p. 109). Awareness is the knowledge and perspectives of the target population and the community regarding the identified areas of concerns and the services provided. Appropriateness refers to the suitability and acceptability of the services to the recipients both culturally and developmentally.

Yuen (1999) further explains: "[A]cculturation refers to the quality and extent of exposure to the dominant American culture and the degree of functioning within the dominant culture" (p. 110). "Ideally, culturally competent service programs are available to meet the identified needs in an appropriate manner. Target populations are aware of the service, and they can geographically and culturally access the services" (Yuen and Terao, 2003, p. 26).

Ideally, culturally specific service programs are available (Availability) to meet the identified needs in culturally appropriate approaches (Appropriateness) that take into consideration the different degrees of acculturation (Acculturation) of the service recipients. Target populations are aware (Awareness) of the needs/ problems and the available services they can access (Accessibility) geographically and culturally.

It is important for service providers to be sensitive to the issue of cultural match versus ethnic match. Ethnic match certainly increases the likelihood of cultural and linguistic compatibility but is no guarantee of cultural match. A youth may agree with her Asian immigrant parents that they all feel more comfortable working with another experienced Asian American worker, because of the ethnic match. She may also feel more connected to a younger African American worker, because the two of them share more aspects of the same youth and contemporary American cultures. In some situations, ethnic minority clients may feel more comfortable working with a service provider of a different background who is from outside their small ethnic community. This is particularly true regarding issues that are controversial or sensitive to the community, such as sexuality, abuse, and violence.

Literature Review

The best way to find a way out of a maze is to look at where one wants to end up—the exit or the finish line. In looking at the end products and figuring out what is required to achieve them, one would recognize what knowledge and skills the job requires. One might also learn from others' experiences and insight how better to develop or chart one's course. The RFA provides the applicant with what the funders are looking for in the proposal. By merging the funder's expectations with what the applicant agency is intending to achieve, the common goals or end products for the applicant's proposal will emerge. This shared goal between the funding source and the applicant will serve as the guiding point for the proposal in the utilization of the logic model to further develop the grant proposal.

Doing a puzzle is always perplexing. Experienced jigsaw puzzlers look first at the proposed end product, group pieces by their similar characteristics, start building the borders, and fill in the pieces. Engaging the human and social service delivery systems is very similar to putting together a jigsaw puzzle, except that we may not have the completed picture in front of us; we may not even have all of the pieces; our partners may be reluctant to play; and the playing field is constantly shaking and changing. Welcome to the exciting world of human and social services!

The literature review section for a grant proposal is an opportunity for the applicant to show a genuine understanding of the needs and problems and capacities to build on current knowledge to promote change and to achieve the desirable outcomes. Its purpose is to prove that the applicant has up-to-date knowledge of the subject matter, understands the various viewpoints, knows how to use the current knowledge to refine the proposed project, and it provides support for the claims made. It is also used to show the areas in which knowledge is lacking. A literature review is a chance for the applicant to demonstrate how it can integrate information with academic rigor and professional quality into the well-developed and practical grant proposal.

> This is not a collection of cut-and-pasted information from unverified sources or personal beliefs. It is a well-developed review of relevant information from creditable sources to lean [*sic*] support to the approaches presented in the proposal. It helps establish and explain the theoretical foundation of the development of the proposal and its intervention. (Yuen and Terao, 2003, pp. 26–27)

Writing a literature review can also be a very confusing process. There is either so much or so little information out there that the question is where one should start and when one should stop. Here is how the jigsaw puzzle example is helpful. The applicant must first decide what he and the funding source want to achieve (i.e., the completed picture and the end product). Then, he must set the borders or the parameters. With these completed, the grant writer has the boundary and the criteria to decide what should be included or discarded. Without that sorting and differentiation, the writer can very likely be overloaded with mountains of information that could impede the writing process. "Where do I start? How much is enough? There is so much (or too little) information!"

Additionally, the writer should group all related information together, connect the dots, and draw his conclusion. Essentially, he must imagine what the finished picture is like, set the borders or the parameters, identify the main themes, develop the theme or arguments through the grouping of related information, link the arguments, and form the conclusions that support the importance and necessity of the proposed program.

People build their puzzle by putting down one or a few pieces at a time. A writer should never try to build the whole thing in his head with complete details of exactly which piece goes where. Some of us may have tried that before, but not too many have been successful. So, the writer should start writing, writing with the end in mind and within the temporary parameters, rewriting, regrouping, rethinking, rewriting, rewriting, rewriting, rewriting, and then STOP.

He is not going to write the final chapter on the subject matter for humankind. His literature review is not intended to set the highest standard and save the world from ignorance. When it is good enough to support his claims, it is time to stop and move on to the next section of the proposal. How does one know whether it is good enough? Certainly, having someone else review it and comment will help. It is also a good idea to set it aside and read it again later to see whether it is comprehensive, comprehensible, has a focus, and is convincing.

Another way to conceptualize the literature review section is as an upside-down triangle. On the top are the general description, historical account, and current thinking of the concerns. The information on the top may include national statistics, reports, and academic literature to establish that the grant proposal addresses a common concern that needs attention. After narrowing down concerns from the national scene, the writer describes the concerns on the state or regional level with relevant information. As the literature review gets narrower, the next level integrates information describing the conditions on the local level, which may be the city, the district, the neighborhood, or a school. Through this process, the needs and concerns for the proposal are established, and the unique or specific situations of the target populations are demonstrated. This review also provides the theoretical backgrounds and practical rational for the design of the program and its interventions.

Target Population: To Whom It May Concern

Who are the beneficiaries or service recipients of the proposed program? Why target these client systems but not others? In the Specific Aims section (Background and Significance, Needs and Problems Statement, Literature Review), the grant writer establishes the demands and necessities for services for certain populations. Here, in this Target Population section, the grant writer is to provide a more comprehensive description of these populations and their unique situations that could benefit from the proposed program. The target populations, by definition, could include several target groups. For instance, a service program for juvenile offenders could focus on the youth as well as their families and communities.

Many populations in the community have equally important and urgent needs that deserve the attention of the service delivery systems. Then, why target this particular group? What exactly are the characteristics of this population? In addition to the basic demographic and socioeconomic information, a proposal writer should highlight conditions that distinguish the target populations from others. The conditions may include whether they are groups at risk, marginalized, neglected, discriminated, or underserved.

In the process of describing the dire situations of target populations—unintentionally or intentionally—a proposal writer may make the target population sound like a desperate and helpless group of people who lack the capacity to succeed; in other words, they need us to save them from their demise. Yes, they are in need of service, but, no, they are not incapable. They may be helpless, but they are not hopeless. Professionally, as social workers and counselors, we employ the strength perspectives that people have the capacity to change and grow. As a result, in describing target populations, we believe it is important to include the target population's strengths and capacities. We should not revictimize target populations just so the agency may receive a grant. After all, in the end, it is the target population that makes the change possible. As service providers, we play the roles of the facilitator, the service broker, the advocate,

Table 5.7 Outline for Writing the Target Populations

1. Define the target populations:
   ➤ Who are the service recipients? Name them up-front and early. Avoid creating the need for the reader to search the proposal to figure out who will be served.
   ➤ Be specific; provide operational (concrete) definitions, not formal (conceptual) definitions. For instance: "500 older adults aged 75 or above who live alone in their own homes in the neighborhood of Seniorvale" is more concrete than "Old people in the area."

2. Describe the environments of the locality of the target population:
   ➤ The locality may include the geographic region, district, city, community, or neighborhoods.
   ➤ Describe the socioeconomic status (SES), race and ethnic compositions, economic status, urban or rural, as well as other descriptors of the populations.

3. Describe the unique conditions and needs of the target populations:
   ➤ Indicate whether the target populations are groups targeted by the RFA.
   ➤ Discuss whether they are high-risk populations, such as victims of violence, youth without support networks, a homeless population, individuals with mental or other disabilities, low-income groups, or other disadvantaged groups.

4. Indicate how many will benefit from or participate in the program activities:
   ➤ How many will be served by each of the intervention activities? How many in each target population will be served? How many will be served during the whole project period? How many will be served annually?

5. Describe the connection between the applicant agency and the target population:
   ➤ No matter what great programs are planned, they are useless unless they can reach the target population. Briefly describe the outreach or recruitment strategies that could bring the proposed program to the populations the services are intending to reach.

the therapist, and the change agent. Table 5.7 provides a general outline for writing the Target Population section of a grant proposal.

Approaches and Methods: What, Why, When, Where, Who, and How

One of the most memorable TV commercials in the 1980s was three older ladies examining a big hamburger bun with one of them repeatedly asking, "Where's the beef?" In a grant proposal, the Approaches and Methods section is the "beef" of the proposal. It is the most read section of the proposal, because it tells what the program will do to bring about change.

Service agencies are passionate about their work and are eager to report what motivates them to provide services that address the serious situation of the service recipients. Although the agency's purpose (i.e., needs and problems) is important, the funding source is more interested in where the proposed program is going and what they are achieving (approaches and methods, and objectives). Similar to a job interview, the employer is more interested in knowing what the applicant can do than why the applicant needs a job! Where you are going instead of where you are coming from.

It has been said that "a fool with a plan is as good as a genius without a plan." Having a good plan, therefore, will make the applicant agency a genius with a plan. Certainly, no agency wants to be caught as a fool without a plan. The Approaches and Methods section lays out the detailed plans about what and how the services will be provided.

From Mission to Action   There are several terms often used in program planning and proposal writing. They are *vision, mission, purpose, directions, aims, goals, objectives,* and *activities.* Every service agency has a vision that reflects the ultimate ideal state the agency can imagine (e.g., world peace, a society free of violence and poverty). That vision is the agency's pot of gold at the end of the rainbow. A vision is very abstract and not easily communicated to others. Putting that vision in writing creates the agency's mission statement. A mission statement describes the reasons for the existence of the agency and what change it intends to achieve (Netting, Kettner, and McMurtry, 2008).

A visionary mission statement is a relatively permanent expression, but it is not static and may change if the social conditions have evolved and modifications are warranted, which is not likely. "Implicit in the relative permanence of a mission statement is an understanding that the problems or conditions of concern to the agency are broad enough in scope and scale that they are not likely to be achieved in the near future" (Kettner, Moroney, and Martin, 2008, p. 122). The elimination of poverty worldwide certainly is most desirable, but it is not likely attainable for a long time. Kettner, Moroney, and Martin (2008) further explain that "a mission statement should focus on what lies ahead for its clients or consumers if the agency is successful in addressing their problems and meeting their needs" (p. 122).

Operationalizing the mission statement, the agency establishes goals for its organizational development and its programs and services. A goal is a general long-term end state or destination. It is general and long term in that it sets the focus and the big picture, but it is not achievable in a short time. Kettner, Moroney, and Martin (2008) define goals as "statements of expected outcomes dealing with the problems that the program is attempting to prevent, eradicate, or ameliorate" (p. 123). Kettner et al. further describe that a goal statement "should flow logically from the agency's mission statement, while providing a framework and sense of direction for the objectives which are to follow" (p. 123). In between the mission statement and goals, there may exist a big gap. An aim is the intermediate focus between mission and goals.

The objective derives from the goal. An objective is a concrete, specific, time-limited, directional, and measurable statement of outcome. "All objectives have a number of elements in common. A good objective is clear, specific, measurable, time limited, and realistic and represents a commitment" (Kettner, Moroney, and Martin, 2008, p. 125). The goal, "promote independence among the target poster youth" would have many objectives, including "60 percent of the 20 foster care youth in the Steps to Success program will attend 80 percent of the program activities and will pass the GED examination in 9 months." As shown in the logic model, objectives could include output (process), immediate outcome (outcome), or end outcome (impact).

Figure 5.1   From Mission to Action

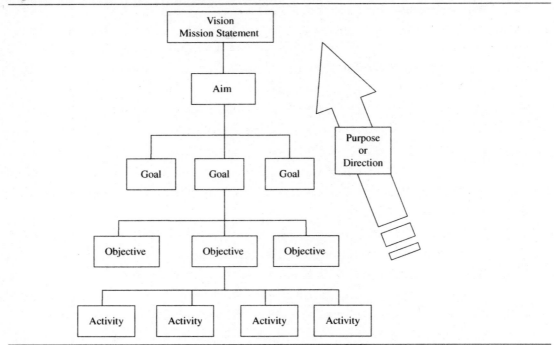

"Activities" are interventions or program tasks implemented to achieve the objective. Activities are implemented by the agency to achieve its objectives, which in turn allows it to attain its goals, and leads to the fulfillment of the agency's mission. As one can see in Figure 5.1, there are logical connections between vision, mission, aim, goals, objectives, and activities. If an agency or a program has this clear and meaningful linkage driven by the mission, one could say the agency or the program has a well-defined purpose or direction. Figure 5.1 shows the meaningful connections among these various elements.

There are many ways to write up the Approaches and Methods section of a proposal. Table 5.8 provides an example of one of the ways to structure the goals, objectives, and activities. Unless it is specified by the funding source, there is no standardized format. Another format we proposed is the use of a Program Planning and Evaluation Worksheet (Table 5.3) that could be used for both program planning (Approaches and Methods) and evaluation.

The general outline would include the following:

1. Introduction and Goals

   ➤ Introduce the goals and a brief summary of the implementation plan of the proposed program.

   For example: The proposed New Beginning program will provide counseling services, support groups, advocacy services, and community events to prevent relapse and to promote sobriety for 300 Spanish-speaking males in Sacramento who have completed residential treatment programs.

Table 5.8 Sample Approaches and Methods

Intergenerational Mentoring Program

Project Goal:

The goal of the Intergenerational Mentoring Program is to promote service and successful aging for the Study Corps, older adult volunteers and to increase academic and personal performances of fourth- to sixth-grade students in the Canusehelp Elementary School. It has three main components: (1) In-Class Facilitation Program, (2) After-School Study Hall, and (3) Out-and-About Learning program.

Component 1: In-Class Facilitation
Objective 1.1 In-Class Support

At least 25 senior volunteers will work with 25 identified fourth-grade students in their math classes to assist and coach them in taking notes and understanding the materials, for a total of 400 hours.

Activity 1.1.1

Twenty-five volunteers will be recruited and trained in the first month of the program. Based on volunteers' and students' preferences, matches will be made during the second month.

Activity 1.1.2

Each volunteer will spend at least four hours per week with the assigned students in class.

Activity 1.1.3

Monthly meeting will be held with the teachers to monitor students' progress.

Objective 1.2 Reading Fun

A total of six volunteers (two per class) will implement the Reading Fun program during the zero-period advisory with interested students, by the group reading from selected books. At least 60 percent of the participating students will fulfill the accelerated reader requirements.

Activity 1.2.1

Based on teachers' recommendations and self-referrals, an open ongoing reading group for each class will be established in the second month. Reading Fun will run at least twice each week.

Activity 1.2.2

Each reading group will select its reading list and reading schedules.

Activity 1.2.3

Each reading group will set its own reward system to promote reading and plan its end-of-the-semester celebration.

Component 2: After-School Study Hall
Objective 2.1 Study Hall

Monday to Thursday every day, at least four of the ten volunteers will staff the school library for a two-hour study hall for 30 fourth- to sixth-grade students. This is to provide academic support and a stable study environment for students who are mostly latchkey children or who could benefit from tutoring.

Activity 2.1.1

Set up the logistics of the study hall program: registration, check-in/check-out, snack schedule, and reward system.

Activity 2.1.2

Implement the study hall program.

(continued)

Objective 2.2 Academic Management

At least 65 percent of the participating students will demonstrate active learning and homework management skills.

Activity 2.2.1

Within the first two months, the students' homework agenda check will move from being done by the volunteers to completion by peers, and then to self-management. In month three, no more than 20 percent of the students will have incidents of an incomplete agenda or missing homework.

Activity 2.2.2

Students will develop a High-Five reward system for students who are able to continuously complete homework assignments for a month.

Component 3: Out-and-About Learning Program

Objective 3.1 Space Shuttle Launching

In cooperation with the Space for Kids program, a Space Shuttle Launching Day Camp will be organized in March for 60 fifth-grade students to provide hands-on learning in math and science.

Activity 3.1.1

Formulate a working committee, including staff from the Space for Kids Program, fifth-grade teachers, and volunteers to coordinate activities and teaching schedules for the day camp.

Activity 3.1.2

Organize day-camp related arrangements: parental approval, transportation, fundraising for the event, and other logistics.

Activity 3.1.3

Five volunteers will develop alternative programs in schools for students who choose to not attend the day camp.

Objective 3.2 Nature Wonderlands

In cooperation with the Outdoor Wonders Association, a Nature Wonderlands program will provide 40 sixth-graders with the opportunity to apply their math skills in doing a wildlife census count in the Delta Wildlife Sanctuary in February.

Activity 3.2.1

Establish working agreements with the Outdoor Wonders Association and the school district for the implementation of the Nature Wonderlands program.

Activity 3.2.2

Include five Big Lake High School seniors in the planning and implementation of the program as their senior project.

Activity 3.2.3

Implement the Nature Wonderlands program with contents that augment the current sixth-grade math and science curriculum.

---

2. Recruitment, Retention, and Community Support

   ➢ Describe how the program will gain access, build connection, and recruit the target population.

   ➢ Illustrate what the program will do to retain participants.

➤ Demonstrate that the program has the cultural and professional competency to reach and serve the target populations.

➤ Explain what barriers or difficulties are expected and the strategies the agency will use to address the anticipated challenges.

➤ Provide evidence of connection, partnership, and cooperation with community groups and collaborating agencies to reach out to the target population.

3. Objectives and Activities

There are many ways to display the program's objective and activities. Two ways are:

➤ They could be listed numerically to show the connection (see Table 5.8).

➤ They could be included in the Program Planning and Evaluation Worksheet (see Table 5.3), if it is used.

4. Timeline

➤ The timeline for individual activity should be indicated when objectives and activities are presented.

➤ The overall activity schedules could also be shown through the use of tools such as the Gantt Chart (see Table 5.9).

➤ Organizing the timeline often helps the proposal writer to become more realistic and practical in the planning of events and activities.

Table 5.9 Sample Gantt Chart

Objectives-Activities/Months	Aug.	Sept.	Oct.	Nov.	Dec.	Jan.	Feb.	Mar.	Apr.	May
Component 1: In-Class Facilitation										
Objective 1.1 In-Class Support										
Activity 1.1.1 Prepare volunteers	X	X								
Activity 1.1.2 Volunteers in class		X	X	X		X	X	X	X	
Activity 1.1.3 Teacher meetings	X				X					X
Objective 1.2 Reading Fun										
Activity 1.2.1 Establish Reading Fun		X								
Activity 1.2.2 Reading List			X	X		X	X			
Activity 1.2.3 Reward and Celebration					X					X
Component 1: After-School Study Hall										
Objective 2.1 Study Hall										
Activity 2.1.1 Set up study hall	X	X								
Activity 2.1.2 Study hall in session			X	X	X	X	X	X	X	X
Objective 2.2 Academic Management										
Activity 2.2.1 Homework check		X	X	X		X	X	X		
Activity 2.2.2 High-five reward		X	X	X	X	X	X	X	X	X

Agency Capacities and Project Management: The Service Providers and Program Management

A private, nonprofit 501(c)3 organization is required to have a board of directors. The board serves many functions, including its fiduciary responsibility. Board members represent the public interests and the citizens, and supervise the organization. They keep the agency accountable.

When a funding source considers the allocation of funding support to an agency, the trustworthiness, creditability, and capacities of the agency are called into question. Could the agency be trusted with the money? Does it have a good record of proper fiscal management? Does it have prior experiences in administrating similar funding? Does it have the organizational and fiscal competencies to manage the awarded funding? Does it have any proof of its claimed abilities? The list of questions could go on and on, until the funding source has the confidence that the agency is capable enough to handle the funding accountably.

Many agencies, voluntarily or by mandate, are using accounting firms to conduct regular independent auditing of their fiscal systems. The audits provide useful information for the agency to improve its fiscal capacities and certify its fiscal soundness to the funding sources and the public. A "management letter," which accompanies the fiscal audit report, provides a summary of the audit, as well as recommendations and comments of interest to the organization and the community at large. Some funding sources request the inclusion of the latest management letter with the grant proposal, as an indicator of the agency's fiscal capacities.

One of the authors has experience helping an outstanding grassroots organization in preparing a major homeless service grant ranked nationally in the top 5 percent among the applications. In the end, the grant was not awarded, because the agency had not been diligent in developing its fiscal management system. The agency was run by several very caring Catholic nuns who had long been living from hand-to-mouth. It was more interested in direct services and doing whatever it could to serve than in formal agency development. Although everyone knew that the agency would do what it proposed to do and more, a sound fiscal system and a formal track record of management was the prerequisite for receiving that multimillion-dollar service grant.

An agency is guided by its vision, which is described in the mission statement. One can learn about the agency by reviewing its mission statement, its history, organizational and managerial structure, programs and services, staff compositions and qualifications, and accomplishments. It is common to hear people suggest going for funding for an additional staff position. The reality is that most of the funding sources for service do not fund a staff or a position. They fund the program and its activities. It is in the implementation of the funded program that a staff member is needed and a relevant position is supported.

Specifically, the funding source is interested in knowing the staffing of the proposed program, their qualifications, their job responsibilities, the agency's management, and its relationship to the agency's other programs. Who reports to whom? Who has the supervisory responsibilities and how are they carried out? In the grant proposal, a project management plan details these concerns. Detailed job descriptions of key positions and resumes for key personnel should be included. An organizational chart is often included (see Figure 5.2).

When a program is proposed, the applicant agency should not fill each position in the proposed program with its current staff. First, not all current staff have the right qualifications for the new program. Second, what happens to their current responsibilities if the new program is funded? Is this new programming just a way to keep this staff employed, or is it a program to meet the needs in the community? However, staff that have expertise in the proposed service and have the established credentials should be named and included. This is particularly true for staff who have special knowledge and training, as well as staff who are culturally competent and linguistically appropriate for the target population. Their involvement could increase the credibility and success of the new program. A mix of existing staff with credentials, and the expected influx of qualified staff as described in the job descriptions, can give the funding source a good sense of the capacities of the service providers.

Beyond these internal considerations, there are equally important concerns for the agency's external connections with the target populations and other organizations in the community. Funding sources and service providers know there is no one agency that can meet the community needs alone. Cooperation, collaboration, and partnership

Figure 5.2 Organizational Chart

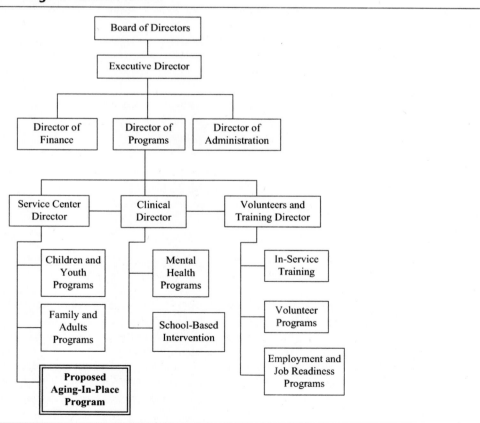

are essential to any program's success. The applicant agency may need to show how it has and can reach the target populations, particularly when they are hard-to-reach groups. Are the recruitment and retention methods culturally appropriate, developmentally suitable, and socially desirable? Are the target populations supportive of this new program? How can other organizations help in making connections, referring clients, providing space or expertise, and collaborating in the implementation of services? Furthermore, is the proposed program supported by politicians and legislators at all levels? One of the ways to show the nature and extent of these supports is to include an appropriate number of support letters from the target populations, partner services, government agencies, and relevant key politicians. This strategy of cooperation also makes the applicant more competitive if other local applicants are applying.

Table 5.10 is a sample outline for preparing the Agency Capacity and Project Management section of the grant proposal. Table 5.11 gives examples of two job descriptions for a program director position and a program evaluator position.

Table 5.10 Sample Outline for Agency Capacity and Project Management

1. Agency Structure
   - Description of Agency: Describe the nature and purpose of the agency, its services and programs. Explain how the proposed program fits in or augments the current program structure, e.g., The Service-for-All Association is a private nonprofit social service agency in the north side of South Park, West Virginia. It is a community-based agency established in 1982, currently with 50 quality staff. Last year, its annual budget was $2.5 million. A total of 3,500 individuals and their families in the community have received services through its various service programs. These programs include an outpatient mental health clinic, substance abuse treatment and prevention programs, domestic violence intervention programs and a safe house, a school-based service team, and a youth center for children and families. The proposed young fatherhood program will be an independent program in conjunction with the school-based program and the youth center.
   - Board of Directors and Organizational Structure: Describe the structure and functions of the board of directors. Attach a list of current directors and the structure of the board in the appendix. The organizational structure of the agency shall also be briefly described, and a copy of the organizational chart should be included in the appendix.

2. Organizational Capacity
   - Provide evidence to show that the agency can effectively implement the proposed service.
   - Highlight the agency's experiences in successfully carrying out similar programs.
   - Draw attention to the agency's staff expertise and qualifications.
   - Emphasize the agency's connections with and understanding of the target populations.
   - Underline the cultural competency of the agency.
   - Display the agency's ability in collaboration and coalition building.

3. Project Management and Project Staff
   - Describe the positions needed and their full-time equivalence (FTE).
   - Include a job description for each key position.
   - If key staff are identified or will be reassigned to this program, highlight their experience, training, and expertise; also include their resumes in the appendix.
   - Describe staff recruitment, training, and retention plan.
   - Explain how, administratively, the proposed project will be able to augment and support current programs.
   - Discuss the general program management structure and approaches, e.g., the component coordinators will supervise each of the project's three components. Together with the project director, they form the management team for the project. Weekly individual supervision will be held between the project director and each coordinator. There will be weekly check-in and biweekly component meetings, and a monthly meeting for project staff. The project director will report to the executive director. The director will also be responsible for organizing the project advisory committee and its quarterly meeting.

Table 5.11 Job Description for Program Director and Program Evaluator

Job Descriptions

Position Title: Program Director

Position Description: The program director is responsible for the planning, development, implementation, and coordination of the Intergenerational Mentoring Program (IMP) project.

The **basic responsibilities** are as follows:

1. Administrative: Plan, develop, and implement the IMP. Develop program strategies for service implementation by staff and reviews by the executive director and the advisory committee. Monitor program implementation and the attainment of program objectives and adherence to administrative guidelines and procedures.

2. Personnel: Develop program personnel procedure and implement agency personnel policy. Recruit and evaluate program staff, and make personnel recommendations.

3. Training: Provide supervision, training, and development to staff and volunteers. Work with staff and executive director in identifying and establishing staff development strategies.

4. Management: Monitor program progress and fiscal control. Ensure proper documentation and reporting by staff. Prepare monthly report to executive director and board of directors. Submit reports to the funding source in a timely manner.

5. Evaluation: Assist the program evaluator in developing and implementing the evaluation plan, reporting out, and using information for program improvements.

6. Public Relations: Represent the program and the agency in establishing linkage with the community and reporting progress.

7. Other duties as assigned by the executive director.

Minimum Qualifications:

1. Graduate degree in social work, sociology, education, psychology, or equivalent experience in program development and management.

2. Two or more years in supervisory roles in program management, staff development, planning, budget management, and reporting.

3. Demonstrated competency in mental health and clinical counseling.

4. Experience in advocacy, case management, and resources in the community.

5. Knowledge in grant writing and program evaluation.

6. Experience and knowledge of the target population in the community.

7. Excellent verbal and written communication skills.

Position Title: Program Evaluator

Position Description: The program evaluator is responsible for the planning, development, implementation, and coordination of the evaluation tasks for the Intergenerational Mentoring Program (IMP) project.

The **basic responsibilities** are as follows:

1. Evaluation: Develop and implement the various components of program evaluation, report findings to appropriate audiences, and prepare deliverables in a timely manner.

2. Training: Train and prepare project staff and volunteers in implementing evaluation tasks and using evaluation findings.

3. Administration: Ensure the evaluation component meets the funding source program, and procedure requirements and deadline. Provide necessary evaluation documents to meet funding source requirements. Monitor the development and implementation of all stages of the evaluation.

Specific Roles and Responsibilities:

1. Meet and communicate with project staff regularly.

2. Develop an evaluation plan that assesses the program.

3. Establish and maintain the information management system.

4. Develop data collection instruments.

5. Conduct or monitor data collection and data entry.

6. Perform data analysis.

7. Report evaluation findings.

8. Produce agreed-upon deliverables (i.e., evaluation plan, midterm report, final report).

Minimum Qualifications:

1. Graduate degree in social work, sociology, education, psychology, or equivalent experience in program evaluation.

2. Demonstrated track record of quality program evaluation.

3. Knowledge in government human service programs and their evaluation.

4. Experience and knowledge of the target population in the community.

5. Excellent verbal and written communication skills.

6. Experience in the types of service provided by the project.

Budget and Budget Justifications: Program Plan in Dollars and Cents

A *budget* is a program plan in dollars and cents. It estimates and allocates the costs for implementing the proposed service. It also reflects the philosophies and emphases of the funding source and the service agency. It is often used as a benchmark for measuring the effectiveness and desirability of the program. To clarify the costs and provide the rationale for the allocations or estimates, an associated budget justification is usually included with the budget. The budget justification could be a separate narrative page, or it could be incorporated into the budget form.

There are many ways to create a budget. The most common one is the line-item budget. In a line-item budget, items are grouped by administrative categories. The total costs/expenses are equal to the total funding requested/income within a particular funding period. A budget form for a grant proposal should, therefore, clearly indicate the budgetary period (e.g., 12 months, 18 months). If a proposed program has several funding sources or contributions for different budget items, some agencies list them on the same budget page to indicate the separation and comingling of funding. Every agency and funding source constructs the template of its line-item budget form differently. In general, the common categories are personnel, benefits, indirect cost, travel and conferences, equipment, supplies, contractual cost, construction, rental/ space, and others (see Table 5.12).

Personnel Cost   Personnel cost is often the most expensive item for a grant proposal budget. It is the salary cost or wages for the permanent staff of the program. Some agencies list the salary range, but others just list the median or mean salary for the position. Some of these staff members are working full-time, and some may only work part-time. The amount of time a staff is employed for the program is reflected in terms of full-time equivalents (FTEs). A staff who works 100 percent or full-time for the program is one FTE; three-quarters time is, therefore, 0.75 FTE; half-time is 0.5 FTE, and so on. Due to the demands of programming or the desire to save salary expenses to pay for other start-up costs associated with funding source approval, the hiring of some staff may be delayed. The number of months of work the program requires is, therefore, used to reflect the length or period of the employment. Depending on the agency or funding source's preference, the amount of money paid for each position can be shown as annual salary or monthly salary.

Employee Benefits   Salary is not the only cost in hiring staff. As many would advise job seekers, take-home money (salary) is important, but fringe benefits are equally important. Employee benefits or fringe benefits are nonsalary compensation or costs for an employee. This cost is usually calculated as a percentage of the employee's salary. The percentage is different from one agency to another. It ranges from 15 percent to 40 percent. In general, it is usually around 30 percent (e.g., $30,000 for a $100,000 position). The employee benefits may include many things, such as Social Security and Medicare taxes (FICA, 8 percent), health insurances (e.g., medical, dental, vision, and mental health, together about 8 percent of the salary), group insurance plans (e.g., life and disability, about 1 percent; unemployment, about 3 percent; and workers' compensation, about 3 percent), and retirement plans (401K, annuity, and others, about 3 percent). They may also include sick leave, vacation, education, day care, awards and incentives, housing, and other items. It would not be unusual for someone to take a lower-paying job because of a more generous benefit package.

Although personnel budget (salary or personnel cost plus employee benefits) often makes up the biggest portion of the budget, normally it is not larger than 65 percent of the total cost of the program (e.g., $65,000 for a $100,000 grant program). [Percentage of personnel budget = (salary + benefit) / total program cost.] An agency that has a personnel budget higher than 65 percent of the total budget should give detailed justification. Certainly, an outpatient mental health counseling program will use most of the cost for hiring mental health counselors, and its personnel budget may exceed 65 percent of the total budget. A meals-on-wheels service program may see more of their expenses in supplies and transportation than in personnel. Its personnel budget is less likely to exceed 65 percent of the total budget.

Indirect Cost   While program staff are working hard on their programs, the executive director is lobbying for additional funding support and briefing the board of directors on the program's progress. The fiscal director is creating the monthly budget report and processing this month's paychecks. The personnel director is busy working on hiring new staff and researching how to legally lay off certain staff. Before everyone comes to work or after everyone leaves, there is the janitor who, along with the maintenance person, works behind the scenes.

There are also social marketing, fundraising, proposal writing, auditing, and other necessary expenses that are not directly related to, or exclusive to, the proposed program. All of these people and expenses have to be paid to keep the agency going. The cost to pay for such organizational support and activities is the indirect cost, also known as overhead.

The calculation of the indirect cost for an agency is not a simple process. It entails specific calculations based on government guidelines, and accounting principles involving direct and indirect expenditures. An organization that has a grant or contract with the federal government has to apply to get a recognized indirect cost rate for the agency. The rate could be a low (e.g., 10 percent) to a high (e.g., 50 percent) percentage of the direct cost. The determination of this rate is a rather important concern. Once the rate is established, it will be applied to all of the agency's future federal grants and contracts. The rate may also apply to state grants and contracts. For various reasons, some states prefer to set up their own rate instead of using the federal rate. Many private funding sources, such as foundations, have made clear that their funding does not pay for the indirect cost. In general, the indirect cost could be 20 percent of the personnel cost.

The indirect cost is normally part of the total grant award. If the grant award amount is fixed, that means the higher the indirect cost, the lower the amount is left for program expenses. It is, therefore, also true that the higher the salary cost, the higher the benefits and indirect cost, and the lesser amount is left for programming. For a few federal grants, the indirect cost is not part of the total award. It is an added amount. For instance, if an agency has a 40 percent federal indirect rate, it will receive $40,000 in addition to the $100,000 grant, for a total of $140,000. For this type of grant, the incentive to keep the personnel budget low is not as strong.

Travel and Transportation   These are costs associated with program staff and service recipients' local transportation and out-of-town travels. For service recipients, there are coach bus rental costs for field trips, as well as bus passes for business and going to appointments. For staff, travel reimbursements are made for mileage driven for official business using personal vehicles. The federal per-mile reimbursement rate changes from time to time. In 2009, the standard mileage rate is $0.55 per mile (IRS, www.irs.gov/newsroom/article/0,,id=200505,00.html). Program staff should check the latest listing for the proper reimbursement rate. While there is a federal rate, a state or an organization may use a different rate, usually less than the federal rate. In addition to local travel, program staff may travel out of town for conferences or meetings. Those expenses should be included in estimating costs.

Equipment and Supplies   Equipment refers to items purchased that cost more than $5,000, or usually last longer than two years. Program apparatus, office furniture, copiers, phone system, or computer system are examples of equipment. Supplies are items that cost less than $5,000, or last less than two years. Materials used for program activities, postage, incentive materials, and office stationery are examples of supplies. While these descriptions are generally correct, different funding sources have different thresholds and definitions of what constitutes supplies.

Contractual or Constant Cost   These are costs for support personnel. They may include part-time instructors, tutors, trainers, computer support persons, and a program evaluator. These personnel are not permanent salaried staff, and they do not get benefits such as health insurance or retirement benefits. To save costs, some agencies increase the use of contractual personnel instead of permanent staff. Every agency has its own definition of whether someone is a permanent employee or a contractor.

Construction and Office Space   Unless the funding source indicates construction is an allowable cost, or it is a construction grant application, construction cost is usually not an allowable item. Construction cost is the expense for new or major renovation, remodeling, or repair of a structure. It is not part of the operation cost for most service-oriented funding. If a new service center needs to add a lobby, office, or bathroom, the agency may need to seek other funding support for such construction. Local charity, foundation, or Housing and Urban Development's (HUD) Community Development Block Grant (CDBG) are some such possible funding sources. Some agencies conduct special fundraising events to support specific construction needs.

Some funding sources may support the use of leasehold improvement or tenant improvement. The owner of the facility may make minor refurbishments to the structure to make it suitable for the particular use by the tenant. The customized alteration of the facility would be included in the lease agreement. Such an agreement may require the tenant to pay higher rent or have a longer lease as part of the agreement.

Office space could be a very expensive item on the budget, depending on the location and local housing demands. To make the service location accessible to target populations, the offices should ideally be located in central locations, easily accessible by public transportation, or within the neighborhood of the service recipients. Sharing space with other agencies or renting from government or charity entities are ways to lower the cost.

Miscellaneous/Other   Miscellaneous expenses, such as staff development, community partnership expenses, reporting out and printing of brochures, janitorial services (many budget people count this as part of the indirect cost), award celebrations, and other minor expenses could be included as miscellaneous or other expenses. A proposal writer should include as many of these items as possible into the identified categories in the budget instead of listing them as miscellaneous or others.

In-Kind Contributions and Matching Funds   In-kind contributions are noncash donations that add value to the proposed program. They could include donated labor, materials, equipments, or space from the applicant agency or its affiliates. Some agencies waive the indirect cost and use it as an in-kind contribution. An agency may donate, as in-kind contributions, licensed clinical social work supervision, 1 FTE of volunteer time, free use of existing office space in the applicant's current office building, or the use of office equipment such as phones, computers, and copiers. It may even waive the indirect cost if the program is funded. Altogether, in-kind contributions could constitute a value equal to, say, 40 percent of the actual cost of the proposed program. With this contribution, the requested amount of funding support is effectively only 60 percent of the actual cost. The funding source, in effect, gets a 100 percent program with only 60 percent of the cost.

It is easy to claim that the agency will share resources among programs. In reality, a service provider has to be realistic about such "robbing-Peter-to-pay-Paul" promises. In the previous example, if the social worker is funded 100 percent of the time by another funding source, will her use of 10 percent of this time for in-kind supervision violate the contract with that funding source? In the end, as she becomes a 10 percent in-kind contribution for 10 different programs, will she, in addition to her real full-time assignment, carry a 200 percent workload? An agency has to be careful about making such promises. Overextended contributions may lead the agency to agree to run a $50,000 program with a $30,000 grant and expect every program to donate their resources, staff, and services to cover the gap. Grant programs in the agency end up working to meet the goals and demands of grants other than their own, and eventually all of them may fail. Comingling, sharing of resources, and cross-training are fine ideas but they have to be managed legally and very carefully.

Matching funds are actual cash contributions coming from another account to support the operation of the proposed program. More and more funding sources are asking applicant agencies to contribute matching funds. This type of cost-sharing approach serves many purposes. It encourages the applicant agency to identify and develop alternative funding and to focus on sustainability and independence. Agencies may use various fundraising events to build up the matching fund account. There are also funding sources that focus on providing matching fund support to agencies to enable and encourage them to apply for funding for which they would not otherwise qualify. To show the inclusion of in-kind contributions and matching funds, some agencies add extra columns on the budget form to highlight such committed support.

Table 5.12 is a sample 12-month budget and justifications for a new program. In addition to a basic budget, it includes delayed hiring, leasehold improvement, a lease-to-purchase option for the copier (a copier is often not an allowable item for purchase with grant funding), and the use of contract monies for the evaluator and part-time staff.

A Word about "Tipping"   "Tipping" is when an agency requests funding that is as big as or bigger than its current budget. The new budget will run the risk of tipping over the existing one and cause all kinds of financial and management issues. Unless it is properly justified, it is a red flag for the funding agency.

Table 5.12 Sample First-Year Budget and Justifications

A. Personnel

	Annual Salary	FTE	Months	Cost	Subtotal	Cum. Total	In-kind
Program Director	$70,000	0.5	12	$35,000			
Coordinator	$60,000	1	10	$50,000			
Counselor	$40,000	3	9	$90,000			
Admin. Assistant	$30,000	0.5	12	$15,000			
		5.0		$190,000		$190,000	

B. Benefits (30% of Personnel Cost/Salary)

1. Payroll taxes (FICA, etc.)
2. Employee benefits (medical, dental, vision, life, disability,
   workers compensation, unemployment, 401K)

					Subtotal	Cum. Total	In-kind
(30% × $190,000 = $57,000)					$57,000	$247,000	

C. Indirect Cost (20% of Personnel Cost/Salary)

	Subtotal	Cum. Total	In-kind
	$38,000	$285,000	$40,000

D. Travel and Conference

1. Local mileage
   ($.55 reimbursement per mile, 5.0 FTE staff, 1 FTE volunteer,
   50 miles/week, 48 work weeks)
   ($.55 × 6.0 FTE × 50 miles × 48 weeks = $7,920)
2. National conference (3 days, 2 nights)
   [($550 Airfare, $150 × 2 nights Hotel, $60 × 3 days per diem,
   $200 registration) × 2 persons= $2,460]

	Subtotal	Cum. Total
3. Local conferences and training ($2,000)	$12,380	$297,380

E. Equipment

1. Computer and printer
   (6 computers × $1,000 + 2 printers × $500 = $7,000)
2. Telephone (6 units × $100 + $500 installation = $1,100)
3. Office and youth center furniture, audiovisual (desks, chairs, couch, TV,
   projector = $10,000)
4. Copier rental

	Subtotal	Cum. Total
[(Rental cost $300 + Service $200 + Operation $300) × 12 months] = $9,600	$27,700	$325,080

F. Supplies

1. General office supplies ($500/mo × 12 months = $6,000)
2. Program/activity supplies ($600/mo × 12 months = $7,200)
3. Printing ($200/mo × 12 months = $2,400)
5. Postage ($50/mo × 12 months = $600)
6. Program incentive and promotional materials

	Subtotal	Cum. Total	In-kind
($100/mo × 12 months = $1,200)	$17,400	$342,480	$2,000

G. Contractual Employees/Consultants

1. Program assistants
   a. Instructors ($20/hr × 80 hrs × 5 instructors = $8,000)
   b. Tutors ($15/hr × 150 hrs × 3 tutors = $6,750)

	Subtotal	Cum. Total
2. Program evaluator $100/hr × 100 hrs = $10,000	$24,750	$367,230

H. Construction

Not applicable

I. Office Space

	Subtotal	Cum. Total	In-kind
1. Main office/youth center (with leasehold improvement) (3,000 sq. ft. × $2.5/mo × 12 months = $90,000)	$186,000	$553,230	$8,000

2. Utilities (Water, sewer, gas, electricity, Internet, phone) ($800/mo × 12
   months = $96,000)

J. Others

	Subtotal	Cum. Total	In-kind
1. Miscellaneous	$1,770	$555,000	
Total Cost	$555,000	$555,000	$50,000
Net Funding Requested	$555,000 − $50,000 = **$505,000**		

Evaluation Plan: Tell the Stories—Successes and Challenges

Depending on the type of proposal and the funding sources, there are various demands regarding the format and rigor for the evaluation component of the grant proposals. Some require a regular reporting or a small-scale periodic output evaluation. Some may demand a more formal evaluation conducted by agency staff or an internal evaluator. A less demanding program evaluation may be a separate section of the proposal or be imbedded as part of the Approaches and Methods. For example, the Program Planning and Evaluation Worksheet (Table 5.3) that was mentioned earlier in this chapter includes the evaluation element for each of the program objectives.

For major funding, a fully developed and independent evaluation plan may be needed to accompany the grant proposal. They may even demand that the evaluation be conducted by an outside evaluator, an external evaluator who has certain credentials and with a separate budget. Detailed discussions and guidelines for developing various types of evaluation plans are included in different parts of this book, particularly in Chapter 6, Program Evaluation, and Chapter 8, Real-Life Samples.

No matter what level of rigor is required, the evaluation component provides a mechanism for the program to tell its stories as well as document its challenges and successes. The evaluation section serves as more than a reporting and accountability requirement. It is also an opportunity for the program to identify strengths, concerns, and ideas for program improvement. For some demonstration or outcome-based grants, a well-designed evaluation component is mandated to test the hypotheses and the utility of the proposed programs.

It is important for a grant proposal to have an evaluation that is program-driven—an evaluation that can assess the degree of goal attainments and the success of the intervention activities. It is dangerous to have an evaluation plan that is excessively dominant that sound intervention activities have to be negatively modified in order to produce the required data for the evaluation. An evaluation-driven program activity serves the needs of the evaluation but not necessarily the service needs of the clients, which is the primary focus of the program activities.

The development of an evaluation plan also serves an amazing function: challenging the program to review and reassess what it has proposed. It is not unusual, during the process of developing the evaluation plan, to spot program inconsistencies and service gaps. As a result, the evaluation plan should be developed during the early stage of the proposal. This helps to refine the proposed program and encourages the development of an evaluation plan that is an integral part of the whole service program.

Proposal Reviews

What happens to the complete grant proposal after it is delivered to the funding source on or before the due date? The answer is simple: "It will be reviewed." However, the review process is not simple. Depending on the nature of the grant proposal and the resources and sophistication of the funding source, the proposal will be reviewed in different formats. Most funding sources form one or several review committees, and each is responsible for reviewing a certain number of proposals. The review committees are made up of individuals of various backgrounds. Most of them are knowledgeable about the subject matter. Their experience in grant proposal writing and program evaluation might be quite different. The reviewers' academic preparation and disciplines might also vary quite a bit.

One review method involves bringing all reviewers together in a meeting room, often for days, to complete the reviews. Technically, they are free from interferences and influences from anyone outside the review group. The size of the review group varies depending on the budget, availability of reviewers, and other factors. An agency staff, usually a program officer, serves as the coordinator and staff for the review groups.

In a formal and large review, each of the reviewers is assigned to do three levels of reviews for a batch of 10 to 15 proposals they are assigned to read: primary review, secondary review, and tertiary review. It is common that each proposal has more than one reviewer for each level of review.

The primary reviewer provides the most in-depth review of the assigned proposal. The primary reviewer not only provides the review group with a written review, but also serves as the presenter of the assigned proposals. Understandably, how the primary reviewer feels about the proposal will frame how the proposal is presented. If both primary reviewers dislike or have difficulties in understanding the proposal, their presentations and comments will certainly not be that positive. Likewise, if the proposal is good and pleasing to the primary reviewer, the primary and other reviewers will likely be the proposal's advocate and cheerleaders.

After the presentations of the primary reviewers, the secondary and tertiary reviewers are called on to share their reviews. Basically, the extent of how they agree or disagree with the primary reviewers is the main framework for the discussions. Review committee members who are not the assigned reviewers are also invited to participate in the discussion and vote on the score for the proposal. For these groups of nonassigned reviewers, the expectation is that they will read the nonassigned proposals with as much detail as their own assigned ones. In reality, some of these reviewers rely on the proposal's abstract or other strategically placed summaries to help them get a general understanding of the proposal, and hopefully help them talk about it in an informed manner.

No matter how in-depth each of the reviewers examine a proposal, each has one vote. A primary reviewer who spent days to dissect the proposal and make comments has one vote, as does another reviewer who only read the abstract and skimmed the proposal briefly. Again, it is very important for a proposal to have a strong, accurate, concise, and convincing abstract.

In the review group, members review and comment on areas they know best. It is not uncommon to have reviewers whose only interests are the budget, the program design, the needs statement, the number of clients served, or even the grammar and style of the writing! Applicants can control the quality of the proposals prepared, but have no control over who will be reviewing their proposals. Nevertheless, applicants with good reputations are well known among the reviewers or have positive prior connections with many or a few of the reviewers or program officers. Such applicants are not likely to receive preferential treatment, but they will at least be respectfully received.

One of the authors (Yuen) often tells his students that whether a grant proposal is funded is 50 percent quality of the proposal, 25 percent luck, and 25 percent connections. He, as well as this book, can only help the applicant agency with the 50 percent quality portion, but it is up to the agency to acquire the 25 percent luck and develop the other 25 percent advantage from connections. Many times, his former students like to remind him that, in reality, the distribution is more likely 30 percent or less quality, 30 percent luck, and 40 percent connections.

No matter what the distributions are, the fact is clear that a quality proposal will get applicants past a key hurdle and give them a solid foundation from which the grant will be considered. Many proposals do not even make it past the first round. An agency should, therefore, be aware of the need for seeking excellence in service, lobbying for community and political support, becoming involved in partnerships, and being hopeful.

It is often said that the best way to learn a subject is to teach that subject to others. In grant writing, the best way to learn to write a good grant is to write one and participate in proposal reviews. The review provides the participants with a chance to see the grant writing and grant making from a different angle, to build connections, and to understand the inner workings of the review process.

Professional Insight 5.1: A Reviewer's Perspective on Preparing Proposals

Betsy Sheldon, MA

What happens after you submit your proposal to the funder? How will your proposal be reviewed? Who will choose the proposals to be funded? What will the proposal reviewers look for in your proposal?

These are questions many applicants ask themselves after having submitted their proposals. Yes, proposal reviewers will be assessing the community need, the proposed activities to address the need, the ability of your organization to implement the services proposed, and the budget. But reviewers will also be looking for other direct and indirect elements of your proposal. Here are suggestions for preparing your proposal so that these other direct or indirect elements will satisfy the reviewer.

1. *Read the instructions and comply with all proposal requirements.* This may seem obvious, but most funding agencies have a multitiered review process that includes an initial review to ensure that certain basic proposal requirements are met. These may include specific requirements for font type and size, page limitations, and assurances. Proposals may get rejected simply because assurances were not signed or the wrong font size was used.

2. *Consider getting an objective person to review your proposal before it is submitted.* Reviewers often are reading lots of proposals and will catch typos and grammatical errors. Although this may not prevent your proposal from scoring well, it does not reflect quality work. It is also obvious when sections have been cut and pasted, resulting in reviewers concluding a rushed process, a project that is not well thought out, or just laziness.

3. *Involve program implementers in the writing process.* They will need to ultimately implement the services being proposed, so include them in the development of the project. Use a logic model process to make sure that what is being proposed is realistic, that strategies link to identified outcomes, and that staffing patterns are adequate.

4. *Resist the impulse to propose more than can be realistically accomplished.* Again, the logic model will assist in this process. Funders usually have ample experience with program implementation and can recognize when a proposal is being unrealistic about what can be accomplished. Proposers should also be aware that if they do propose more than what can be accomplished, they will be held accountable for achieving stated outcomes or risk being defunded.

Summary

The first important step in getting grant-funding support is to submit a proposal. Getting a major grant would provide needed services and improve the infrastructure for more effective services. Grant writing is a labor-intensive and energy-draining activity. It is also one of the most interesting and satisfactory tasks in social services. It requires input from the community, research to identify needs and conduct the program evaluation, creativity in program design, attention to detail to complete the proposal, and many other great professional qualities. Grant writing is an ongoing process.

A 1983 Far Side comic by Gary Larson depicts two little spiders standing at the end of a children's slide that is covered by a big spider web. The spiders say to each other, "If we pull this off, we'll eat like kings." The reality is that even if your web lands a big catch, service providers do not eat like kings. The receipt of a grant funding only signifies the beginning of hard work, but this is customized work that serves the community.

The first grant is the most difficult one to write. Once it is done, many of the proposal sections are boilerplate write-ups that only need updates and minor modifications and can be used for other proposals. Take advantage of the comments from the reviewers. Modify and revise the proposal and service delivery. Soon a great funded program will emerge.

References

Coley, S., & Scheinberg, C. (2008). *Proposal writing* (3rd ed.). Thousand Oaks, CA: Sage Publications.

IRS announces 2009 standard mileage rates. Retrieved February 14, 2009, from www.ninds.nih.gov/funding/differences.htm.

Kettner, P., Moroney, R., and Martin, L. (2008). *Designing and managing programs: an effectiveness-based approach* (3rd ed.). Thousand Oaks, CA: Sage Publications.

NINDS funding opportunities: Know the differences. Retrieved February 14, 2009, from www.ninds.nih.gov/funding/differences.htm.

Netting, F. E., Kettner, P. M., and McMurtry, S. (2008). *Social work macro practice* (4th ed.). Boston: Allyn and Bacon.

Yuen, F. K. O. (1999). "Family health and cultural diversity" In J. Pardeck & F. Yuen (Eds.), *Family health: A holistic approach to social work pratice.* (pp. 101–114) Westport, CT: Auburn House.

Yuen, F. K. O., and Terao, K. (2003). *Practical grant writing and program evaluation.* Pacific Grove, CA: Brooks/Cole–Thomson Learning.

Simply proposing a program design and describing how proposed services will be implemented will no longer result in a strong proposal. Funders also want to know how the applicant will determine whether the proposed services benefited the participants. How will the organization evaluate the services to show participants gained from their participation?

> Funding sources are no longer willing to allocate resources for human services and expect merely a report on whether or not the program and service providers did what they said they would do. Funders want to know what benefits are gained from the services provided. Programs are now required to evaluate their services and show the results (process, outcome, and impact) of the services provided. (Yuen and Terao, 2003, p. 3)

In addition to reporting outcome results to the funding source, the organization can utilize program evaluation to help with:

➤ Gathering information for continuous program improvement

➤ Collecting useful data for management and decision making

➤ Assembling information for grant writing to pursue additional funding

➤ Assessing the effectiveness of the program design

Program evaluation should be viewed as a positive process to improve the program's services and showcase its successes; it should not be viewed as a process that implies "checking to see if the program did something wrong." This chapter discusses how organizations can develop an evaluation plan for their proposal that responds to the question, "What difference did our services make?" and can be implemented in a cost-effective manner. This plan should yield results that are helpful not only to the funder but also to the organization.

The Level of Rigor

Program evaluations can be defined as "individual systematic studies conducted periodically or on an ad hoc basis to assess how well a program is working. They are often conducted by experts external to the program, either inside or outside the agency, as well as by program managers" (GAO, 2005, p. 2). On one side of evaluation, the design can be high rigor and research-focused, while on the other side, evaluation can be less formal and conducted internally within the program, using an empowerment or participatory evaluation approach.

Chapter 3, Basic Research Methods and Program Evaluation, describes the various types of evaluation designs; some of these designs will require a professional evaluator, but other designs can be conducted by program staff with guidance from a coach (i.e., evaluator). The level of rigor depends on the validity and reliability of the instrument, how the subjects are selected, how the instruments are administered, how the data is aggregated, and how the data analysis is conducted. The cost of the evaluation is generally in direct relation to the level of rigor (i.e., the higher the rigor, the higher the cost for an evaluation).

When writing a proposal, at what level should the rigor of the evaluation be? A few guidelines can help answer this question. The level of funding available for a proposal can be used as an indicator. If the funding is substantial (e.g., $500,000 or more annually), then the funding source may expect an evaluation design that is comprehensive, abides by sound evaluation practices, and is driven by a qualified evaluator. Allocating $50,000 (about 10% of the total budget) or more for an evaluation may be acceptable and, in some cases, expected. However, some programs with lesser amount of funding may have very little or no money available for evaluation. In some cases, the Request for Application (RFA) may use key words that indicate the funder expects an evaluation entailing a high level of rigor. It may require a separate evaluation plan using particular research designs. It may simply ask how the proposed service activities will be evaluated.

Generally, most funders understand the challenges programs face when evaluating program services. They understand the cost of conducting an evaluation, especially one that requires high rigor versus one conducted internally within the program. Funders expect the majority of program dollars to be used for program implementation, not evaluation. However, funders still want to know whether the program services made a difference. A less demanding evaluation, or a performance-measurement process, may be suitable for most proposals. "Performance measurement is the ongoing monitoring and reporting of program accomplishments, particularly progress toward pre-established goals. It is typically conducted by program or agency management" (GAO, 2005, p. 2).

Even though a performance-measurement process may be viewed as a less rigorous evaluation, do not underestimate the usefulness of this evaluation process as a tool for managing program services. It allows program staff and other stakeholders to be actively involved in tracking the progress of their program and identifying program strengths and possible areas for improvement.

> Regular measurement of progress toward specified outcomes is a vital component of any effort at managing-for-results, a customer-oriented process that focuses on maximizing benefits and minimizing negative consequences for customers of services and programs. . . . A particularly crucial outcome characteristic for public programs—often neglected in discussions of the uses of performance measurement—is equity. A well-designed measurement system

enables agency managers to assess the fairness of a program and make appropriate adjustments. (Hatry, 1999, pp. 3–4)

Performance measurement does not measure whether the services caused the change, only whether change occurred. "Performance data do not, by themselves, tell why the outcomes occurred. In other words, they do not reveal the extent to which the program caused the measured results" (Hatry, 1999, p. 5). Although performance measurement does not measure change by causation, measuring change because participants were involved in the program services (i.e., by association) can be very helpful to stakeholders. It ensures program accountability and can help improve services and client outcomes. It is also cost effective and user-friendly.

Outcome–Focused Evaluation

Outcome-focused evaluation is one approach to conducting a simple internal evaluation. This approach measures whether change occurred because of participants' involvement in the service activity or by association.

Outcome-focused evaluation informs funders and other stakeholders that a difference did occur after program services were provided. These changes can be particularly meaningful for program improvement, especially when these changes are identified before the program service is conducted. Programs that developed a logic model before implementing program services will have identified these expected changes, or anticipated outcomes. As discussed in Chapter 4, Program Planning and Evaluation, the logic model helps to build the program design not only by aligning the community needs to the service activities, but also by aligning the anticipated results such as program outputs and outcomes.

Empowerment Evaluation

What is empowerment evaluation? Empowerment evaluation is the process of having program staff and beneficiaries participate in the planning, development, implementation, and data analysis for reporting results. In most cases, program staff may need or want a coach or consultant to assist in this process. A coach is a professional evaluator who will provide technical assistance and guidance as program staff move through the evaluation process. In the case when program staff have evaluation experience, a coach may not be needed.

The purpose of empowerment evaluation is to allow program staff to set their own terms for measuring the effectiveness of their services for program improvement. One important nugget of empowerment evaluation is that the process of planning for and developing an empowerment evaluation contributes to program improvement almost as much, if not more, than using the results for revising or modifying program services.

Empowerment evaluation is necessarily a collaborative group activity, not an individual pursuit. . . . As a result, the context changes: The assessment of a program's value and worth is not the end point of the evaluation—as it often is in traditional evaluation—but part of an ongoing process of program improvement. . . . Program participants learn to continually assess their progress toward self-determined goals and to reshape their plans and strategies according to this assessment. (Fetterman, Kaftarian, Wandersman, 1996, pp. 5–6)

Other benefits of empowerment evaluation include the delivery of information to stakeholders on the difference the program services make after beneficiaries participate in the services. In addition, program staff self-assess, or self-evaluate, their program services; this eliminates the high cost of hiring an evaluator to evaluate the program.

There are challenges to empowerment evaluation as well. The benefit of program staff being informed because of their involvement in conducting the evaluation also places a burden on staff. They have an added responsibility of assisting in planning for the evaluation, as well as conducting the evaluation (e.g., collecting the data).

Program administrators and staff need to learn how to aggregate and analyze the data as well as write an evaluation report. Depending on the complexity and rigor of the evaluation design, data aggregation and analysis can be challenging, requiring additional resources such as time, technology, or an evaluation consultant.

Outcome-Focused Empowerment Evaluation

Combining the concepts of outcome-focused evaluation and empowerment evaluation allows program staff to be part of the evaluation process and to understand how the evaluation results are directly linked to the services provided. This connection can help program staff use these results for program improvement.

The logic model process described earlier (Chapter 4, Program Planning and Evaluation) allows stakeholders to identify program services based on the community need, and link these services with the anticipated results, both outputs and outcomes. The use of these anticipated results will ensure that the alignment of what is being evaluated will be directly associated with the service activities and community needs. Based on these anticipated outputs and outcomes, program staff could identify indicators that are to be collected, and the data source from whom or where the information will be obtained. At the same time, the methods of data collection and the associated instruments should also be determined.

Indicators

Indicators are the information that can be documented to determine whether the program services accomplished what they set out to do. They are the specific, measurable items of information that specify progress toward achieving the result. They may be measures that reflect the condition and the change of one's knowledge, attitudes, and behaviors.

Outputs have straightforward indicators. Generally, outputs are the counts of beneficiaries served or the number of units being addressed (e.g., number of acres of a watershed that will be restored, number of houses weatherized). For a literacy tutoring program, for example, if the program design is to provide one-on-one reading skills tutoring to youth, the outputs can include number of youth tutored, number of sessions each youth was tutored, and amount of time tutoring was provided. These counts or numbers measure the effort made in the program service delivery. They do not measure change in the participants or change in the units after service activities were provided.

Indicators are needed to measure outcomes and to show what change has occurred. To measure students' increased positive attitude toward reading through a literacy tutoring program, documenting the increased number of books read, the increased amount of time spent in a library, or the increased amount of time reading or browsing through books can be the indicators. To measure increased reading skills, the indicators could include results of student reading assessments, reading test scores, or teachers' assessment of students' reading ability over the course of the school year.

Data Source

In selecting the indicators, one should also consider the *data source* for each of these anticipated results. The data source identifies the origin of the information to be collected. It is the location of the data or the identified persons who will provide the information containing the indicators. For example, the data source for outputs of a literacy tutoring program can be the tutors or the site supervisor of the tutoring program.

The data sources for collecting outcome information are not always as clearly defined as with outputs. For example, one may think that the data source for measuring increased interest in reading would be the tutor who counts the number of books the student carries with him. However, it is not just the number of books that needs to be tracked, but also whether those books were actually read by the student. Therefore, the person who can track whether the youth read the books is the data source: the teacher, the tutor, or other adult (e.g., parent). In some situations, the data source may not be an individual who collects the data, but a location from where information can be obtained. For example, if the indicator for increased reading skills is grades, then the data source may be the school office where the grades reside. For a neighborhood watch program that organizes neighborhood watch groups, the data source for obtaining crime statistics to determine if there is a reduction in burglaries in a neighborhood (the indicator) would be the police station. The data source for the sense of safety in the neighborhood would be from the residents.

The feasibility, availability, and accessibility of data from the date sources should be seriously considered. For example, teachers may be an ideal data source for obtaining student reading grades; however, teachers may not have the time to look up the grades, or school policy may not allow teachers to provide grades to outside sources. The police station is an ideal location where one can obtain crime statistics on burglaries; however, police stations may track burglaries only by citywide statistics and not by neighborhoods. Therefore, it is good practice to pilot the data collection process; collect sample data from the data source or minimally ask the data source if they are legally and ethically able to provide the information needed to meet the evaluation requirements.

Instrument Type and Method of Evaluation

Instruments are the tools used to document the information that will be aggregated and analyzed to determine if the outputs and outcomes were reached. The research design used for the evaluation and data to be collected will determine the type of instrument (e.g., pre-post survey questionnaires, observation rating form, phone interview protocol) employed. When preparing for a proposal, at a minimum, the instrument type needs to be determined so that the data collection process can be described. Specific information about the instrument (e.g., the questions to be asked in a survey or the list of items to be rated in an observation scale) may not be needed at this time. However, knowing whether the instrument type will be a pre-post survey questionnaire or an observation rating-scale is critical to describing the method of evaluation.

After identifying the indicator and data source for each anticipated result, the data collection instrument can be further developed. Common instruments such as attendance sheets, participant rosters, or activity logs can be used to track the number of participants, amount of service provided, and length of time service was provided, both by individual service unit (e.g., minutes of each tutoring session) and by length of time with the program (e.g., student tutored for four months). How these instruments are formatted and the type of information collected will depend on the indicator and data source.

Before identifying common types of instruments that can be used to measure outcomes, the term *baseline data* needs clarification. Anticipated outcomes are statements that propose what kind of change will occur after service activities are provided (e.g., "increased" reading skills or "reduced" incidents of crime). Therefore, to determine whether a change has occurred, information needs to be collected *before* service activities are provided. The information collected before the service activities occur is called *baseline data.* This data is then compared with information collected *after* the service activities or interventions have occurred to determine change.

Generally, there are two methods by which baseline data can be obtained. The first method is to collect *existing baseline data*, information that has been collected over time for other purposes. If this data is available, it can be compared with information collected after service activities are conducted. For example, a student's average grade for the past three years can be the baseline data for a literacy tutoring program, to be compared to the student's grade in reading after participating in the program. The average incidence of burglary (crime statistics) during the past three years before a neighborhood watch group was formed can be baseline data, which will then be compared to the burglary crime statistics after the neighborhood watch group has been in existence for a program year. The challenges with existing data include gaining access to it and having the ability to collect it in a timely manner when the data is needed.

If existing data is not available, the other alternative to obtaining baseline data is to collect the information from the person or location before the service intervention begins. The timing of collecting baseline data in this situation is critical; if data is not collected before or early in the service delivery, participants will already have been exposed to the intervention and may have benefited from service during this time lapse of delayed data collection effort. It will then be difficult, if not impossible, to collect accurate baseline information. Once baseline information is collected, the same information can be collected again after services are provided and a comparison made.

The common types of instruments for collecting outcome information are pre-post surveys, post-only surveys, retrospective surveys, observation rating forms, observation checklists, transfer data forms, phone interview protocols, in-person interview protocols, and focus group protocols. These instrument types are described as follows:

Pre-post surveys. Generally used when information is needed from individuals before participating in a service activity, the pre-survey (baseline data); then again collecting the same information after participating in the service activity, the post-survey.

Post-only surveys. Generally used when existing data is available as baseline data; therefore, information needs to be collected only after beneficiaries participate in the service activity, the post-only survey.

Post-only retrospective surveys. Post-only surveys can be used without baseline data when the questions are crafted in a manner that requires the respondent to reflect the level of change that occurred since participating in the service activity; this is called a retrospective survey. Here is an example of a question and a choice of responses: "To what extent did the student increase his or her reading skills since participating in the tutoring program? not at all; made little progress; made progress, made substantial progress."

Observation rating forms. Observing attitudes or behavior of participants generally occurs over time, during the term of a service activity. Documentation is conducted after sufficient time has passed (e.g., midterm or at the end of service). In most cases, an Observation Rating Form asks the data source, usually a person who has regular contact with the participants during the time of the service activity (e.g., teachers, staff of an organization, parents/guardians), to rate attitude or behavior changes of participants after their participation in the program. Observation rating forms operate similarly to post-only retrospective surveys;

baseline data may not be necessary because the questions are crafted in a manner that indicates rating the level of change that occurred since the beginning of the service activity.

Observation checklists. Observation checklists ask the data source to document whether the participants or outcome products accomplished benchmarks during/after the implementation of the service activity. For participants, observations of skills developed and/or successful completion of tasks can be measured in this manner. Observation checklists are popular for product-driven outcomes. For example, an environmental program that focuses on watershed restoration may use an observation checklist to determine the extent to which watersheds have been cleaned. Checklist items might include removal of invasive plants or canal clean-up efforts. Pre-checklist observations can be made before the service activity begins to collect baseline data and then again after the service activity to determine outcomes.

Transfer data forms. Even when existing data is available and the program does not have to administer instruments to collect the needed information, instruments may still be needed so information can be transferred from secure records that are not physically available to the evaluator to a document that will become the record for the evaluation. For example, if the indicator for improved reading skills is the reading grade of students during a school year, evaluators may not be able to take or copy school records; however, they can transfer the reading grades of student participants (e.g., anonymously) to a summary form or instrument.

Phone interview protocol. The phone interview data collection process is very common with marketing research. However, phone interviews can also be used to collect data for a program evaluation. Because phone interviews are conducted remotely, the person administering the interview must be prepared before making the calls. Generally, the phone interviews are short, 15 to 20 minutes maximum. A phone interview protocol instrument is needed to serve two functions: (1) it provides a guide on how the questions should be asked; and (2) it allows the interviewer to document the responses quickly and accurately. Generally, the questions are predetermined, focusing on specific issues and looking for specific responses (e.g., how did increasing your reading skills help you with other school subjects?). The protocol is formatted in a manner that allows the interviewer to quickly document the responses.

In-person interview protocol. As with the phone interview protocol, the in-person interview protocol acts as a guide for what questions will be asked of an individual. However, because an in-person interview is conducted face-to-face and is usually longer (e.g., 30 to 60 minutes), the questions may not need to be as focused, allowing the participant flexibility in responding to the questions (e.g., please describe how your increased reading skills changed your attitude toward school).

Focus group protocol. A focus group protocol is used when interviewing a small group of people. This data collection method allows the evaluator to collect rich qualitative data, information generated by the interaction between individuals in the group. A focus group protocol acts as a guide for what questions to ask; however, these questions are used to generate discussion. The group is allowed to expand the discussion beyond the questions.

Bringing Together the Indicator, Data Source, and Instrument Type

Developing the method for collecting data takes an approach of bringing together the indicator, data source, instrument type, and service activity. Consider all four areas when determining how data is to be collected.

➤ Always connect your instrument type and data source to your activity and outcome indicator. For example, a questionnaire (instrument) that collects information from new parents (data source) regarding *satisfaction* with a parenting class would not measure increased parenting skills (indicator). However, a focus group, using a focus group protocol (instrument) that collects information from new parents (data source) on *how they resolved child tantrums*, will provide information on improved parenting skills (indicator).

➤ When identifying the data source and instrument, consider the feasibility of collecting the type of information, or indicators, associated with the instrument from the data source. For example, if you need to gain access to data on crime rates, you will want to know if the police department will allow you to transfer crime data to your Crime Rate Summary Log.

➤ Identify your data source and instrument type in the evaluation plan. In some cases, you may not have identified an instrument during the early planning of your program, but know where you would get the information. If so, state the data source from which you will obtain your information (indicator); identifying the specific instrument type to be used may become necessary later.

Evaluation Section of a Proposal

In writing a proposal, almost all Requests for Applications (RFAs), especially government-related RFAs, will include a section requiring you to describe how the proposed program services will be evaluated. What should be described in this section? Where should you begin? If you developed a logic model, it will provide the key information on program services and the expected outcomes. This information, in addition to describing the indicators, data source, instrument type, and targets, can provide the basis for a solid description of your program's service evaluation.

You can state how you plan to evaluate the proposed services by following these three sections:

> ➤ Evaluation questions
> ➤ Methodology
> ➤ Target for success

Evaluation Questions

The purpose of an evaluation is to identify and respond to questions that can help stakeholders make informed decisions about the project and/or assist staff to improve program services. These evaluation questions might ask whether the program services made a difference with the individuals who participate in the program services. The outputs and outcomes identified in the logic model can help to formulate the evaluation questions. For example, evaluation questions for a literacy tutoring program might include:

> ➤ To what extent did the literacy tutoring program operate as intended and serve the target audience identified in the community needs assessment?
> ➤ To what extent did the literacy tutoring program increase the reading ability of youth participating in the program?

The process of developing evaluation questions follows the theme of this book, "begin with the end in mind." By focusing on the end results of the program activity for evaluation, the anticipated outputs and outcomes, evaluation questions can be formed. The logic model can be a helpful resource for obtaining this information. Not only does it state the anticipated results, but it also aligns the results with the proposed service activities and community needs.

Methodology

Guided by the evaluation questions, a plan on how the evaluation will be organized and implemented needs to be thoughtfully considered. This is the methodology that describes the approaches and methods of the evaluation. It includes the evaluation questions, indicators, data source, instrument type, timeline, and other evaluation processes. A description of the evaluation methods should provide an accurate and complete picture of how the service activities will be measured, as well as a description of the anticipated outcomes of the evaluation. An example of the core elements of an evaluation description may look like this:

A commercially developed reading assessment measuring phonetics will be identified as the instrument for evaluating increased reading ability of students. Tutors will be trained on how to administer the instrument and will administer the instrument to the students three times per year—at the beginning of the school year, after the first semester, and again at the end of the school year.

The data will be sent to the company providing the commercial assessment for data aggregation. The aggregated data will be submitted to the project director who will analyze the data and develop an evaluation report.

Of course, this description will need to be expanded and include details of the service activities related to the evaluation, so readers who are not familiar with the proposed program services can connect the intent of the program services with the evaluation.

Targets for Success

When conducting an outcome-focused evaluation, target statements for each anticipated outcome might need to be stated to show what the program designers minimally hope to achieve. Targets are the level of success the program expects to gain over a particular period of time, often expressed as an integer or percentage. For example, if the outcome is "tutored students will improve their reading skills," the target might be "60 percent of the students tutored will improve their phonetics by at least three assessment category levels. Students improving their phonetics by three or more levels will indicate they have increased their reading skills." Here are a few guidelines to help identify targets:

➤ Be realistic! You are the best judge of how much change to expect over a given time period as a result of your program's activities. If this is the first time you are collecting data for this measure, usually the target is considered a guesstimate.

➤ Consider the amount of service or dosage (e.g., once a week for three hours) and length of time (e.g., three months) beneficiaries will receive. The target may be higher for an activity offering a large dosage of service to beneficiaries as compared to an activity whose beneficiaries receive a lower dosage.

➤ Targets need to reflect what you hope to see as change, given the level of resources (e.g., staffing, funding, material). Does the target justify the resources invested? Do not underestimate the target, but also try not to be overly optimistic.

➤ Beneficiaries with more challenges may require more resources or dosage of service for change to occur, resulting in a target that is not as high as compared to beneficiaries with fewer challenges (e.g., tutoring youth in literacy whose primary language is other than English versus tutoring English-speaking youth who are behind in reading ability). What are the characteristics of the beneficiaries you plan to serve?

Evaluation Worksheet and Evaluation Plan

An *evaluation worksheet* is a working document that can be used as a tool to help in program planning and developing an evaluation plan. If the logic model was developed, it can play an important role in creating the evaluation worksheet. The components of the logic model can be transferred to the evaluation worksheet, then detailed information can be included in each of the logic model components to complete the evaluation worksheet. The evaluation worksheet allows you to enhance the information of each of the anticipated results (i.e., outputs and outcomes) stated in the logic model, including the indicators, data sources, type of instruments, and targets. As illustrated in Chapter 5, Grant Proposal Writing, Table 5.3 shows how the information in a logic model can be transferred to an evaluation worksheet.

The evaluation worksheet and a description of its components may be all that is needed for an RFA. The worksheet can act as an evaluation plan for a proposal; a comprehensive evaluation plan may not be necessary. The worksheet provides the key components of the methodology and targets for success as described earlier.

An *evaluation plan* is a written document that describes the purpose, approaches, and strategies/steps of the program evaluation. It could be a stand-alone document. For example, it may include the following:

1. An overview of the evaluation plan

2. An explanation of the purpose of the program evaluation

3. Identification of methods for capturing the following general evaluation contexts:

    a. Record-keeping of program planning and development

    b. Description of program activities and interventions

    c. Development of evaluation data management and data analysis

4. Utilization of a particular format such as a Program Planning and Evaluation Worksheet to detail the expected results and evaluation approaches for each of the identified objectives

5. Attention to human subjects' protection (ethical considerations)

There is no one standard format or template for developing an evaluation plan. The plan can be a basic summary (one page) to a very detailed description (10 to 15 pages) of the proposed evaluation. An RFA might ask for a basic summary of how the proposed program services will be evaluated, whereas in other cases, especially if the funding is substantial, the funder may require a higher-rigor evaluation and request a detailed evaluation plan be included in the proposal. The following outline provides another example of the components that might be included when developing an evaluation plan:

1. Program summary

2. Evaluation plan overview
    a. Evaluation classification

    b. Role of the evaluator

    c. Evaluator qualifications

    d. Evaluation timeline and completion of evaluation report

  e. Participants who developed the evaluation plan

  f. Purpose of the evaluation

  g. Projected use of findings

3. Audiences
 a. Primary stakeholders
 b. Secondary stakeholders

4. Evaluation questions

5. Evaluation design
 a. Summary
 b. Data types
 c. Ethical considerations

6. Data collection (methods and instruments)

7. Data management and analysis

8. Strategies for using evaluation findings

9. Budget

An example of a completed evaluation plan that follows this outline can be viewed in Chapter 8, Real-Life Samples.

Beyond the Grant Proposal

After an organization is awarded the grant, the work is just beginning. Not only will the organization need to begin planning for and implementing the proposed program services, but the organization will also need to begin planning for and implementing the program evaluation. The following basic steps describe the continuum for implementing a program evaluation:

1. Identify and develop program objectives

2. Use a logic model and a program planning and evaluation worksheet to develop each objective

3. Design data collection instruments

4. Collect the data

5. Analyze the data

6. Report evaluation results

The planning and implementation of an evaluation should begin as the program year begins, not at the end when results are needed for reporting to stakeholders. Therefore, in reviewing the basic implementation steps outlined previously, steps one and two were most likely completed when planning for and writing the proposal. In some cases, an evaluation worksheet or an evaluation plan may have already been developed as part of the proposal. If so, this document should be reviewed and revised as necessary. The next four steps in developing and implementing an evaluation include selecting/developing instruments, getting prepared for data collection, planning for data analysis, and knowing what information is needed for reporting results.

Select/Develop Instruments

The most likely next step in the evaluation process is to select or develop instruments that will collect the data needed to address anticipated outcomes. Several topics need to be addressed when selecting or developing an instrument.

What Are Instruments? Program evaluation uses instruments to collect service data and the results of the service. These data are aggregated and analyzed to determine if the outputs and outcomes identified were reached. The output data provides justification for the amount of service conducted, whereas outcome data determines the extent to which change occurred to beneficiaries because of the services provided. The development and the application of the data collection instruments are the integral and critical part of the evaluation process.

When deciding what instrument to use, keep in mind the following issues:

➢ Will the instrument collect the data needed to address the anticipated outcome?

➢ What data collection procedures need to be considered?

  ➢ Who will complete the instrument (data source)?

  ➢ Will the data source be willing, or have the ability to use and complete the instrument?

  ➢ Will the data source be able to complete the instrument in a timely manner?

➢ What data analysis procedures need to be considered?

  ➢ After the instrument has been administered, how will you aggregate the data (e.g., database)?

  ➢ Do you know how to aggregate the data so it will provide the information needed to analyze the data?

  ➢ Data analysis takes a certain level of skill; do you have or is there someone who has these skills?

  ➢ Does the data collected allow more advanced statistical analyses (e.g., t-test, chi square, regression)? Is there a person who knows how to run these statistical analyses?

➢ What resources need to be considered?

  ➢ Has a person been identified who has the time and knowledge to oversee the evaluation process, from ensuring that the instruments are administered correctly to knowing what to do when data becomes available?

  ➢ Does the program have a budget for the evaluation?

What Type of Instrument Is Needed?   The purpose of the instrument is to collect information to determine the amount of effort the program accomplished (outputs), as well as the amount of change the beneficiaries participating in the services made (outcomes). The type of instrument will depend on the information needed to respond to the outputs and outcomes identified. The following are questions to consider when choosing an instrument:

- ➤ Do you need to document the number of beneficiaries or participants served or the number of times service was delivered? Then consider using a participation roster or a service activity log.
- ➤ Do you need information from existing records? Then consider using a data documentation sheet.
- ➤ Do you need to know whether something (an idea, opinion, or behavior) exists or not? Then consider a checklist or yes-no format.
- ➤ Do you need to assess knowledge or skills? Then consider using a test or observation instrument (e.g., rubric).
- ➤ Do you need to get a rating, such as quality or satisfaction? Then consider a survey using a scale of numbers or phrases.
- ➤ Do you need details about something? Then consider asking an open-ended question.
- ➤ Do you need to be able to ask follow-up questions? Then consider using an in-person format such as an interview protocol, phone survey protocol, or focus group protocol.

The type of instrument selected also depends on the data source, the person expected to complete the instrument, and the kind of information to be collected. For collecting data from existing records, the data source may be a place (e.g., police department for burglary incidents, school office for standardized test scores). For change of knowledge, attitude, or behavior, the data source will most likely be people (e.g., service recipients, teachers, mentors). Therefore, both the data source and the information to be collected are important factors to be considered when selecting the type of instrument.

How Do I Find an Appropriate Instrument?   Evaluation instruments can be obtained by identifying an existing instrument that will collect the data needed, or by developing an instrument to fit the data collection needs specified in the evaluation worksheet or plan. There are advantages and disadvantages to each of these approaches.

Identifying an Existing Instrument.   Many instruments that have been developed for other evaluation studies are available to the public. Many commercial instruments that measure a variety of community and educational service areas are also available. These instruments can be found on Web sites and in publications. However, finding an existing instrument that will collect the data you want can be a challenge. If you can find one, consider the advantages and disadvantages of using an existing instrument.

Advantages

> ➤ Do not need to develop an instrument
> ➤ Instrument, in many cases, has been tested for validity and reliability
> ➤ May provide instructions on how to analyze the data or a data aggregation/ analysis service may be offered

Disadvantages

> ➤ May require buying the instrument and/or its services
> ➤ May require training before one can administer the instrument
> ➤ May require that program services meet minimum criteria (e.g., dosage of service, trained staff in program services)

Program staff searching for an instrument need to make sure they are thorough in their review process. They may feel they have found an appropriate instrument, because the title of the instrument reflects the services they are providing, describes similar outcomes the program has identified, or the subject area falls under the same service area the program provides. However, if the program feels it has identified an existing instrument, then review the instrument in detail and consider the following cautions:

> ➤ Does the instrument measure what you want to measure?
> ➤ Is the data source available and willing to complete the instrument?
> ➤ What degree of burden will be placed on program staff in administering the instrument?
> ➤ Will you know how to aggregate and analyze the data after it is collected?
> ➤ Will the results of the analysis respond to the anticipated outcomes and address the community needs?

In some cases, the program may find an instrument that will collect the data needed to measure its program services if modifications or revisions are made to the instrument. For example, questions may need to be added or deleted, the wording of the questions may need to be simplified, or formatting and/or layout design may need to be altered. Modifying or revising existing instruments are a common practice; however, a few potential problems need to be considered before doing so.

> ➤ Does the instrument have a copyright?
> ➤ Will revising the instrument affect the validity or reliability?
> ➤ Will modifications affect the analysis plan?

Developing an Instrument.   Depending on the evaluation questions and/or anticipated outcomes of the service activities, an existing instrument may not be available. If this is the case, an instrument may need to be developed. This is more common than people may think. For example, the authors of this book have worked with organizations receiving AmeriCorps program and Senior Corps program grants funded by the federal Corporation for National and Community Service. They provide training and technical assistance to assist these community organizations in planning, setting up, and implementing their performance measurement systems. In more than 90 percent of the cases, they are asked to assist programs on developing instruments specific to their evaluation needs.

Consider the following steps when developing an instrument:

Step 1: Determine types of questions. The types of questions asked will depend on the type of instrument to be developed and who will complete the instrument (i.e., data source). Keep in mind that the responses to questions need to provide information that reflects the outcomes being measured. Examples of how questions can be framed include open-ended questions, fill-in-the-blank questions, yes-no questions, multiple-choice questions, or ranking and rating questions (GAO, 1993).

Step 2: Clearly state questions. Questions need to be clear and not confusing to the respondent. Avoid questions that:

➤ Are not relevant to the evaluation considerations or anticipated outcomes (e.g., asking middle school students in a child abuse prevention workshop, "What are the benefits of taking Algebra?").

➤ Cannot or will not be answered correctly (e.g., asking grade school students, "What was your family income last year?").

➤ Are not geared to the respondent's ability to provide the information or perceptions (e.g., asking a recently arrived refugee child questions that are relevant to growing up in suburban America).

➤ Are threatening or embarrassing. (e.g., asking a teenage male victim of bullying, "Were you too scared to stand up to the bully and fight back like a real man?").

➤ Are vague or ambiguous (e.g., "What do you think?").

Step 3: Arranging the layout design of the instrument. The layout design of an instrument is almost as critical as the questions being asked. If the design is not seen as user friendly (i.e., if the format of the instrument makes it difficult to respond to questions), or if the design provides little space to respond, respondents may choose not to complete the instrument, or they may make mistakes when completing the instrument.

The following are critical items to consider when designing an instrument:

> ➤ *Instrument title.* Is the name of the program stated and type of service indicated?

> ➤ *Introductory statement.* What is the purpose of the instrument? How will the data be used? Is there a statement on ethical considerations such as confidentiality or anonymity?

> ➤ *Demographics.* Are there questions about the respondents' relevant information and their background?

> ➤ *Directions.* Are there directions that describe how to complete the instrument?

> ➤ *Questions.* Is the language used understandable to the respondents?

> ➤ *Format.* Is the instrument pleasant to the eye? Does it have enough space between questions? Does it use a font type that is clear? Does the layout cover the entire page?

An example of how an instrument can be designed is available in Chapter 7, Learning by Doing.

Will the Questions Collect the Information Needed for the Evaluation?   Does this instrument collect the information that is meant to be collected? Will the information answer whether the anticipated outcome met its target? One way to ensure that the instrument collects the information needed to measure the anticipated results is to create a table that matches the needed information with the questions in the instrument. This table is called a Table of Specifications. The Table of Specifications can be used for one instrument at a time or for a group of instruments that address similar issues. Table 6.1 provides a basic Table of Specifications template.

An example of the Table of Specifications is demonstrated in Table 6.2 for a pre-post questionnaire for an Independent Living Mentoring Program for Foster Youth;

Table 6.1 Table of Specifications Template

Table of Specifications for "Instrument Development Survey PRE/POST"	
What is the information you need?	**Which questions collect this information; when should the information be collected?**
Can participants identify the parts of an instrument?	#2 Pre and Post
Do participants know the difference between Selection and Supply Questions?	#3 Pre and Post
Can participants identify sensitive questions?	#7 Pre and Post
Can participants identify different types of questions?	#4 Pre and Post
Can participants identify steps in pilot testing?	#5 Post only
Who are the participants? (demographic information)	#8a Post test only

Table 6.2 Example of a Table of Specifications for a Pre–Post Questionnaire for an Independent Living Mentoring Program for Foster Youth

What is the information you need? (Focus)	Which question(s) collect this information(Contents and Indicators?)	(Targets)	What data analysis method(s) will you use?
Demographic data	# 1 (name), #2 (gender), #3 (age), #4 (class level), #5 (living condition)	Match at least 25 target youth with mentors	Frequency count
Self-confidence level	# 16, #17, #18, #19, #20 (Self-confidence items) # 21 (Self-confidence composite score Pre-mentoring). # 22 (Self-confidence composite score Post-mentoring).	40% of the youth who spent at least 100 hours with their mentors will show a significant improvement in their self-confidence score or in at least 3 of the 4 items.	Frequency count Percentage distribution Comparison of pre/post score, t-test
Proficiency of Independent Living Skills	Pre/Post Scores for #6, #7, #8, #9, #10—living skills assessment checklist	90% of the participating youth will demonstrate mastery of all five of the identified living skills on the checklist.	Frequency count Percentage distribution
Advanced Analyses			
Case Management and Counseling	#11, 12, 13 (frequency, hours, and outcomes of counseling) #14, 15 (frequency and outcomes of case management)	60% of the youth will remain active in receiving counseling and case management. 30% will achieve intervention goals.	Frequency count Percentage distribution
Examination of Correlations (intervention outcomes)	Self-confidence & Independent Living Skills Case management & Independent Living Skills Counseling & Independent Living Skills		Test of correlation, i.e., X^2, Rho, Pearson's r

Important considerations:

➤ Is this instrument appropriate to age, reading level, culture, and other concerns?

➤ Is this instrument being formulated and implemented in a least burdensome and most efficient manner?

a second example can be reviewed in Table 6.3 for a post-survey questionnaire for an Aging In Place Senior Program.

An exercise on how to use the Table of Specifications when developing an instrument is included in Chapter 7, Learning by Doing.

Pilot Testing Instruments   The purpose of pilot testing instruments is to determine if the instruments will collect the information needed to respond to the anticipated outcomes. Instruments should be pilot tested whether existing instruments were selected or instruments were developed. Pilot testing the instruments can address uncertainties, such as: Will the data source, the persons who will complete the instruments, be able to complete the instruments? Are the questions asking for the appropriate information needed to address the outcomes identified in the evaluation plan? Table 6.4 outlines the following steps on how instruments can be pilot tested.

Table 6.3 Example of a Table of Specifications for a Post–Service Survey Questionnaire for an Aging In Place (AIP) Senior Program

Table of Specifications for Social Connectedness with Analysis Methods

Variables/Information	Items/Questions	Target	Analysis
	As the result of my participation in AIP in the last three months . . .		
Linkage to Others (socializing, participation, knowledge of neighbors)	1. I have come to know at least three new neighbors. _____ Yes _____ No 2. I have phone numbers of at least two neighbors I recently met. _____ Yes _____ No 3. I feel more comfortable with greeting and chatting with my neighbors. _____ Agree _____ Disagree 4. I have visited one of my neighbors for the first time. _____ Yes _____ No	Know at least three new neighbors and have two additional phone numbers. Accomplish three of the four results.	fq, %
Knowledge of Resources	5. If I need assistance, I know I could call on my neighbors without feeling I am putting a burden on them. _____ True _____ Not true 6. I learned more about how and where to get help for my social security benefit. _____ Agree _____ Disagree 7. I store the emergency safety kit I received from Emergency Training in a proper place in the house. _____ Yes _____ No 8. I have the Community and Emergency Service Contact Information Sheet posted/stored close to my phone. _____ Yes _____ No	75% participate in emergency training; 65% know where and how to seek assistance; 30% would seek help if needed.	fq, %
Social Involvement	9. I signed up to be visited by a Senior Companion volunteer. _____ Yes _____ No 10. I have become more active in clubhouse activities. _____ Strongly Agree _____ Agree _____ Disagree _____ Strongly Disagree 11. I am out of my house meeting people more than before. _____ Strongly Agree _____ Agree _____ Disagree _____ Strongly Disagree 12. I have been to or plan to go to one of the neighborhood parties. _____ Strongly Agree _____ Agree _____ Disagree _____ Strongly Disagree 13. All these activities have disturbed the quiet and calm life I enjoy. _____ Strongly Agree _____ Agree Disagree _____ Strongly Disagree 14. I would rather be left alone for the time being. _____ Strongly Agree _____ Agree _____ Disagree _____ Strongly Disagree	55% give at least three positive responses to items 9 to 12. No more than 5% respond positively to items 13 and 14, and their desire is honored.	fq, %, mean
Demographics	15. Gender: _____ Male _____ Female 16. Age: _____ 60–69 _____ 70–79 _____ 80+ 17. County of Residence:		

Basic Considerations:

➤ Is this tool culturally competent?
➤ Would accessibility be a concern?
➤ Is this tool age appropriate?

Table 6.4 Steps to Pilot Testing Instruments

a. Find some participants in the group of people to be surveyed/interviewed. *(Usually four to five people are sufficient for this type of pilot test.)*

b. Arrange for the participants to take the survey/interview. Try to make the pilot test conditions match the actual administrative conditions whenever possible. (If it is a phone survey, pilot test over the phone; if it is a mail survey, have them fill it out without any assistance, or even mail it to them.)

c. If the instrument is written, ask participants to record the time it takes them to complete it.

d. After each participant completes the instrument, set up a time as soon as possible to talk with him or her. Ask the following questions to determine if this instrument will collect the information needed:

For individual items:

➤ Are the directions clear?

➤ Do participants understand how to answer each question?

➤ Are there any sensitive questions?

➤ Are there any questions that do not make sense?

➤ Are participants interpreting the questions in the way you intended?

Overall:

➤ What do participants think the survey/interview is about?

➤ What problems, if any, did participants have in completing the survey or interview?

➤ Do participants understand, from the information provided, how their responses will be used?

➤ Do participants understand how to return the survey?

e. Collect the answers and write up the results from the pilot participants. Try to analyze the data and present the results in the manner you intend to use when presenting them to the stakeholders.

f. Share the pilot results with other people who will be using the data. Will this data provide answers to their questions?

g. Modify the survey/interview based on the pilot results you have gathered.

Professional Insight 6.1: Tips for Anticipating Criticism and Planning Accordingly

Edie L. Cook, PhD

Sometimes you don't hear the actual criticism, but someone tells you it was a quality issue. Or you may be told that the evaluation section in your application wasn't strong enough. Then again, you might be informed very specifically why your renewal is in jeopardy, but, alas, it's too late to redo your evaluation study. How can you take steps to avoid this situation?

Your best bet is to anticipate possible criticism of your evaluation efforts before you start collecting data, so you can address the issues before they become real problems. Get started with these three common criticisms, and tips for prevention:

1. "There's little evidence of the validity of your measures."

"Wait a minute!" you say, "We selected our measures from a reliable source." Although reliability estimates are important and contribute to a validity case, evidence for reliability is not sufficient reason to claim any degree of validity. When you are criticized about the validity of your measure, it is usually about your choice of measure for the purpose and population involved, or the appropriateness of your claims based on data you have gathered. So what's the best prevention strategy?

Brainstorm

Spend some time thinking about possible validity concerns people might have. For example, take into account that measures can become outdated. Wouldn't you question a "sexual risk behavior" inventory developed in the 1950s, no matter how reliable it may have seemed at one point in time? Or could your measure be more applicable to a different population? Not too long ago, a widely used preschool vocabulary test included pictures of farm animals and gardening tools, as well as culturally distinct objects such as teacups and saucers. To be sure, this test eventually raised validity concerns after it was implemented for children in urban areas.

Find Out If Your Measure Has Been Tested Elsewhere

Have results from your measure been correlated with an objective measure (i.e., comparing physical samples to self-reported tobacco or drug use)? Or, if your measure includes questions related to participants, "intent to use" certain skills, has there been any testing that indicates that your measure helps predict behavior? Does your questionnaire fit into a known treatment model?

Test It Yourself

You could do an initial pilot study of your evaluation tools and/or process with the aim of improving the quality of the questions, or to assess the method of inquiry for your purpose. Or you might consider conducting some follow-up, like in the instance of "intent to use" statements, to see if you can show how well intent correlated with actual behavior (predictive validity).

Why is the search for a valid measure so difficult? Partly because it is such an important question, and also because validity relates to each use of a particular tool or measure. Perceived validity not only relates to the instrument itself, but also to your claims based on your use of it. Validity will change depending on when it is administered, how it is administered, with whom, as well as how it is analyzed. This means that you should be wary of claims that any measure is proven valid.

2. "Your measures were not sensitive enough to show program effects."

Ouch! Measures commonly used in evaluation studies are often vulnerable to difficulty showing strong program effects, a problem compounded by low sample sizes. What might help you?

Look at Pretest Results Right Away

If you want to demonstrate change in knowledge, skills, attitude, or behavior using pre- and post-tests, you can be in for an unwelcome surprise if you don't look at your pretest data when it comes in. Failing to analyze your pretest data right away is a common and unfortunate mistake, because even a few moments glancing at your pretest results can usually tell you whether your post-test measure is sensitive enough to show gains.

For example, let's say your program's purpose is to teach kids cultural appreciation. Once your pretest is administered, you look at the overall average scores. It turns out that your pretest cultural appreciation scale averaged 4.6 on a 5-point scale. This should set off warning bells! Your students have scored so high already on your measure of cultural appreciation that you have a very low likelihood of showing substantial gains on that dimension.

Use More Than One Measurement Tool and/or Method

Don't put all your evaluation eggs into one basket. Data collection is sometimes a tricky endeavor. Data sources have been known to become unavailable, and computers can crash. Criticism can be leveled at your primary source of data. Many programs have been saved by data results from extra evaluation efforts.

3. "Your response rate is too low."

This is a big, big deal, yet it is one of the most overlooked issues by evaluation planners. Why is response rate so important? Because your conclusions carry less weight if only a small percentage of your population responds. If you asked 10 people if they liked your new haircut and three people answered affirmatively, but the rest didn't respond, how confident would you be with your new hairstyle? Now what do you need to do?

Invest in Strategies for Higher Return

Many researchers heavily invest time and money to create measures and materials for evaluation purposes but drop the ball when it comes to maximizing their return rates. They then risk having their conclusions questioned because of the lack of power to show program effects.

Make It Easier to Respond, and Be Creative

Arrange for participant time to complete the measure. Format your questionnaire in a user-friendly manner. Follow up by sending reminders. Wear a bunny suit and entertain the little tykes while the parents fill out your survey, if that's what it takes.

Finally, a general tip about criticism: Welcome criticism early on, and you will be amply rewarded.

Criticism may not be agreeable, but it is necessary. It fulfills the same function as pain in the human body.
—Winston Churchill

Getting Prepared for Data Collection

A summary of what the instrument is and a description of how it should be administered will help in the data collection process. This summary is a snapshot of the preparation that will need to occur before the instrument is administered as well as when the instrument is administered. Table 6.5, Instrument Review and Data Collection, summarizes the preparation for administering the instrument and collecting data.

When completing this Instrument Review and Data Collection form, be as specific as possible when responding to the identifiers.

Name of Instrument. For example, if the exact name of the instrument in not known, the instrument type can be described (i.e., pre-post questionnaire, survey).

Who Should Administer the Instrument. For example, rather than stating the program coordinator will administer the instrument, state the name of the coordinator and describe his or her responsibilities in administering the instrument.

Purpose of Instrument. Describe the purpose of the instrument; what it will measure, outputs or outcomes. In some cases, one instrument can measure two or more anticipated results (e.g., intermediate outcome, end outcome). For example, if the respondent (i.e., data source) will be asked questions that will measure both the intermediate outcome and the end outcome, these questions can be placed on one survey (i.e., instrument). If so, describe this in this section.

Data Source. Describing the data source is a very important section of this guideline. As described earlier, if the person will not or cannot complete the

Table 6.5 Instrument Review and Data Collection

Name of Instrument	*One instrument per Instrument Summary Form (examples of instruments):* ➤ Roster/Log—Data Documentation Sheet ➤ Checklist—Observation Instrument ➤ Test—Survey with scale numbers ➤ Open-Ended Questions—Interview/Focus Group Protocol
Who should administer this instrument	*Is the person in charge, the:* ➤ Program Administrator ➤ Program staff ➤ Other Involved Person
Purpose of Instrument	*Most instruments will measure only one of the following results:* ➤ Output ➤ Intermediate outcome ➤ End outcome
Data Source	*The information will come from one of these data sources:* ➤ Place ➤ Person
Training for person(s) administering this instrument	*For example:* ➤ That responses are confidential ➤ That honest responses are essential ➤ When and to whom to return the instrument
When to complete this instrument	For example: ➤ Six weeks after mentoring has begun, and again at nine months
Other instructions or issues to consider	For example: Verify with the data source that the place or persons will provide you with the information being collected by the instrument. Other?

instrument, or the location at which the data resides is not accessible, different indicators, data sources, and/or instruments need to be identified. Therefore, the data source stated in this guideline, whomever or wherever that may be, needs to be verified.

Train the Person(s) Administering This Instrument. Make sure you plan for training the person(s) who will administer the instrument. Training can vary from formal (workshop) training to an informal (conference call) training effort. The key is to provide training appropriate to the difficulty of administering the instrument.

Key areas to consider for training those who will administer the instruments include:

➤ Provide written directions to survey respondents and interviewers.

➤ Train those who will conduct phone surveys, face-to-face interviews, and focus groups on the special skills needed for these types of data collection methods.

➤ Walk through the instrument with those administering the instrument.

➤ Provide a completed instrument example.

➤ Allow time to practice.

When to Complete This Instrument. Determining the time when the instrument will be administered ensures that the data source is available to provide the information at the time the information is being requested. In some cases, the instrument will be administered two or more times within an evaluation cycle. For example, if you will be administering a pre-post survey, you will need to plan a time at the beginning of the program year (pre-survey), then again a time at the end of the program year (post-survey). Timing for when data is collected can be critical to the entire evaluation process. In some cases, only a small window exists as to when the data can be collected; if data is not collected within that window, the data collection may need to wait until the following cycle (e.g., program year).

Other Instructions or Issues to Consider. The last part of this guide suggests other instructions or issues to consider when preparing for and collecting data. For example, there might be a need to emphasize the amount of time needed to administer a survey, what to do with the instruments after they have been administered, or a process of aggregating data onto a summary form.

Planning for Data Analysis

Data analysis is the process of taking the collected data and, as stated by Worthen and Sanders, making sense out of this data.

> Evaluations involve processing mountains of information that—if not organized in a form that permits meaningful interpretation—is often worthless, or worse yet, misleading.

> The aim of *data analysis* is to reduce and synthesize information—to "make sense" out of it—and to allow inferences about populations. The aim of *interpretation* is to combine the results of data analysis with value statements, criteria, and standards in order to produce conclusions, judgments, and recommendations. (Worthen and Sanders, 1987, p. 328)

As a result of this effort, statements can be made that produce conclusions and recommendations. Chapter 3, Basic Research Methods and Program Evaluation, provides a detailed discussion of data analysis. It states that data analysis is a key component of program evaluation and that statistics are used to achieve this task. Statistics can be categorized into *descriptive statistics*, which summarize and present data as what they are, and *inferential statistics*, which attempt to infer from the samples about the population, draw conclusions, give an explanation, or make predictions. For empowerment evaluation, descriptive statistics will most likely be used. The tasks under this statistical category are doable by program staff, requiring basic mathematical skills for calculating frequency distributions, graphic presentations, and/or summarizing the data on what attributes are typical (i.e., mean, median, and mode).

Each instrument should have an analysis plan. This could be a simple narrative page or part of the Table of Specifications. This documentation will ensure that the person who will analyze the data has a clear picture of what needs to be done and why. The plan identifies the statistical techniques, or the mathematical tool that will help describe and summarize the features of the data collected. These statistics need to consider the evaluation questions and the type of data being collected. "Methods for data analysis and interpretation should be selected at the time decisions are being made about how information will be collected and which questions or issues will guide the evaluation. All these evaluation activities work together" (Worthen and Sanders, 1987, p. 329).

Data collected could be managed by database software such as Microsoft Access or Statistical Package for the Social Sciences (SPSS) for storage and analysis. In a literacy tutoring program, staff may want to know the percentage of students by gender whose primary language is other than English and who are reading below grade level, as compared to students who speak only English and are also reading below grade level. Plan ahead so resources are available for the development and use of this technology, if it is needed.

Reporting Evaluation Results

Effective reporting is tailored to address the issues of greatest interest for the primary user of the report. Remember that different users may need different information. *Primary users* are the individuals who will use the results to make decisions or promote the program; these people are your chief audience and often your funders (e.g., community partners providing matching funds). *Secondary users* are individuals who may be associated with the program or have an interest in what the service activities offer (e.g., city council, internal organization, neighborhoods, and service recipients).

Turning Your Data into an Evaluation Report

Before beginning to develop an evaluation report, gather the following material:

- ➤ Copy of your evaluation plan
- ➤ Record of accomplishments (e.g., number of individuals served)
- ➤ Results of your data analysis transferred to an easy reference format (e.g., in a table, or recorded onto a copy of the original instrument)
- ➤ Stories collected from members or statements from service recipients

After gathering the information needed for an evaluation report, the report writing can begin. An example of how a basic evaluation report can be developed is outlined here.

1. Executive Summary

   Provide a brief summary of the evaluation process and its key findings and recommendations. It could be in a narrative format with bullets or numbers to highlight key points. It is short, one to two pages in length.

2. Restate your objective.

   Rewrite the complete objective: what is the community need, what service activities were implemented to address the need, what were the anticipated outputs and outcomes, and what targets were set toward the anticipated outputs and outcomes. Here is where the purpose of the evaluation can be described and/or the evaluation questions restated.

3. Describe the progress made toward achieving the objectives during this reporting period.

   Refer to the evaluation worksheet and/or evaluation plan developed when preparing the evaluation section of the proposal to make sure the service activities, beneficiaries, and the number of people served are aligned with the report. What did you do relating to this objective during this period? Who did you serve or impact? How many beneficiaries did you serve or impact this period? Describe your anticipated outcomes and indicators used to measure the desired result. A description of progress toward achieving the objectives during this reporting period might be stated like this:

   > Ten volunteers were placed at two middle schools, five members at each school, to provide tutoring in reading literacy three days per week for each high-risk student tutored during a school semester. Each volunteer tutored four high-risk students each semester for a total of 80 students during this school year. Our desired result was for students to increase successful completion of their homework, thereby increasing their literacy skills.

4. Note evaluation activities in which you have engaged.

   Refer to the evaluation worksheet and/or evaluation plan developed when you prepared the evaluation section of the proposal to make sure that the anticipated outcomes measured reflect the evaluation results being reported. Describe the types of instruments used (e.g., survey, test, observation, etc.). Provide this information for every instrument that was used. (Do not forget to report the baseline data collected during early reporting periods.) Describe who administered each instrument and when it was administered. Describe to whom, as well as how, each instrument was administered. Describe which, and how many individuals, completed each instrument. A description of evaluation activities in which the program engaged might be stated in this manner:

   > Volunteers used a Homework Assignment Form to describe and document successful homework completed for each student during a semester. Volunteers documented successfully completed homework assignments daily and gave copies of their Homework Assignment Forms to their supervisor weekly. Documentation of successfully completed homework assignments was recorded for all 80 students. Data for two previous years on homework

completion with reading literacy was recorded for each student who began participation in the tutoring program and was used as baseline data.

5. Describe relevant evaluation data.

Describe the results of the analysis based on the anticipated evaluation results stated in your objective. What quantitative statistics did you find? What qualitative information did you find? What stories do you have that relate to your quantitative or qualitative data? Compare the results of the evaluation with the target set in the objective. Did the program meet the target stated in the objective? What is the importance of the quantitative or qualitative information? How did this service address the existing need (relate this to baseline data)? What does this imply about the success of the program services? A description of relevant evaluation data might look like this:

> The worksheet target stated: 50 percent of the students who participate in the Tutoring Program will successfully complete 80 percent of their homework during this school year. By the end of the year, the program succeeded in assisting 40 percent of the students tutored to successfully complete at least 80 percent of their homework assignments, 10 percent less than the target the program hoped to reach. However, of those students who met the target, the average completion rate of homework assignments for each student during the school year was 95 percent, 15 percent more than was originally expected.

6. State ideas for program improvement, or any next steps.

How do the evaluation results inform the program in terms of next steps for program improvement? Should the program expand its service? Can the evaluation results be helpful to other stakeholders (e.g., the schools)? Can the evaluation results be used for other purposes? A description of reporting results might look like this:

> Those students who successfully completed at least 80 percent of their homework (the target set in the evaluation worksheet), actually successfully completed 95 percent of their homework, a 15 percent increase in homework over the target that was set at the beginning of the year. Therefore, the program will review how tutoring was provided to these students reaching the target and compare the services with those students who did not reach the target. Areas that will be under review will include, but will not be limited to, the training the tutors received, the manner in which tutoring was provided, the environmental conditions under which tutoring was provided, and the level of supervision. The program plan for next school year will be to increase the number of students (e.g., greater than 50 percent) who meet the homework completion target.

The examples provided demonstrate only the key elements of an evaluation report. It is recommended that more detail be included in the final evaluation report and that it should be more robust than shown here.

References

Fetterman, D. M., Kaftarian, S. J., & Wandersman, A. (1996). *Empowerment evaluation: Knowledge and tools for self-assessment and accountability.* Thousand Oaks, CA: Sage Publications.

Hatry, H. P. (1999). *Performance measurement: Getting results.* Washington, DC: Urban Institute Press.

United States Government Accountability Office (GAO). (1993). *Program evaluation and methodology division, developing and using questions.* GAO/PEMD-10.1.7

United States Government Accountability Office (GAO). (2005). *Performance measurement and evaluation: Definitions and relationships.* GA/05–739SP.

Worthen, B. R., & Sanders, J. R. (1987). *Educational evaluation: Alternative approaches and practical guidelines.* White Plains, NY: Longman Group.

Yuen, F. K. O., & Terao, K. L. (2003). *Practical grant writing and program evaluation.* Pacific Grove, CA: Brooks/Cole–Thomson Learning.

CHAPTER 7

Learning by Doing: Exercises, Templates, Samples, Checklists, and Training Ideas

Samples and Self-Help Materials

The seven sections of this chapter contain practical tools to apply in developing the key components of a grant proposal and program evaluation. Figure 7.1 diagrams the connections and flow of these seven sections as they relate to the grant writing and evaluation processes, that is: using the needs assessment to develop a program logic model; proposing programmatic initiatives to meet the need while developing evaluation plans and tools; using the evaluation data to assess the impact of the program; and feeding back the findings of the evaluation into needs assessment and program planning in order to improve service delivery.

Each section presents opportunities for readers to further their understanding of the evaluation and grant-writing process by building on information presented in the

Figure 7.1 Grant Proposal and Evaluation Plan Flow Chart

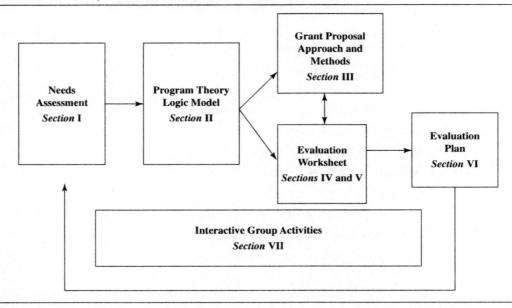

previous chapters and moving from theory to practice. The learning opportunities in Sections 1 to 6 include the use of templates or forms, checklists, and learning exercises. Readers can develop the components of an evaluation plan or a grant proposal by employing the included templates and then check their progress using self-administered checklists. Sample documents help illuminate important concepts. Small- and large-group interactive exercises in Section 7 at the end of the chapter provide targeted learning experiences to enrich collaboration and skill building with colleagues and partners. In total, the activities presented in this chapter will enhance the skills of those involved and ultimately contribute to a stronger grant proposal and evaluation plan.

Each section begins with a brief description of the learning opportunities and the self-help materials. The sections provide instructions on how to use the materials and exercises. Forms and self-help material in each section may include the following:

➤ *Template*. The template is a ready-to-use form to employ as you create your own evaluation and grant-writing pieces.

➤ *Checklist*. Check how you did. Was anything missing? The checklist is self-administered and gives you the assurance that key elements are included.

➤ *Exercise*. Two sections, basic terminology and instrument development, include exercises that can be worked on individually (self-guided) or in a training situation to assess mastery and practice with the material.

➤ *Sample document*. Especially when you are stuck, a sample can jump-start creative juices or illuminate elements in ways that the text cannot.

At the end of the chapter, Section 7 presents eight interactive activities that can be used within large and small group settings:

➤ *Interactive group activities*. Whether you are trying to motivate a new grant-writing working group or train staff to carry out data collection tasks, interactive exercises can support and strengthen the learning and skill-building process.

Table 7.1 (on the following page) lists the learning opportunities and self-help materials included in each of the seven sections.

Section I: Needs Assessment

Template: Needs Assessment   The needs assessment establishes and describes the compelling problem and target population in the community that an existing or new service plans on addressing. The needs assessment form outlines the key components of a needs assessment plan and report (see Chapter 4, Program Planning and Evaluation, for more information on needs assessments). Given the proposed intervention, needs assessments vary greatly in scope and level of detail. By adapting this form, the user creates a clear reference for implementing a needs assessment appropriate for the unique context. Furthermore, the form can be used in training settings.

Table 7.1   Seven Key Sections and Materials List

Key Sections	Forms and Self-Help Material
1. **Needs Assessment**	**Template:** Needs Assessment Template **Checklist:** Needs Assessment Checklist **Sample:** Naturally Occurring Retirement Communities
2. **Results Terminology and Logic Model**	**Exercise:** Identifying Results (with Answer Key) **Template:** Logic Model Worksheet **Checklist:** Logic Model Checklist **Sample:** Temporary Assistance for Needy Families
3. **Grant Application**	**Template:** Grant Application Format **Checklist:** Grant Application Checklist **Sample:** See Chapter 8, Real-Life Samples
4. **Program Planning and Evaluation Worksheet**	**Template:** Program Planning and Evaluation Worksheet Template **Checklist:** Program Planning and Evaluation Worksheet Checklist **Sample:** Parent Skills Training
5. **Instrument Development**	**Checklist:** Instrument Formatting Checklist (with instrument) **Exercise:** Table of Specifications (Answer Key) **Template:** Table of Specification **Sample:** Emergency Financial Assistance Client Follow-up Interview (Telephone)
6. **Evaluation Plan**	**Template :** Evaluation Plan Outline **Checklist:** Evaluation Plan Checklist **Sample:** See Chapter 8, Real-Life Samples
7. **Interactive Group Activities**	**Exercises:** Everyday Evaluation Gaining Perspective The Importance of Focus From Table Conversation to the Award Speech The Right Fit Picture This! Sort It!

Checklist: Needs Assessment Checklist   The needs assessment checklist is a ready-to-use tool to review the needs assessment plan for completeness. In addition, it provides prompts and tips for key elements. Once you have drafted the needs assessment plan, review each component. Given the needs assessment requirements, all components may not be pertinent to the project, so they can be adjusted accordingly.

Sample: Naturally Occurring Retirement Communities   The scenario describes a senior community, Naturally Occurring Retirement Communities—Home Forever Project, and along with materials for three sample data collection tools, offers insights on how one project conducted a needs assessment. Three methods are employed to assess the need of the community:

1.   Document studies/key informants (use to generate "Mrs. Turner—A composite resident")

2.   Agenda, discussion questions, and guide for focus group meeting

3.   Needs assessment survey form

Table 7.2   Needs Assessment Template

Program/Initiative name:

I.   Purpose and Planning

Describe purpose:

Identify population:

Describe current social service program (if program already exists):

Demonstrate program theory and organizational capacity fit
(if organization exists):

Describe working groups and partners (roles, profiles):

II.   Target Population and Service Environment

Define target population (individual, community, systems):

Describe target population (e.g., demographics,
dispersion, geographic, socioeconomic, language):

Describe current or proposed service environment
(e.g., eligibility, dosage, service capacity):

III.   Need Identification: Scope of Problem/Social Condition

Describe problem/social condition
(e.g., rates, estimates, prevalence/incidence, etc.):

Source of data (e.g., existing data, social indicators, social research,
agency records, survey/censuses, focus group, community forum,
on-site observations, key information, forecasting):

IV.   Need Assessment: Character of Service Need

Describe extent of social condition/problem:

Describe key outcomes:

Provide qualitative and quantitative data:

Propose possible solutions:

Offer recommendations:

VI.   Communication and Reporting

Identify reporting venues and audiences
(e.g., oral presentations to potential clients, written report to funders):

Table 7.3   Needs Assessment Checklist

Due Date	Done	I. Purpose and Planning
	☐	**Purpose.** Describe what you need to know. Why is the needs assessment necessary? What question do you want to answer?
	☐	**Population.** Identify the target population. Is the target a system, group, or individual?
	☐	**Current service status.** Describe the current service intervention, if applicable. What does the program attempt? Describe clients (demographic information—economic status, age group, languages, etc.).
	☐	**Organizational scan and program theory fit.** Talk with staff members and current clients about services. Describe how this new or expanded service fits into mission of organization. Are there or will there be staff and funding resources available?
	☐	**Working group.** What is needed and who can help? How are staff and potential clients able to participate? Identify roles of participants.
	☐	**Partners.** Who else is providing services like those proposed? Identify other organizations offering complementary or competitive services and possible partnerships.

Due Date	Done	II. Target Population and Service Environment
	☐	**Target population.** Define (individual, group, etc.) and describe the target population (demographics, language, dispersion, etc.).
	☐	**Criteria.** Describe target population specification (how included or excluded), need, or demand rates of occurrence.
	☐	**Current or proposed service environment.** How are clients currently accessing service? Use and appropriateness of current services? Gaps in service? Accessibility?

Due Date	Done	III. Need Identification: Scope of Problem/Social Condition
	☐	**Problem or social condition.** Describe the social condition.
	☐	**Source of data.** Is data available to collect from existing sources (agency records, social indicators)? Will you need to customize research (focus group, community forum, etc.)?
	☐	**Gaps in service, resource inventory.** Describe service gaps, complementary and competing programs. What resources are available?

Due Date	Done	IV. Need Assessment: Character of Service Need
	☐	**Extent of social condition/problem.** Provide estimates of the condition and distribution. Provide estimates, rates of occurrence. What are the key areas?
	☐	**Outcomes.** Describe key outcomes from the assessment.
	☐	**Qualitative and quantitative data:** Gather and describe the nature of problem based on findings.
	☐	**Analyze and interpret.** Describe what the data indicates about the new or expanded program. What are the strengths of an intervention? Weaknesses?
	☐	**Possible solutions.** Interpret data and determine potential action.
	☐	**Recommendations.** Given what you know about the data and possible solutions, what do you recommend as a service intervention for target population?

Due Date	Done	V. Communication and Reporting
	☐	**Report.** Identify who needs to know what and the best way to share the information. Generate reports or presentations appropriate to audience.
	☐	**Plan.** How will the information help with decision making? What are the steps?

Needs Assessment Sample Scenario
Naturally Occurring Retirement Communities—Home Forever Project

In this scenario, documentary studies, key informants, focus group, and a community survey are used to assess the needs of a community. More than 75 percent of the residents in Sunshine Park are older adults who live alone or with their spouses. The majority of them is living off their savings, retirement benefits, or support from children. While it is a moderate-income community, most of the residents are financially limited and vulnerable. The median age for the park is 70 years old, and the average level of education is community college to college education. Sunshine Park has 100 small- to medium-sized townhouses built about 35 years ago. For a long time, it was a prime location for local working-class families to own their first homes and to raise a family. In the last 15 years, younger people have steadily moved out, and more older adults have moved in. Many of them are families of retirees from the nearby manufacturing and technology companies. Sunshine Park's proximity to a major regional hospital 15 minutes away is believed to be a draw for its popularity among older residents.

The last three reports by the Area Agency on Aging on medical and social services and a recent newspaper special investigation raise concerns regarding the early institutionalization of the elderly residents in this community. An increased number of residents from Sunshine Park have moved into nursing homes or been hospitalized, although they are relatively self-sufficient and are not seriously ill.

Journey Family Services (JFS) is a local social service agency that is part of the local elderly service coalition. The agency is located just a few blocks away from Sunshine Park. During several occasions, the agency's elderly service has worked with Sunshine Park's two organizations: Caring Family and Friends and Concerned Neighbors, on a number of health and home-safety activities.

JFS is cooperating with the Area Agency on Aging on developing a Home Forever project. This project aims to prevent premature institutionalization and promote successful aging in one's home. It is based on the aging-in-place concept that through proper facilitation and assistance, older adults can remain healthy and active in their own homes. It is particularly appropriate for a naturally occurring retirement community (NORC), such as Sunshine Park.

Before any program activities are developed, it is necessary to better understand the conditions and needs of the community, specifically from the perspectives of the residents. The agency also believes it is important to set up the program evaluation from the very beginning of the project. With the assistance of a program evaluator, JFS staff conducted a sequence of needs assessment activities to further their understanding of the community and the target population. These activities included the following:

1. Documentary studies
2. Focus group meetings using nominal group process
3. Mailed questionnaire survey

   1. *Documentary studies and key informants interviews*. Recent academic and applied research and service reports, U.S. Census statistics, and news media reports related

to Sunshine Park and the general region were collected and carefully organized. Contents of these documents and their findings were analyzed using methods such as sorting and pairing. Patterns, trends, focuses, and critical incidents were identified. A narrative summary report was developed. Additionally, the program evaluator interviewed three longtime residents, who have been active in volunteering or organizing in the community, on their views about the needs of the residents. The program evaluator summarized the findings and put together a composite resident, Mrs. Turner (Box 7.1), who has most of the characteristics of a typical resident and a few unique issues. Mrs. Turner would then be used for the focus group meeting.

2. *Focus groups.* Several focus group meetings were scheduled to solicit input and understand the needs directly from the residents. The focus groups used a nominal group process to help direct the discussions, generate group summary, and make recommendations. Box 7.2 is the agenda or group meeting plan for the focus meeting and the description of a nominal group process. Box 7.3 is the focus group discussion questions and guide. Focus group meetings provided the agency with a wealth of information on the needs of the community and necessary interventions.

3. *Surveys.* A summary report of these focus group meetings was compiled and the findings were used to inform the development of the needs assessment survey form (Table 7.4).

Box 7.1 Mrs. Turner—A Composite Resident

JFS Home Forever NORC Composite of Sunshine Park Resident

My name is Edith Turner, and I am a 73-year-old widow living in Sunshine Park. In general, I am happy with my condition, although I am not in very good health. I have no major disabilities. Most of the time, I do not have any difficulty in completing daily chores. If I need any medical attention, I rely on Medicare or my HMO. My home is paid off, and I have moderate monthly expenses. I enjoy meeting with friends and family, but that does not happen too often. I know I have been blessed, because many of my friends in the neighborhood are not doing as well as I am. They do not want to let other people know about their problems. That may be why they refused to participate in any survey or activities. The lack of money, deteriorating health, absence of family and friends, and diminishing independence are the usual things that we deal with every day. As to the people who have moved in within the last 10 years, I don't know many of them. I do, however, know they are struggling like my friends.

If I need help with something, I feel comfortable asking for assistance or speaking up for myself. I can either ask a friend or I figure out how to contact someone who can lend a hand. The things I seem to need the most assistance with are home repairs for problems such as plumbing and appliance malfunction. It costs so much to get a simple problem fixed, and you never know who you can trust to avoid being ripped off! Of course, there are always problems of getting to medical appointments, knowing my medications (there are a lot of them!), and having someone guide me through the medical and service bureaucracy and explain to me my options. I could drive my own car, but I prefer not to do that. If I need to take the bus, I know where the stops are, although they are not close. I could use a ride to the grocery store or to run some errands, but I do not want to trouble people. They always refuse to take my money for gas. If, for some reason, I could no longer take care of myself, I know there are assisted living communities nearby. I want to stay in my own home as long as I can. I wish our neighbors could come together more often and socialize.

Box 7.2 Agenda for Home Forever (JFS NORC) Program Planning Focus Group Meetings

The Agenda for the Group Meeting:

1. Welcome and explain the purpose of the meeting

2. Self-introduction

3. Discussions using the focus group discussion questions and guide

4. Conclusion

5. Thank you for your participation

Process and Logistics:

Each group will have no more than 12 people. Each meeting will last about 60 to 90 minutes. Meetings will take place in the mornings or evenings at a location convenient for the participants. Each meeting will have a group facilitator and at least two co-facilitators/recorders. JFS will recruit participants through its current contacts. Light refreshments will be provided. There will be a sign-in form to document who participated in these meetings. Audio or video recording and photographs will be prohibited.

Methods Used for JFS Program Planning Focus Group Meeting:

1. Use the focus group discussion questions and guide (Questions 1, 2, and 3) for the whole group.

2. After Question 3, break up into two smaller groups. Employ nominal group techniques for some of the questions (Questions 4, 5, 6, 7, 8, 9, 10, and 11).

3. Use a short questionnaire to explore interest (Questions 12 and 13).

The Five Possible Focus Groups:

1. Caring friends and families group

2. Concerned neighbors and volunteers group

3. Men group

4. Women group

5. Social group (mixed group)

Key Nominal Group Procedures:

1. Individual thoughts in response to statements and questions

2. Collect responses

3. Vote

4. Discuss

(Continued)

The JFS Nominal Group Process

1. After Question 3, form small groups of three to four persons. Each person will have a sheet that has Questions 3 to 12.

2. Ask each person to write down his or her individual response to Question 5. (Provide assistance if needed.) (Use big paper on the wall or a flip chart to help remind participants which topic is being discussed and to write down responses.)

3. Take turns, each person tells his or her first, then second, and third choice responses. List all of them on a flip chart. No discussions or comments; all responses are equally important and included.

4. Cluster responses.

5. Repeat above procedures 2, 3, and 4 for Questions 7, 9, and 11.

6. Allocate 10 points to reflect their views, 10 being the item about which they feel most strongly. Use sticky notes (with participants' initials) to indicate assigned points and to increase participation, if mobility is not a problem. Otherwise, participants could take turns calling out their allocated points.

7. Discuss the top choices or all of them, depending on available time.

8. Each group comes up with its top five choices.

9. Reassemble into one big group, and summarize or further narrow down the list with general discussion or another round of nominal group process.

10. Expand discussions if appropriate.

Box 7.3 Focus Group Discussion Questions and Guide

Big Group Process

1. Meet Edith Turner. In your opinion, how much does Mrs. Turner represent the characteristics of older adult residents of Sunshine Park? What are your immediate comments about this description?

2. What else is important but not being captured in this description?

3. Some have claimed that "driving/transportation," "information about alternatives to living at home," "home repair assistance," and "lack of social connections" are the four main areas of concern for older adults in Sunshine Park. Do you agree? Should anything else be added to this list?

Nominal Group Process

4. Is transportation or your ability to drive a concern to you? Do you agree that older adults' driving and transportation is a concern?

5. If so, please list three possible solutions that could address those concerns.

6. Is a lack of information about alternatives to living in your own home a concern to you?

7. If so, please list three possible solutions that could address those needs.

8. Is getting home repair assistance a concern for you?

9. If so, please list three possible solutions that could address those needs.

10. Is a lack of social connection a concern to you?

11. If so, please list three possible solutions that could address those concerns.

Big Group Process

12. If Journey Family Service was to organize activities to serve residents in Sunshine Park, would you be interested in participating in any of the following proposed activities? (Provide participants the one-page proposed activities list.)

13. Specifically, the possibility of an intergenerational mentoring program is being explored. Would you be interested in completing the short, one-page questionnaire?

Table 7.4   Needs Assessment Survey Form

Naturally Occurring Retirement Communities (NORC) Home Forever

Needs Assessment Survey Form

Community: Sunshine Park

Agency: Journey Family Services

Please tell us what you think of your community by circling the answer that reflects your opinion.

1. Overall, as a place to live, I would rate my community as
   Very Poor   Somewhat Poor   Good   Excellent

2. People in my neighborhood generally try to help each other out
   Never   Occasionally   Often   Almost Every Day

3. If I need a ride I could call a neighbor, friend, or family member
   Never   Occasionally   Often   Almost Every Day

4. If I need help with something around the house, I could call a neighbor, friend, or family member
   Never   Occasionally   Often   Almost Every Day

5. Generally speaking, I feel safe in my neighborhood
   Never   Occasionally   Often   Almost Every Day

6. Other people in the neighborhood ask me for help
   Never   Occasionally   Often   Almost Every Day

7. I have regular contact with my family
   Never   Occasionally   Often   Almost Every Day

(Continued)

Social Involvement

Please tell us about your social activities and involvement by circling or checking the statement that reflects your answer.

8. In the past 8 weeks, have you volunteered for any civic, service, or religious organization?

   Yes   No

9. If Yes, please list organization(s) _____

10. In the past 4 weeks, did you do any of the following? (Check all that apply)

   _____ Get together socially with friends, relatives, or neighbors
   _____ Talk on the telephone with friends, relatives, or neighbors
   _____ Go to a place of worship for services or other activities
   _____ Go to a show, movie, sports event, club meeting, class, or other group event

11. Would you like to participate in any of the following activities, if they are available in your community? (Check all that apply)

   _____ Reading club _____ Investment club _____ Walking club
   _____ Movie club _____ Exercise club _____ Service club

12. Who do you depend on if you need help? (Check all that apply)

   _____ Friend _____ Religious organization _____ Relative
   _____ Neighbor _____ Social service organization _____ No one

Transportation

In the past 4 weeks, were there any times when you were unable to go somewhere because you did not have transportation? _____ Yes   _____ Does not apply to me (skip to Question 18)

How often is it a problem for you to get transportation to ...	Daily	Weekly	Twice per month	Once per month	Less than once per month	Never been a problem
13. Buy groceries						
14. Run errands						
15. Receive medical or dental care						
16. Visit friends, other social activities						
17. Visit a place of worship						

Specific Services

Please help us identify the services most important to you by circling "yes" or "no" in the two columns. If it does not apply, check the third column, "does not apply to me".

Service/Need Area	I currently receive this service	I am in need of this service	Does not apply to me
18. Transportation: Someone to take you where you want or need to go and pick you up afterward	Yes No	Yes No	Does not apply to me
19. Shopping Assistance: Someone to shop with you or for you	Yes No	Yes No	Does not apply to me

20. Housekeeping or Laundry: Someone to come to your home on a set schedule to help you take care of your house or do your laundry	Yes No	Yes No	Does not apply to me
21. Home Maintenance: Help with minor home repairs or seasonal tasks	Yes No	Yes No	Does not apply to me
22. Home-Delivered Meals: Delivery of lunch and/or dinner to your home	Yes No	Yes No	Does not apply to me
23. Respite Care: Someone to come to your home to stay with a loved one who can't be left alone, so you can get out for a few hours	Yes No	Yes No	Does not apply to me
24. Case Management: Help you coordinate care, access services, and community services	Yes No	Yes No	Does not apply to me
25. Volunteer or Companion Visits: Someone to spend time with you on a one-on-one basis	Yes No	Yes No	Does not apply to me
26. Personal Care: Someone to come to your home on a set schedule to assist you with medication management, bathing, grooming, dressing, etc.	Yes No	Yes No	Does not apply to me
27. Adult Day Care: A daytime activity program that provides caring supervision	Yes No	Yes No	Does not apply to me
28. Legal Assistance: Estate planning, end-of-life issues, identity theft, etc.	Yes No	Yes No	Does not apply to me

Health and Safety

In your home, do you have . . .		
29. A working smoke detector	Yes	No
30. A working fire extinguisher	Yes	No
31. A working carbon monoxide detector	Yes	No
32. Grab-bar in your bathroom	Yes	No

33. Generally speaking, I feel in control of my life: (please circle)

   Never   Occasionally   Often   Almost Every Day

34. I feel lonely

   Never   Occasionally   Often   Almost Every Day

35. Most of the time, my outlook on life is

   Very Poor   Somewhat Poor   Good   Very Good

(Continued)

36. Overall, I would say my physical health is

Very Poor   Somewhat Poor   Good   Very Good

37. I consider my activity level to be

Very Poor   Somewhat Poor   Good   Very Good

38. I worry about money

Never   Occasionally   Often   Almost Every Day

39. I worry about the future

Never   Occasionally   Often   Almost Every Day

General Information

Please tell us about yourself. This information is collected for information and planning purposes only. It will be kept confidential and reported only in summary form.

40. What is your age? _____

41. Gender: _____ male _____ female

42. How long have you lived in your current residence?

_____ Less than 1 year _____ 1 to 5 years

_____ 6 to 10 years _____ 10 years or more

43. How would you describe yourself?

_____ White/Caucasian _____ Black/African American _____ Latino/Hispanic
_____ Asian Pacific Islanders _____ Other (Please specify) _____

44. What is your highest level of education?

_____ Less than high school graduate _____ High school graduate

_____ Some college/Associate degree _____ College graduate

_____ Master's degree _____ Doctoral degree

45. Approximately what was your total household income last year before taxes?

_____ less than $10,000

_____ $10,000–$49,999

_____ $50,000–$99,000

_____ Over $100,000

46. Are you currently working for pay?

_____ Yes, full-time _____ No, but I would like to work

_____ Yes, part-time _____ No

47. What is you marital status?

_____ Married _____ Widowed

_____ Single, divorced _____ Single, never married

48. What are your living arrangements?

_____ Live alone _____ With spouse only _____ With children only

_____ With spouse and children _____ With relative

_____ With friend(s) _____ Other (please specify) _____

49. Do you participate in activities at a place of worship?

_____Yes _____ No

50. Do you want to be informed about JFS NORC activities?

_____ Yes (please fill out the attached address slip and mail in the self-addressed, stamped envelope in back)

_____ No

Thank you for completing this survey. Please return it in the self-addressed and stamped envelope provided. Your responses will be used to help make our community a better place to live for all residents.

Section II: Results Terminology and Logic Model

The materials in this section support a basic understanding of the types of results and the creation of a logic model for program planning and as the basis of an evaluation.

Exercise (self-guided or pairs): Identify Results (Answer Key) (Tables 7.5 and 7.6)

The identifying results exercise gives you a chance to practice recognizing different result types: outputs, intermediate outcomes, and end outcomes. (Refer to the logic model in Chapter 4, Program Planning and Evaluation, for the review of results.) This exercise can be done individually or in pairs as part of a training workshop or meeting. After completing the exercise, participants discuss why they identified each result as an output, intermediate outcome, or end outcome. Prudent people will disagree on the type of result for some activities, depending on what they believe to be the program's theory of change. This exercise demonstrates how important it is to understand program assumptions when determining results. The answer key is included.

Template: Logic Model Worksheet (Table 7.7)   This logic model worksheet is a concise, visual display of the basic components of a logic model. Each component (e.g., activity, input, output) is linked to the next and supports program planning, evaluation, and parts of the grant-writing experience. The logic model displays may vary; however, the linkage of the components does not. The logic model worksheet is effective for teaching the core components. Use a paper copy to brainstorm each of the elements, or build your logic model electronically (e.g., Word document) by setting up a simple grid and populating the cells.

Checklist: Logic Model Checklist (Table 7.8)   The information in this logic model checklist is organized in the same order as a logic model worksheet. The checklist describes each component of the logic model. Use the logic model checklist as a prompt when developing a program logic model or to review a draft logic model. Using this checklist will ensure that the key elements for each component of a logic model are considered.

Sample: Temporary Assistance for Low-Income Families   Table 7.9 illustrates what one program's complete logic model looks like and how it reads. Samples are especially helpful for stakeholders who are being introduced to program logic models for the first time and want to develop their own.

Table 7.5 Identifying Results Exercise

Direction: For each activity, mark the results as output, intermediate outcome, or end outcome.

Neighborhood Watch	Output	Intermediate Outcome	End Outcome
Property crime rates decline.	☐	☐	☐
Volunteers organize informational meeting with neighborhood residents.	☐	☐	☐
Neighborhood watch committees are established.	☐	☐	☐
In-Home Service			
Seniors with disability can perform daily tasks with assistance from home-help workers.	☐	☐	☐
Seniors with disability receive weekly visits from home-help workers.	☐	☐	☐
Seniors with disability are able to stay in their homes.	☐	☐	☐
Mentoring Youth Offenders			
Mentored youth demonstrate increased self-understanding.	☐	☐	☐
Youth received mentoring services from the program's mentors.	☐	☐	☐
Recidivism rates decline among mentored youth.	☐	☐	☐
Respite Care			
Family caregivers have more time for themselves.	☐	☐	☐
Family caregivers have less stress.	☐	☐	☐
Patients with Alzheimer's disease receive weekly visits from a member of the service team.	☐	☐	☐
Special Needs Children	☐	☐	☐
Children with special needs demonstrate improved academic performance.	☐	☐	☐
Children with special needs receive biweekly visit from the school social worker.	☐	☐	☐
Children with special needs demonstrate improved coping skills.	☐	☐	☐

Based on document by Aguirre Division, JBS International.

Table 7.6 Identifying Results Exercise (Answer Key)

Neighborhood Watch	Output	Intermediate Outcome	End Outcome
Property crime rates decline.			✓
Volunteers organize informational meeting with neighborhood residents.	✓		
Neighborhood watch committees are established.		✓	
In-Home Service			
Seniors with disability can perform daily tasks with assistance from home-help workers.		✓	
Seniors with disability receive weekly visits from home-help workers.	✓		
Seniors with disability are able to stay in their homes.			✓
Mentoring Youth Offenders			
Mentored youth demonstrate increased self-understanding.		✓	
Youth received mentoring services from the program's mentors.	✓		
Recidivism rates decline among mentored youth.			✓
Respite Care			
Family caregivers have more time for themselves.		✓	
Family caregivers have less stress.			✓
Patients with Alzheimer's disease receive weekly visits from a member of the service team.	✓		
Special Needs Children			
Children with special needs demonstrate improved academic performance.			✓
Children with special needs receive biweekly visit from the school social worker.	✓		
Children with special needs demonstrate improved coping skills.		✓	

Table 7.7 Logic Model Worksheet

Step 1	Step 3	Step 4	Step 2 Results		
Community Need	Inputs	Activities	Outputs	Intermediate Outcomes	End Outcomes
In our community, we have identified the following problem:	In order to accomplish our activity, we will need the following:	In order to address our problem or asset, we will conduct the following activity:	We expect that once completed or underway, this activity will produce the following evidence or service delivery:	We expect that if completed or ongoing, this activity will lead to the following intermediate changes:	We expect that if accomplished, this activity will lead to the following end changes:
	⇨	⇨	⇨	⇨	⇨

Table 7.8 Logic Model Checklist

Due Date	Done	I. Community Need
	☐	**Problem or Condition.** Describe the condition in the community (include community name) that needs to be improved. Include key factors that contribute to or cause the problem.
	☐	**Target Population/Community.** Describe who is most affected (e.g., individuals, families, ethnic group, children with incarcerated parents). Include demographic information, relevant characteristics.
	☐	**Research.** Cite research or other reliable data sources that document this need.

Due Date	Done	II. Inputs
	☐	**Human resources.** Describe the number of staff/volunteers participating in the activity and the total hours of the intervention.
	☐	**Support.** Describe any training for volunteer/staff. Include topic and scope (how long), frequency (how often).
	☐	**Material resources.** Describe resources needed including equipment, structure, vehicles, curriculum, travel expenses.

Due Date	Done	III. Activities
	☐	**Scope of Activity.** Clearly describe the service or intervention that will address the need, including who will provide service, how often, and for how long.
	☐	**Target population.** Describe the direct recipients of the service and how they come to program (i.e., criteria for selection: self-selected, mandated to participate).
	☐	**Address need.** Describe how this service will address the identified community need. Is it reasonable and logical that this service could affect the community need?

Due Date	Done	IV. Outputs
	☐	**Well defined.** Clearly describe who will be served or what will be created.
	☐	**Aligned.** Does the output flow logically from the activity? Will it occur because of this activity?

Due Date	Done	V. Intermediate outcomes
	☐	**Milestone change.** Describe the milestone that will occur for the recipients within the program year. Who or what directly changes (short or medium) because of this activity?
	☐	**Knowledge, skill, attitude behavior.** Clearly describe what benchmarks will be achieve by recipients.
	☐	**Aligned.** Does the intermediate outcome flow logically from the activity? Will it occur because of the intervention?

Due Date	Done	VI. End Outcomes
	☐	**Ultimate change.** Describe the long-term change that will occur for the recipients within the program year (or longer). Who or what directly changes because of this activity?
	☐	**Knowledge, skill, attitude behavior.** Clearly describe what benchmarks will be achieve by recipients.
	☐	**Aligned.** Does the intermediate outcome flow logically from the activity? Will it occur because of the intervention?

Table 7.9 Logic Model Sample: Temporary Assistance for Low-Income Families

Need	Inputs	Activities	Outputs	Intermediate Outcomes	End Outcomes
In San Marcos, California, approximately 26% of the population depends on seasonal agricultural work or variable service jobs for household incomes. According to the annual report published by the Community Services Council (CSC) of San Marcos, 525 working families and individuals requested temporary assistance in 2008 to help pay for rent or mortgages due to unexpected financial crisis through temporary loss of wages or health problems. They are the working poor who usually do not qualify for government general assistance, but are at risk of homelessness when a crisis occurs. The CSC helps these families by providing temporary (one month) payment of rent or mortgage, financial skills classes, and individual budget counseling for up to six months after they receive this aid. The CSC is able to provide more services and keep its overhead costs low because of the volunteers who commit their time.	Twenty community volunteers will provide 10 hours of services each for 46 weeks during the year, for a total of 9,200 hours of service. Initial orientation and training will be provided by the United Way of greater San Marcos County and the CSC of San Marcos. Ongoing training and supervision, office space, equipment (desk, telephone, copier, etc.), and supplies will be provided by the CSC.	Twenty community volunteers will serve for one year at the Community Services Council office in San Marcos. The volunteers will provide service to approximately 500 low-income families by responding to inquiries about the rental/ mortgage assistance program, taking appointments, screening applicants to determine need and eligibility, and collecting documentation. Volunteers will also assist case managers with budget counseling and tracking client data.	Families seeking help at the SC will receive assistance with the rigorous application process.	Families who applied for funding will receive financial assistance.	Families who received financial assistance, financial skills classes, and case management will remain in their homes/apartments for at least six months.

187

Section III: Grant Application

Template: Grant Application Format   The grant application format is a general outline containing common components required for most proposals (see Chapter 5, Grant Proposal Writing, for more information). Each funding agency will have its own requirements and in many cases, the Request for Application (RFA) will include an outline of content the funder wants and how it is to be organized. This should be followed to the detail. Familiarize yourself with this sample grant application format—the tasks to complete and documents to gather—to expedite the preparation and writing process. In most cases, an applicant has only six weeks from the date that an RFA is released to the proposal due date. By developing an understanding of the expectations and tasks early on, you will be more successful in completing the proposal within the tight time frame.

Checklist: Grant Application Checklist   The checklist for completing a grant application supplies a list of key tasks associated with the grant application preparation process (Chemise 2000, Cozzan retrieved 2009, Kluge retrieved 2009). In addition to preparing the proposal, this grant application checklist can be used beforehand to gauge interest in and the capacity of potential applicant to respond to the RFA. Many tasks may need to be carried out simultaneously, and it can be easy to forget a step. Other tasks require an ordered step-by-step completion before beginning the next task. Keep the grant application checklist before you while working to ensure that all steps are completed.

Sample Grant Proposals in Chapter 8   Two samples of completed grant proposals can be reviewed in Chapter 8, Real-Life Samples. These simple proposals offer you an idea of what a completed proposal may look like.

Table 7.10 Grant Application Outline

I. Abstract and Table of Contents

Describe purpose:
Identify population:

II. Specific Aims

Needs and problem statement (Describe why the program is needed):
Literature review (Report information that informs proposal):

III. Target Population

Describe the target population (Include how you will recruit and sustain beneficiary population):

IV. Approaches and Methods

Describe program plan, activities, and objectives (Include how the program plan will be implemented):

V. Agency Capacity and Project Management

Describe the organization's capacity:
Describe the project management (Name staff positions and resources):

VI. Budget and Budget Justification

Provide a line-item budget:
Budget justification (In narrative format, describe how the budget supports the project):

VII. Evaluation Plan

Describe how the identified results will be measured (instruments, data collection):

VII. Assurances and Appendices

Sign and supply assurances (e.g., assurance concerning civil rights, handicapped, sex and age discrimination):
Include all requested appendices (e.g., organizational chart, board of directors list, program evaluation plan, sample consent forms, resumes/job descriptions):

Table 7.11 Grant Application Checklist

Due Date	Done	I. Gather Information for Decision Making
	☐	**Know internal processes.** Who gives the go-ahead and signs off on writing grants? How long will it take to write the proposal?
	☐	**Gather helpers.** Who is available to assist? Identify those who can help gather information, prepare proposal, edit documents (colleagues, experts, community leaders, representative stakeholders).
	☐	**Identify partners (optional).** May be required or may improve strength of proposal if applicant partners are with another agency, especially if there are gaps in organizational expertise or capacity.
	☐	**Review documents carefully. Repeat.** Read again. Copy and distribute: complete copy of RFP, statement of interest, guidelines, application, budget, assurances, and previous grants. Do you have all pages including attachments? Do you understand the grantor's needs?
	☐	**Requirements and eligibility.** Understand the requirements and regulations. Don't apply if the scope of work is beyond the capability of the organization and its resources.
	☐	**Prepare questions.** Gather questions to submit to contracting officer for bidder conference call or electronic submission.
	☐	**Decision making time.** Can you match the expertise of your organization/project with the grant-making agency? Can you complete the proposal and gather the necessary documents by the deadline? Does it make sense to go forward?

Due Date	Done	II. Preparing to Write the Grant
	☐	**Letter of intent.** Complete and submit by deadline.
	☐	**Collect references.** Contact and pass on information to references, review for accuracy, completeness.
	☐	**Define roles for helpers.** Meet with group and assign tasks. Arrange for technical support in preparing and submitting proposal (graphics, technical read of funders' statement of need or interest). Provide writers with formatting guidelines, instructions, character limits/page limits, draft deadlines. Determine review, feedback, and editing process.
	☐	**Collect resumes/Curricula Vitas, partner information.** Identify number and type of consultants /staff and gather documents. If partnering, develop scope of work with partner.

Due Date	Done	III. Proposal Development (Writing the Grant)
	☐	**Prepare draft outline. "Lift" RFP format and goals.** Use the format provided in RFA to determine headings and organize proposal.

(Continued)

Table 7.11 Grant Application Checklist *(Continued)*

☐ **Abstract/Executive summary.** Once other sections complete, write summary of project.

☐ **Table of contents.** Make your document as organized as possible.

☐ **Needs and problem statement.** Describe community need to be addressed and how needs were identified. Use and cite data (local, state, national) to support your statement. Note how the plan will meet the community need and benefit clients.

☐ **Literature review.** Pull information to justify the project need (needs assessment) and chosen strategies. Use needs assessment information, also pertinent local, state, and national research.

☐ **Target population.** Describe population of beneficiaries (unique qualities, locale). Why target these clients but not the others?

☐ **Approaches and methods.** Introduce goal, brief summary of implementation plan, recruitment and retention of target population. Describe proposed project design: objectives, activities, and how objectives will be accomplished and measured. Include timeline. Often the longest section.

☐ **Evaluation plan.** Describe project accountability and evaluation procedure, including criteria to be used to evaluate the results, and the data to be collected, instruments, and timeline.

☐ **Organizational capacity and management:** Describe agency's capacity to manage project, current projects and personnel strengths.

☐ **Identify staff capacity.** Who will head up the service? Describe project director/staff education, experience, qualifications and roles relevant to project development/delivery. Address equal access and treatment concerns.

Due Date	Done	IV. Budget and Justification
	☐	**Calculate budget detail.** Develop line-item spreadsheet to calculate cost of each budget line item. Common items are:
		☐ **Personnel.** Include all positions, consultants, evaluator
		☐ **Travel.** In-state, out-of-state, fuel costs, per diem for meals, lodging, flights
		☐ **Indirect cost.**
	☐	**Match or in-kind.** If required, describe sources for matching in-kind or monetary resources.
	☐	**Overall budget justification.** In narrative form, describe budget line items and how they are related to the plan.

Due Date	Done	V. Support Material/Appendices
	☐	**Adequacy of organizational resources.** Describe resources present and needed to carry out service activities (facilities, equipment, and supplies)
	☐	**Edit and attach.** May need to reformat and edit: Letters of support/references, key personnel and CV.
	☐	**Assurances.** All should be signed. Assurances may concern civil rights, handicapped, and sex and age discrimination.
	☐	**Appendices.** Include all requested. Examples include project structure, organization chart, board of directors list, sample consent forms, letters from collaborating agencies, bibliography.

Due Date	Done	VI. Final touches—Packaging/submission
	☐	**Cohesive writing.** Put in required format, cover pages, format check (margins, font, etc.). Spell check.
	☐	**Review and editing.** Have a third party proofread the proposal. Is it easy to read? Intelligible language to the nonspecialist? Major points stand out?
	☐	**Determine how proposal is to be packaged.** Are hard copies needed, and if so, how many copies? Cover sheet?
	☐	**Prepare transmittal letter.**
	☐	**Delivery.** Make sure the proposal is at the funding office before the deadline date/times. Should it be hand-carried? Use a courier service?
	☐	**Submit required copies.** Ensure proper signature throughout documents.

Section IV: Program Planning and Evaluation

Template: Program Planning and Evaluation Worksheet (Table 7.12)   As discussed in previous chapters, the Program Planning and Evaluation Worksheet is a working document that can be used as a tool in program planning and developing an evaluation plan. If the logic model was developed, it will supply key components that can now be elaborated in the worksheet. Use the Program Planning and Evaluation Worksheet to enhance the information for each of the anticipated results (i.e., outputs and outcomes) stated in the logic model by including the indicators, data sources, type of instruments, and targets. Completing the worksheet together is an excellent exercise for program staff as they define and clarify their program evaluation goals.

Checklist: Program Planning and Evaluation Worksheet Checklist (Table 7.13)   The Program Planning and Evaluation Worksheet checklist lists components (each with prompts and questions) to consider when preparing for and creating the worksheet. After trying your hand at completing the Program Planning and Evaluation Worksheet, the checklist can be used to ensure that all key elements are accounted for and complete.

Sample: Parental Skills Training (Table 7.14)   The parental skills training Program Planning and Evaluation Worksheet sample demonstrates how the worksheet can capture important information in a precise format for implementation. Samples are particularly helpful when training staff and orienting members of an evaluation working group.

Table 7.12 Program Planning and Evaluation Worksheet Template

Program Name:					
Objective Title:			Date(s) Developed and Changes Made:		
Activity Start Date:		Activity End Date:		Staff:	
1. Identified Needs					
2. Target Population/ Service Recipient					
3. Activities/Interventions					
4. Desired Results (Outputs, Outcomes)	Output:				
	Intermediate Outcome:				
	End Outcome:				
5. Method of Measurement					
6. Indicators/Benchmarks					
7. Targets/Standards of Success					
8. Resources and Inputs					
9. Data Collection, Aggregation, Analysis, and Reporting					
Objective Statement:					

Based on document by Aguirre Division, JBS International.

Table 7.13 Program Planning and Evaluation Worksheet Checklist

Due Date	Done	I. Identify Needs
	☐	**Problem or condition.** Describe the condition in the community (include community name) that needs to be improved. Include key factor that contribute to or cause problem.
	☐	**Target population/community.** Describe who is most affected (e.g., individuals, families, ethnic group, children with incarcerated parents). Include demographics and relevant characteristics.
	☐	**Research.** Cite research or other reliable data sources that document this need.

Due Date	Done	II. Target Population
	☐	**Size of population.** Describe how many beneficiaries will be serviced.
	☐	**Selection criteria.** Are beneficiaries self-selected, or is participation mandated? Describe how participants are recruited or identified for the service.

Due Date	Done	III. Activities
	☐	**Scope of activity.** Clearly describe the service or intervention that will address the need, including who will provide service, how often, and for how long.
	☐	**Target population.** Describe the direct recipients of service and how they come to the program (i.e., criteria for selection: self-selected, mandated to participate).
	☐	**Address need.** Describe how this service will address the identified community need. Is it reasonable and logical that this service could affect the community need?

Due Date	Done	IV. Desired Results: Outputs
	☐	**Well defined.** Clearly describe who will be served or what will be created.
	☐	**Aligned.** Does the output flow logically from the activity? Will it occur because of this activity?

Due Date	Done	Intermediate Outcomes
	☐	**Milestone change.** Describe the milestone that will occur for the recipients within the program year. Who or what directly changes (short or medium) because of this activity?
	☐	**Knowledge, skill, attitude, behavior.** Clearly describe what benchmarks will be achieved by recipients.
	☐	**Aligned.** Does the intermediate outcome flow logically from the activity? Will it occur because of the intervention?

Due Date	Done	End Outcomes
	☐	**Ultimate change.** Describe the long-term change that will occur for the recipients within the program year (or longer). Who or what directly changes because of this activity?
	☐	**Knowledge, skill, attitude, behavior.** Clearly describe what key change will be achieved by recipients.
	☐	**Aligned.** Does the end outcome flow logically from the activity? Is it connected to the intermediate outcome? Will it occur because of the intervention?

Due Date	Done	V. Method of Measurement for Each Result (Output, Intermediate Outcome, End Outcomes):
	☐	**Data source.** Has an appropriate data source been identified and confirmed? Is it the most direct possible to measure results?
	☐	**Instrument.** Identify the instrument by name method. Is it connected to indicator and target?
	☐	**Coordinator of data collection.** Describe who will coordinate and administer instruments. Include timeline and any necessary training.
	☐	**Baseline data.** If you are going to measure an increase or decrease in something (skill, attendance, test scores), baseline data is needed. Include where/when it will be collected for comparison.
	☐	**Clarity.** Would someone unfamiliar with your program understand your method of measurement?

(Continued)

Table 7.13 Program Planning and Evaluation Worksheet Check List *(Continued)*

Due Date	Done	VI. Indictors/Benchmarks
	☐	**Concrete evidence.** Describe what will be looked at to gauge progress toward the result.
	☐	**Service criteria:** If appropriate, describe minimum dosage of service to expect results (e.g., students who receive at least 40 hours of tutoring per month will . . .).
Due Date	**Done**	**VII. Targets/Standards of Success**
	☐	**Quantifiable level of change.** Does each target respond to the specific result indicator?
	☐	**Specificity.** Does the target identify who or what will change, the specific change that will occur, the amount of change and over what time period?
	☐	**Realistic number.** Does the target identify a numerical achievement (percent or integer) that is realistic and ambitious?
Due Date	**Done**	**VIII. Resources and Inputs**
	☐	**Human resources.** Describe the number of staff/volunteers participating in the activity and the total hours of the intervention.
	☐	**Support.** Describe any training for volunteer/staff. Include topic and scope (how long), frequency (how often).
	☐	**Material resources.** Describe resources, including equipment, structure, vehicles, curriculum, travel expenses.
Due Date	**Done**	**IX. Data Collection, Aggregation, Analysis, and Reporting**
	☐	**Data collection.** Describe who will be collecting the data and how often data will be collected.
	☐	**Aggregation and analysis.** Describe who will be aggregating and analyzing the data and how often.
	☐	**Reporting.** Describe who will write the report and how often the report is due. Include report deadlines. Describe other forms of reporting performance measurement information (newsletter, press release), who will write these reports, and how often it occurs.
Due Date	**Done**	**X. Objective Statement**
	☐	**Objective statement.** Restate the complete objective statement by combining the target with the result statement.

Table 7.14 Program Planning and Evaluation Worksheet Sample: Parental Skills Training

Program Name: School–Based Youth Development Project

Objective Title: Parenting Program   **Activity: Parental Skills Training**

Activity Start and End Date: 09/01/2015   05/31/2016   **Staff: Ed Jucate, MSW, Dee Valarman, BA**

1. Identified Needs Describe what identified needs are to be addressed. (The Why)	One in five students in this school dropped out last year (*Ridgeway School District Annual Report*). Parents have indicated they need help to support their children through high school (*Survey of Ridgeway Parents,* conducted by the School District and City of Ridgeway).
2. Target Population/Service Recipient Briefly describe the target groups (and the estimated number) your activity will serve. (The Whom)	Fifty current students and their parents who are referred by the child welfare judge, teachers, or self-referred.
3. Activities/Interventions Describe the service or interventions. (The What) (Also include who, when, and where that are involved.)	Program staff will implement a dropout prevention program including an eight-week class for parents. The class activities will prepare parents with the skills they need to support their children and keep them in school.
4. Desired Results (Outputs, Outcomes) Explain what results will be achieved because of the described activity. (The Products and Effects) (Number and type of results vary from, e.g., Output only, Output and Intermediate outcome, etc.)	*Output*: Twenty parents enrolled and 75 percent completed the training. *Intermediate Outcome*: Among the parents completed the course, at least 60 percent of them will demonstrate effective parenting skills as measured by the assessment form. Their children will also be at least 8 percent lower in reported behavioral problems according to the school records. *End Outcome*: Twelve percent lower dropout rate compared to students of parents who are on a waiting list (if available) for the program according to school record and parent survey.
5. Method of Measurement Describe the method and the instrument used to assess results (e.g., record, questionnaire)	School records, parenting skills assessment form, attendance record, roster, survey questionnaire.
6. Indicator/Benchmarks Describe the concrete and observable evidences.	Dropout statistics, attendance, student behaviors report, and responses on the survey questionnaire.
7. Targets/Standards of Success Define a level of success expected. (How good is good enough? At least X% show improvement.)	20 enrolled, 75% completed, 60% demonstrate skills, and 12% lower drop out.
8. Resources and Inputs Briefly describe the resources/input needed.	Program staff, school district staff and teacher support, parent support, parenting skills curriculum
9. Data Collection, Analysis, and Reporting Describe when and who will be collecting, aggregating, and analyzing the data and how often.	Program staff and teacher, before and after training.
Objective Statement: Combine 1–7 into a single statement of objective.	*Example:* Among the parents of the 50 identified students, 20 parents will enroll in the positive parenting program and 75% will complete the program. It will lead to the increase of parenting skills and the decrease in student behavior problems and dropout rate.

Section V: Instrument Development

Checklist: Instrument Formatting Checklist   Whether you are creating your own instrument or borrowing and adapting one, the instrument formatting checklist points out formatting practices and offers tips to strengthen instrument rigor. The checklist includes an instrument at the end to diagram the format tips. Once you have created or identified an instrument, go through each of the seven formatting areas (e.g., demographics, directions, questions), and use the checklist to make sure your instrument addresses the items. This will ensure that your instrument is understandable to the respondents and yields high quality data.

Exercise (individual or small group): Table of Specifications Exercise   This three-part exercise walks the learner through an alignment process; moving from the program outcome (and its variables and indicators) to the questions in a questionnaire meant to address the outcome. After completing the exercise, an example of a complete table of specification for the Post-Service Survey Questionnaire for an Aging in Place (AIP) Senior Program is included to compare with your effort. This exercise can be tackled as a self-guided activity or as part of a group training that emphasizes the close alignment between instruments and indicators.

Template: Table of Specifications (Tables 7.15, 7.16, 7.17, and 7.18)   The table of specification template assists in the development of an instrument by noting the information or variables that define the outcome, and then identifying the questions that deal with those variables.

Sample: Emergency Financial Assistance Program—Client Follow-Up Interview (Telephone)   A simple sample performance measurement instrument and data analysis instructions from the files of Project STAR (technical and training assistance provider in internal program evaluation to National Service programs) illustrate the main elements to consider when selecting or developing an instrument:

1. Recap of the program activity and outcome

2. Instrument administration instructions

3. Instructions for the interviewer

4. Emergency Financial Assistance—Client Follow-Up Telephone Interview

5. Data analysis instructions

As programs select or develop their own instruments, this complete, albeit simple, packet identifies the materials and processes for successful data collection and, ultimately, reporting.

Instrument Formatting Checklist

Consider the following items when you develop your valuation instrument. The end of the checklist contains a sample survey illustrating many of these tips.

1. Instrument Title:

   ☐ Use clear and concise words.

   ☐ State the program name.

   ☐ Indicate the type of service provided (e.g., tutoring, mentoring).

   ☐ Reflect the instrument method and content (e.g., survey, checklist).

   ☐ Make sure the instrument type is identical to the one listed in the Performance Measurement worksheet/work plan/project plan.

2. Introductory Statement:

   ☐ Include information about the instrument's purpose.

   ☐ Include information about how the data will be used.

   ☐ Include information about the level of confidentiality that will be arranged (e.g., who will see their responses, how responses will be reported). *Always provide the confidentiality you promise.*

3. Demographics:

   ☐ Include questions that ask respondents for relevant information about themselves and their background (e.g., student's name, grade, age).

   ☐ If necessary, include questions that ask about the person administering the instrument (e.g., teacher's name, observer's name).

   ☐ If appropriate, identify the length of respondent participation in the program.

4. Directions:

   ☐ Include general directions on how to complete the instrument (e.g., when, where, and how to return the instrument).

   ☐ Include specific directions on how to complete each section of the instrument.

   ☐ Make sure specific directions appear before each appropriate section.

5. Questions:

   ☐ Use language that respondents understand (e.g., "pedagogical" vs. "way to teach").

- ☐ Avoid double-barreled questions (e.g., "Has your student's *classroom behavior* and *homework habits* improved?").

- ☐ Allow enough space for participants to write when using open-ended questions.

- ☐ Avoid biased and value-laden words or phrases.

- ☐ Include only questions asking for *needed* information.

- ☐ Keep question-and-answer options on the same page.

- ☐ Allow space for comments, concerns, or suggestions.

6. Format:

- ☐ Use icons or graphics as clarifiers (e.g., *Please place a check ☑ in the appropriate box.*).

- ☐ Use a clearly legible font (e.g., Arial, Times New Roman, Courier) and appropriate font size (at least 10 pt).

- ☐ Lay out text and graphics using an entire page. Separate sections of the survey with spacing and bold headings.

- ☐ Allow enough space between the questions.

- ☐ Develop an instrument that is pleasing to the eye (e.g., not busy).

- ☐ Indicate the date of test administration.

- ☐ Identify whether it is a pre-, post-, or ongoing survey.

- ☐ Note the name of the program/organization that *developed* the instrument at the bottom of the page.

- ☐ Include a computer file location path of where to find a copy of the instrument in the footer (e.g., C:\My Documents\STAR\survey).

- ☐ Include the date of each new version in the header/footer.

7. Pilot Testing:

- ☐ Clearly label a draft instrument **DRAFT**.

- ☐ Be mindful that advance permission to conduct the pilot test may be necessary.

- ☐ Arrange for the pilot test participants and conditions to be as close to the actual administration conditions as possible (e.g., time of day, location, methods, respondents).

1

READY-TO-READ SURVEY

DRAFT

7

Our Tutoring Program

6

This is a: ☐ pre-test ☐ post-test

2

Dear Tutor:

This instrument will help measure school readiness and listening skills for students participating in the Our Tutoring Reading program. All data will remain confidential and results will be reported anonymously.

4

Please indicate above if this is a pre- or post-test. The pre-test should be conducted within the first month of the program. The post-test should be conducted after the students have participated in the program for at least seven months.

3

Your Name: _____ Date: _____

School: _____ Student's Name: _____

6

6

School Readiness

Directions: Please check all items that you observe for each student.

4

1. *Before tutoring session begins:*

☐ Student is prepared for tutoring session (e.g., read assigned material, completed homework).
☐ Student has materials (e.g., pencils, paper).
☐ Student arrives on time.

2. *During tutoring session:*

☐ Student follows ground rules.
☐ Student participates in tutoring session activities (e.g., participates in discussions/ answers questions, completes seatwork, works cooperatively with other students).
☐ Student asks for assistance when needed.

5

Listening Skills

Directions: Based on your observations, please check the items that best describ your perception of this student.

☐ Student pays attention to whoever is speaking.
☐ Student does not interrupt the person speaking.
☐ Student actively listens and tries to answer questions.
☐ Student is able to reiterate clearly what the speaker said.
☐ Student demonstrates the ability of recognizing the main idea of discussions.

4

If there are any comments you would like to add, please do so on the back of this page.

Thank you. Please return the completed form to the Program Manager.

Table of Specifications Exercise

Objective:

✓ Practice using the table of specifications to organize and develop a questionnaire or any data collection tool.

✓ Learn how to use the table of specifications to ensure balance of items and organize data analysis methods.

Instructions: Read the Scenario Background and then try completing the following three tasks:

Scenario Background

Your task: Develop a questionnaire to measure the success of the social connectedness component of the Aging-In-Place (AIP) program in a senior community.

Program goal: This program aims to help older adults stay in their own residences and maintain appropriate involvement in the community life.

Target population: There are 250 older adults living in the senior housing community.

Program services: The program goals and objectives are to be achieved through supportive activities and events that promote health and safety, as well as social and neighborhood connections between older adults and their neighbors. Program activities include meals on wheels, home safety and healthy living education, home maintenance inspection and repair assistance, provision of disaster preparedness supplies, regular social activities at the clubhouse, which is also a drop-in center, transportation, and case management services. A local service organization built this senior housing community and rents out houses to qualified seniors. Several human service organizations provide various health, welfare, and mental health services in the community.

Main focuses: There are three main focus areas of AIP: (1) Health and Safety, (2) Social Connectedness, and (3) Access to Services.

Social Connectedness is defined as (i.e., indicators):

1. Knowledge of neighbors and community resources

2. Extent of participation in social activities as allowed by one's conditions

3. Attitude toward socializing and social involvement

4. (add your definition here) _____

Activity Instructions: Individually or in a small group, complete the following tasks:

➤ Task 1. Read the attached Table of Specifications for Social Connectedness. **Consider questions you might want to add or modify.**

➤ Task 2. Review how the Table of Specifications is used to develop a questionnaire. **Add or modify items.**

➤ Task 3. Review the new order of numbered items from the modified questionnaire and put them back into the Table of Specifications. **Add target and data analysis methods.**

Task 1:

    a. **Read** the Table of Specifications below.

    b. Are there any items or variables you would like to **add or modify?**

Table 7.15 Table of Specifications for Social Connectedness

Variables/Information	Items/Questions
As the result of my participation in AIP in the last 3 months . . .	
Linkage to others (socializing, participation, knowledge of neighbors)	➢ I have come to know at least three new neighbors. ___ Yes ___ No ➢ I have phone numbers of at least two neighbors I recently met. ___ Yes ___ No ➢ I feel more comfortable to greet and chat with my neighbors. ___ Agree ___ Disagree ➢ *(Add your new items below at blank bullet points)*
Knowledge of resources	➢ If I need assistance, I know I could call on my neighbors without feeling like I'm a burden. ___ True ___ Not True ➢ I learned more about how and where to get help with my social security benefits. ___ Agree ___ Disagree
Social Involvement	➢ I have become more active in clubhouse activities. ___ Strongly Agree ___ Agree ___ Disagree ___ Strongly Disagree ➢ I signed up for visits by a senior companion volunteer. ___ Yes ___ No
(Added Variable)	
Demographics	➢ Gender: ___ Males ___ Female ➢ Age: ___ 60–69 ___ 70–79 ___ 80+ ➢ County of residence: _____

Task 2:

    a. Review how the Table of Specifications above is used to develop items for a questionnaire (below). **Add or modify items.**

    b. **Organize, format, and refine this questionnaire.** For instance, sequence questions and assign numbers to items, add introduction and directions, etc.

Social Connectedness Questionnaire

Instructions:

_____ I have come to know at least three new neighbors. ___Yes ___ No

_____ I have phone numbers of at least two neighbors I recently met. ___Yes ___ No

_____ I feel more comfortable to greet and chat with my neighbors. ___ Agree ___ Disagree

_____ If I need assistance, I know I could call on my neighbors without feeling like I'm a burden. ___ True ___ Not true

_____ I learned more about how and where to get help with my social security benefits. ___ Agree ___ Disagree

_____ I have become more active in clubhouse activities. ___ Strongly Agree ___ Agree ___ Disagree ___ Strongly Disagree

_____ I signed up for visits by a senior companion volunteer. ___ Yes ___ No

_____ Gender: ___ Male ___ Female

_____ Age: ___ 60–69 ___70–79 ___ 80+

_____ County of residence: _____

(Add your new items here . . .)

_____

_____

_____

Task 3:

 a. Review new order of numbered items put back into the Table of Specifications.

 b. Add target and data analysis methods in the right-hand columns. Check your responses against the complete samples in Table 7.17.

Table 7.16 Table of Specifications for Social Connectedness with Target and Analysis Methods

Variables/Information	Items/Questions	Target	Analysis
	As the result of my participation in AIP in the last 3 months . . .		
Linkage to others (Socializing, participation, knowledge of neighbors)	4. I have come to know at least three new neighbors. ___ Yes ___ No 5. I have phone numbers of at least two neighbors I recently met. ___ Yes ___ No 6. I feel more comfortable to greet and chat with my neighbors. ___ Agree ___ Disagree # # #	Ex. *200 of 250*	Ex. *frequency*
Knowledge of resources	14. If I need assistance, I know I could call on my neighbors without feeling like I'm a burden. ___ True ___ Not true 15. I learned more about how and where to get help with my social security benefits. ___ Agree ___ Disagree # #		
Social involvement	8. I signed up for visits by a senior companion volunteer. ___ Yes ___ No 9. I have become more active in clubhouse activities. ___ Strongly Agree ___ Agree ___ Disagree ___ Strongly Disagree # #		
#(New Variable)	#		
Demographics	18. Gender: ___ Male ___ Female 19. Age: ___ 60–69 ___ 70–79 ___ 80+ 20. County of residence: _____		

Table 7.17 Example of a Completed Table of Specifications: Post–Service Survey Questionnaire for an Aging In Place (AIP) Senior Program

Variables/Information	Items/Questions	Target	Analysis
	As the result of my participation in AIP in the last 3 months . . .		
Linkage to others (socializing, participation, knowledge of neighbors)	4. I have come to know at least three new neighbors. ___ Yes ___ No 5. I have phone numbers of at least two neighbors I recently met. ___ Yes ___ No 6. I feel more comfortable to greet and chat with my neighbors. ___ Agree ___ Disagree 7. I have visited one of my neighbors for the first time. ___ Yes ___ No	Know at least three new neighbors and have two additional phone numbers. Accomplish three of the four results.	fq, %,

Table 7.17 Example of a Completed Table of Specifications: Post Service Survey Questionnaire for an Aging In Place (AIP) Senior Program *(Continued)*

Knowledge of resources	14. If I need assistance, I know I could call on my neighbors without feeling like I'm a burden. ___ True ___ Not True 15. I learned more about how and where to get help with my social security benefits. ___ Agree ___ Disagree 16. I store the emergency safety kit that I received from Emergency Training in a proper place in the house. ___ Yes ___ No 17. I have the Community and Emergency Service Contact Information Sheet posted/stored close to my phone. ___ Yes ___ No	75% participate in emergency training 65% know where and how to seek assistance 30% would seek help if needed	fq, %
Social Involvement	8. I signed up to be visited by a senior companion volunteer. ___ Yes ___ No 9. I have become more active in clubhouse activities. ___ Strongly Agree ___ Agree ___ Disagree ___ Strongly Disagree 10. I am out of my house meeting people more than before ___ Strongly Agree ___ Agree ___ Disagree ___ Strongly Disagree 11. I have been or plan to go to one of the neighborhood parties. ___ Strongly Agree ___ Agree ___ Disagree ___ Strongly Disagree 12. All these activities have disturbed the quiet and calm lives that I enjoy. ___ Strongly Agree ___ Agree ___ Disagree ___ Strongly Disagree 13. I would rather be left alone for the time being. ___ Strongly Agree ___ Agree ___ Disagree ___ Strongly Disagree	55% would give at least three positive to response items 8–11. No more than 5% would respond positively for items 12 and 13 and their desire would be honored.	fq, %, mean,
Demographics	18. Gender: ___ Male ___ Female 19. Age: ___ 60–69 ___ 70–79 ___ 80+ 20. County of residence: _____		

Table 7.18 Table of Specifications Template

Table of Specifications			
Variables/Information	**Items/Questions**	**Target**	**Analysis**

✓ *Are you covering major variables or information areas?*

✓ *Will you be able to respond to your target?*

✓ *Do you know what analysis method you will help you respond to your target?*

Emergency Financial Assistance—Performance Measurement Instrument and Analysis

---

Activity Description: Volunteers/members provide support at a financial assistance program (counseling and emergency assistance for utilities, rent/mortgage). Volunteers/members respond to inquiries, set appointments, screen applicants, collect documentation, and track client data as they go through the program.

Outcome: Clients who receive assistance are able to avoid eviction and maintain utilities (water, gas/electric) for at least three months, and credit the program's help.

Indicator: Percentage of clients who report they were able to avoid eviction and maintain utility services uninterrupted for three months due, in part, to the program's assistance.

Target: *(Enter your specific number)*% of clients report they were able to avoid eviction and maintain utility services uninterrupted for three months due, in part, to the program's assistance, by responding positively to four questions in a follow-up interview.

Instrument: Client Follow-Up Interview

About This Instrument

What is the purpose?	To determine the extent to which clients have been able to maintain utilities after receiving assistance.
Who should complete this instrument (data source)?	Clients who have received financial assistance
When should we administer this instrument?	Three months after the client has received assistance
What else should we do to prepare?	✓ Be sure you have a system in place to keep interview data *confidential* and that anyone handling the data (staff or volunteers) understands the system.
	✓ Interviewers should *practice* with the instrument before calling clients.
	✓ Interviewers should know to whom to refer a client if the client indicates they need additional help.
	Optional
	✓ Since this is a follow-up interview, make a note of the *specific services* the client received before calling.
	✓ If needed, ask *demographic* questions (e.g., age, ethnicity, income level) at the end of the interview.
	✓ For *program improvement*, consider asking about how people learned about the program and whether they had any difficulty getting to the office or making an appointment.

Emergency Financial Assistance—Client Follow-Up Interview

Instructions for Interviewer

Once you have made telephone contact and greeted the client who received the assistance, read the script included at the beginning of the interview form. It explains who you are, your connection to the service, and the purpose of the interview. Assure clients that the interview is confidential and voluntary, and that their responses will not affect their access to future services.

Read each question to the client, and repeat as needed. For questions 1 to 5, check the client's response on the interview form. Question 6 is an open-ended question; try to record the client's response verbatim, in his or her own words. Notes to the interviewer are in italics.

Interviewing Tips:

➤ Do a few practice interviews before calling a client. Find a partner and role-play an interview until you feel well prepared.

➤ This interview asks the client about services he or she received recently. Before you call, make a note of the specific services the client received so you can remind him or her if needed.

➤ Use a neutral tone. Be sure you are not inadvertently leading the client to answer one way or another.

➤ Be aware of when to discontinue an interview. If the client sounds fatigued, upset, or confused, do not push; thank the client and politely end the interview. Make a note of what happened on the interview form.

➤ Have the name and phone number of a counselor available in case the client indicates he or she needs immediate assistance. For example, if the client tells you that he or she was evicted or has had utilities turned off, can the program offer assistance or another referral? What is the next follow-up step with this client?

[Put your program name here.]

Emergency Financial Assistance
Client Follow-Up Interview

Client Name: **Date of Interview:**
Interviewer:

Interviewer: Please read this script to the client before you begin the interview:

My name is *(name)* and I am a *(position)* at the *(project name)*. About three months ago, you received emergency financial assistance that included *(briefly describe)*. I would like to ask you a few questions about your experience with this program. Your answers are confidential and will help us understand how our clients use the service and how it can be improved. Your participation is voluntary and will in no way affect your access to the program's services in the future. Do you have about 5 minutes right now to answer some questions?

(If yes, continue. If no, ask if there is a more convenient time when you might call.)

First, I would like to ask you if the assistance has helped you.

1. **Did the assistance you received help you to remain in your house or apartment for the last three months?** *(If needed, prompt by reading the responses.)*

   ❑ Yes, it was helpful.   ❑ No, it was not helpful but I am still in my home/apartment.

   ❑ No, I had to leave my home/apartment. *(If this response, skip to Question 6.)*

2. **Did the assistance you received help you to maintain utility services (that is, water, gas, and electric) for the last three months, without services being shut off during that time?** *(If needed, prompt by reading the responses.)*

   ❑ Yes, it was helpful.   ❑ No, it was not helpful, but I still have service.

   ❑ No, my service was shut off at least once during that time.

   I am going to read two short statements. For each one, please tell me if you *strongly disagree, disagree, agree,* or *strongly agree* with each statement.

3. **I believe I received helpful financial counseling and support.** *(Check one.)*

   ❑ Strongly Disagree   ❑ Disagree   ❑ Agree   ❑ Strongly Agree

4. **Because of the assistance I received, I am better able to manage my household budget and finances.** *(Check one.)*

   ❑ Strongly Disagree   ❑ Disagree   ❑ Agree   ❑ Strongly Agree

5. **Overall, how satisfied are you with the assistance you received?** Would you say you are *very dissatisfied, dissatisfied, satisfied,* or *very satisfied*? *(Check one.)*

   ❑ Very dissatisfied   ❑ Dissatisfied   ❑ Satisfied   ❑ Very Satisfied

6. **Do you have any other comments about the service you received, including how we might improve the service?**

Interviewer: If the client answered "I had to leave my home/apartment" (Question 1) or "My service was shut off . . ." (Question 2), recommend that he or she talk to a program counselor and provide a name and phone number.

Program counselor's name and phone number:

Notes:

Thank the client for their time and end the interview.

Client Follow-Up Interview

SUMMARIZING THE RESULTS

Analysis Instructions

Following are step-by-step instructions for aggregating and analyzing information collected with the Client Follow-Up Interview. To do this, you will need the completed interviews and your work plan/worksheet that states the target for this performance measure. You may also want a calculator and extra writing/scrap paper.

Your target may be different than the suggested target criteria in the box below. If so, you will need to adjust the analysis steps accordingly.

> **Suggested Target Criteria:** Clients must answer Questions 1 to 4 positively: "yes" to questions 1 and 2, and "agree" or "strongly agree" to Questions 3 and 4.

Step 1. Count the number of interviews and note that number.

Total number of completed interviews: _____

Step 2. Look at each completed interview and divide them into two piles:

Pile 1: Interviews in which the client answered positively to all questions 1 to 4 ("yes" to Questions 1 and 2, and "agree" or "strongly agree" to Questions 3 and 4).

Pile 2: Interviews in which the client did *not* answer positively to all Questions 1 to 4.

Step 3. Count the number of interviews in Pile 1 and note the total. These are the clients that met the target criteria.

Total number of clients that met the target criteria: _____

Step 4. Determine the percentage of clients who met the target. Divide the number that met the target criteria (in Step 3) by the total number of completed interviews (noted in Step 1). Multiply this number by 100.

EXAMPLE: Calculating the Percentage

Of the 70 Client Follow-Up Interviews collected, 58 met the target criteria (58 clients responded positively to Questions 1–4). Divide 58 by 70, and multiply by 100: **58 / 70 = .83 (or 83%)**

Percentage of respondents that met the target criteria: _____ %

Step 5. Compare the percentage of clients who met the target with the anticipated target in your work plan/worksheet.

EXAMPLE: Anticipated Target Statement

Seventy-five percent of clients who receive emergency financial assistance will report they were able to avoid eviction and maintain utility services uninterrupted for three months due, in part, to the program's assistance, by responding positively to four questions in a follow-up interview.

Did you meet your target? Write a results statement.

EXAMPLE: Results Statement

Eighty-three percent (or 58) of the 70 clients interviewed who received emergency financial assistance reported that they were able to avoid eviction and maintain utility services uninterrupted for three months due, in part, to the program's assistance, by responding positively to four questions in a follow-up interview. We exceeded our target of 75 percent.

Step 6. Don't stop there! Responses to Question 5 can corroborate your results, and responses to Question 6 may provide feedback for improving services.

In general, the respondents who met the target should also report that they were satisfied with the service (Question 5). If not, this may be an indication that respondents did not understand the interview questions or they had expectations about the service beyond the financial counseling and support provided.

Additionally, Question 6 asks respondents to provide comments on the service. Remember that for respondents who were not able to stay in their homes, this is the only other question they were asked about the service. This feedback can help you improve your service, but you may also find complimentary quotes you can use in reports, newsletters, and recruitment materials.

Step 7. Last, when you report results, always include these important details about how you collected your data and who was responsible for aggregating and analyzing it:

- ➤ The name of the instrument (in this case, an interview)
- ➤ Who conducted the interviews, and if appropriate, training they received
- ➤ When and how often the interview was conducted
- ➤ The number of attempted interviews and the number of completed interviews
- ➤ If the interviews were not collected as planned, explain what you did differently
- ➤ Who aggregated and analyzed the data

EXAMPLE: Explanation of Data Collection/Processes

The client follow-up interview was conducted by the program supervisor with individual clients three months after they had received financial counseling, support, and assistance. Of the 90 clients who received assistance, 60 clients completed the interview (19 could not be reached after five attempts, and 11 chose not to do an interview). The program supervisor aggregated and analyzed the interview data for this report.

Section VI: Evaluation Plan

Template: Evaluation Plan Outline (Table 7.19)   The evaluation plan is a written document that describes the purpose, approaches, and strategies/steps of the program evaluation (see Chapter 6, Program Evaluation, for more information on evaluation plans). Evaluation plan designs vary and this sample outline can be modified or adapted to fit the needs of your program and evaluation. Funding organizations sometimes provide a template of their own but all evaluation plan outlines share the main elements found in this evaluation plan. Share it with staff and others to familiarize them with the expectations in describing the evaluation process.

Checklist: Evaluation Plan Checklist (Table 7.20)   Following the format of the evaluation plan, the checklist prompts—and even offers tips—to assist with the completion of a comprehensive evaluation plan. The evaluation plan checklist can be used to review a draft evaluation plan or to help create one. With your evaluation plan in hand, review the thoroughness of the document.

Sample Evaluation Plans in Chapter 8   Two completed sample evaluation plans can be found in Chapter 8, Real-Life Samples.

Table 7.19 Evaluation Plan Template

I. Program Information

Date:

Program Name:

Organization name/Applicant:

Contact person:

Phone/e-mail:

II. Program Summary

Program description and primary activities:

III. Evaluation Plan Overview

1. Evaluation classification:

2. Role of the evaluator:

3. Evaluator qualifications:

4. Evaluation timeline and completion of evaluation report:

5. Participants who developed the evaluation plan:

6. This evaluation plan aims to serve the following purposes in addition to meeting funding requirements:

7. Projected use of findings:

IV. Audiences

1. Primary stakeholders for this evaluation:

2. Use of evaluation results for these primary stakeholders:

V. Evaluation Questions

Key evaluation questions to be answered by this evaluation:

VI. Evaluation Design

1. Summary:

2. Data types:

3. Ethical considerations for this evaluation:

VII. Data Collection (Methods and Instruments)

1. Proposed data collection methods:

2. Instruments be to used:

3. Person responsible for data collection:

4. Data collection timeline:

VIII. Data Management and Analysis

1. Data management:

2. Data analysis strategies:

3. Person responsible for data analysis:

IX. Strategies for Using Evaluation Findings

1. Reporting:

2. Evaluation debriefing:

3. Post-evaluation action plan:

X. Budget

Evaluation staff/consultant salary/benefits or consultant fee

Travel

Communications

Printing/duplication

Supplies

Indirect costs

Other: Data entry

Other:

TOTAL

Budget justification:

Table 7.20 Evaluation Plan Checklist

Due Date	Done	I. Program Information
	☐	**Contact information**. Name of the program/service that is being evaluated; legal applicant name; address and contact information (e-mail, phone), date.
	☐	**Table of contents**. Often optional but helps reader follow document.

Due Date	Done	II. Program Summary
	☐	**Background about organization**. Describe the organization, history, capacity.
	☐	**Service/Program activities and overall goal**. Describe primary activities being evaluated, how the service is developed and delivered.
	☐	**Problem statement**. Describe the target population and community need that is being met by the service/program.
	☐	**Staffing.** Describe the number of personnel and roles in the organization that are relevant to developing and delivering the service/program.

(Continued)

Table 7.20 Evaluation Plan Checklist *(Continued)*

Due Date	Done	III. Evaluation Plan Overview
	☐	**Evaluation type.** Identify the classification of evaluation to be conducted, timeline; completion of report.
	☐	**Evaluator role, evaluation plan designers/committee.** Who will conduct the evaluation? Determine role, qualifications of key players. Describe who develops/assists in preparation of plan and their credentials.
	☐	**Purpose of the evaluation.** What decisions will be aided by the findings of the evaluation? Who is making the decision?

Due Date	Done	IV. Audiences
	☐	**Primary stakeholders.** Who are primary stakeholders, and how will they use results? Which other groups will use results?

Due Date	Done	V. Evaluation Questions
	☐	**Evaluation questions.** Identify overall evaluation goals. What questions will the evaluation answer?

Due Date	Done	VI. Evaluation Design
	☐	**Summary.** Note evaluation approach used (e.g., exploratory, quasi-experimental, experimental, etc.).
	☐	**Data types: Outputs and outcomes.** Describe the type of data/information that will be collected: process, outcomes (performance measures can be measure as indicators toward the outcome).
	☐	**Ethical considerations.** How will privacy and confidentiality be protected? Describe consent documents, human subject review approval.

Due Date	Done	VII. Data Collection (Methods and Instruments)
	☐	**Proposed data collection methods and instruments.** How will data/information be collected? Identify instruments by name (if possible). Include timeline.
	☐	**Person responsible to data collection.** Identify the coordinator for data collection process. Include training issues and timeline.

Due Date	Done	VIII. Data Management and Analysis
	☐	**Data management.** Describe any database or software systems (SPSS, SAS, Excel spreadsheet) you will use for data.
	☐	**Data analysis strategies.** How will data/information be analyzed? What key descriptive and/or inferential statistics will be employed?
	☐	**Person responsible for data analysis.** Identify the person or position handling the data analysis; setup of system, data entry. Include timeline.

Due Date	Done	IX. Strategies for Using Evaluation Findings
	☐	**Reporting.** Identify primary audiences and appropriate formats to share the information. Be ready to report methods, finding, limitations of the evaluation (e.g., cautions about findings) and recommendations on how to use the findings. Identify deadlines for drafts and final reports.
	☐	**Evaluation debriefing.** Describe debriefing opportunities or presentations and appropriate audiences.
	☐	**Post-evaluation action plan.** Provide an action plan (program improvement) based on findings.

Due Date	Done	X. Budget
	☐	**Line item.** Provide line-item budget (staff/consultant fees/salaries [include benefits], travel, communication [phone, printing Internet]).
	☐	**Overall budget justification.** In narrative form, describe budget line items, how they are related to the plan and why they are needed.

Section VII: Interactive Group Activities

Whether you are trying to motivate a new grant-writing working group or train staff to carry out data collection tasks, interactive exercises support and strengthen the learning and skill-building process. There are many different kinds of interactive exercises—icebreakers, energizers, closers, role-plays, brainstorms—all aspiring to heighten the effectiveness of group training or meetings. They can:

➣ Create a positive group atmosphere and cohesion

➣ Help people to relax and break down social barriers

➣ Energize, engage, and motivate

➣ Support creative thinking and help people to think outside the box

➣ Help people to get to know one another and build trust

Most of the exercises in this section meet these goals; moreover, they focus on interactive experiences to broaden participant knowledge or perspective on evaluation and grant-writing components.

By employing engaging activities that anchor the evaluation and grant-writing concepts, we recognize that adult learners seek practical information and skills they deem as important and applicable to real-life situations—in this case, real-life grant-writing and evaluation situations. The interactive exercises support the participant's understanding of relevant information through positive and encouraging processes (Knowles, 1980).

These eight exercises support participant exploration of evaluation and grant-writing concepts and lay the foundation for key content areas. For each activity, there is a brief sentence on the context/purpose, topic area, materials needed and the flow or steps. Questions and possible responses, in parenthesis, are provided. Maurie Lung imparts professional insight using an interactive exercise with a struggling staff.

I. Title: *Everyday Evaluation*

Topic Area: General evaluation or needs assessment

Purpose/Context: To tie topic [evaluation, needs assessment] to the ordinary life of group participants.

Material: None needed

Participants: Small or large group

Time: 10 to 20 minutes

Flow:

1. Ask the group the following questions and let them respond by a show of hands: "How many of you looked in the mirror today? How many of you looked at your hair first? Checked out your teeth? Looked for new wrinkles? Looked at your nose? Mouth?"

2. Debrief with the following questions: "It seems as though we all have developed some habits over the years because we look in the mirror so regularly. Does it make any difference if the mirror is this size (indicate size with hands) or full length? How? What are we learning each day when we evaluate our appearance by passing by a mirror? How could you increase the likelihood of learning more about yourself?" (Systematically look at different parts of self, asks someone else to help evaluate our appearance.)

3. Ask the group: "How is this related to thinking about a needs assessment?" (Needs assessment assist us in examining anew the social condition or problem of the target population, appropriate service strategies gaps in service, cultural competencies.) or "How is this related to thinking about an evaluation?" (Evaluation pushes us to focus on what we are trying to change, look closely to see if we achieved the impacts.)

II. Title: *Gaining Perspective*

Topic Area: General evaluation

Context: To encourage a broad perspective as team members prepare to work on evaluation or proposal tasks

Materials: Enough copies of one of the suggested perceptual illusions, one for every two participants.

Young girl–old woman (http://mathworld.wolfram.com/YoungGirl-Old WomanIllusion.html)

or the rabbit-duck (http://mathworld.wolfram.com/Rabbit-DuckIllusion.html)

Participants: Small or large group

Time: 10 to 15 minutes

Flow:

Pass out a copy of one or more of the perceptual illusions.

1. Ask the group to examine the picture for a minute or two.

2. At the end of two minutes, ask a few people in the group (or the entire group) for their thoughts. "What do you see?" Typically groups quickly see one image first, and it takes longer to find the second image (young girl–old woman; rabbit-duck)

3. Debrief with the following questions: "What keeps us from seeing the other image?" (Sight influenced by past perceptions and beliefs.) "What do you have to do to see something differently?" (Look at it in a new way, shift attention or body.) "How is this connected to an evaluation? (A good evaluation plan [report, or any part of evaluation] sometimes needs a fresh perspective, without the baggage that often comes with evaluation.) "Does it help to have someone else's ideas?" (Yes, can point out what isn't obvious to you.)

III. Title: *The Importance of Focus*

Topic Area: Theory of change, logic model, evaluation plan, instruments, report or grant proposal

Context: A very quick demonstration that highlights the need to prioritize (activities, results, questions on an instrument, key report items, etc.)

Materials: Small items (approximately 30) that can be thrown without damaging people or property (e.g., small, wrapped candy or corn), three midsize objects that can be thrown (e.g., oranges, large candy bars, foam balls, small baskets), and one large item, also to be thrown (e.g., beach ball, large basket)

Participants: Small or large group. If you use an edible small item (e.g., candy), adjust the quantity so the entire group can have a piece later.

Time: 15 minutes

Flow:

1. Each time, advise the group to pay attention, and hide the item(s) until you are ready to toss it.

2. Warn the group to pay attention and then shout "Catch!" Immediately toss out a large handful of small items, at least 30 items (small, wrapped candy is popular).

3. Repeat the directions and shout "Catch!" Once again, immediately toss out three to five larger objects (e.g., small foam balls, large candy bars, oranges).

4. One final time, shout "Catch!" This time toss out one large item (e.g., beach ball, large basket).

5. Debrief with the group. "What was dropped?" (usually the smallest item.) "Why?" (e.g., couldn't catch them, too many, too small, not enough time) "What did you catch? Why?" (large item, only one, could focus on it and had better chance of being successful, more prepared the third time) "What was the difference between each of the experiences?" (small items were dropped as everything came at us too fast, felt overwhelmed) "How does this tie into your evaluation plan [or outcomes, instruments, report, etc.]?" (If you try to catch too much, you might miss everything; don't try to catch everything, focus on the most important pieces.)

Assumption: The group will be more successful at catching fewer and more defined items. As an added part, you can even calculate the percentage of items caught for each toss.

IV. Title: From Table Conversation to the Award Speech

Topic Area: Moving from program activities to evaluation plan to reporting

Context: To demonstrate the need for alignment among program activities, results (evaluation plan), and reporting

Materials: Scrap paper for participants

Participants: Small or large group; exercise done in dyads

Time: 15 to 20 minutes

Flow:

1. Ask the group to pair up. Each individual in the pair will have an opportunity to play the part of an estimated older relative at a family gathering and ask the question, "So, what is it that your program does?" The other partner has 2 minutes to briefly describe their program.

2. Switch roles.

3. Debrief in small (3 to 5 participants) groups or large group. "How was the experience?" (Difficult to contain program description, didn't know what to say first, felt good to have someone listen.)

4. Now, tell the group to flash forward and imagine themselves 10 years from now. They are being presented with a special award and have been asked to deliver a 15-minute speech about what has been accomplished, the challenges, the rewards, and the people that contributed to the effort.

5. Ask the participants to write down two or three accomplishments that they would want to be able to tell the group that the program has achieved.

6. Debrief with the following questions: "What is the difference between what you said to your esteemed relative about your program and what you outlined in your speech?" (One is a list of activities and the other involves successful outcomes/results.) "How are the two connected?" (Activities link up with the results you hope to brag about in the future.) "What does this tell us about what we are getting ready to do? How can the logic model [evaluation plan, etc.] help us?" (Make sure the two are related, that we should check on our outcomes and adjust the activities to get there; use tools like logic model, evaluation worksheet focus on alignment.)

V. Title: *The Right Fit*

Topic Area: Instruments

Context: Program staff may try to shoehorn an instrument into the program evaluation despite the fit. This quick activity reflects on appropriate instrument fit.

Materials: None needed

Participants: Small or large group; exercise done in dyads

Time: 10 to 15 minutes

Flow:

1. Tell the group to "Pair up. Take something that you have on your person (not your nametag!) and switch it with another person." Participants pair up and exchange.

2. Now ask the group to put on that object and ask them the following questions: "Does it fit? Is it appropriate? Is it the best fit?"

3. Discuss: "How is this experience similar to selecting an instrument?" (Instruments that look good don't necessarily fit our program services or population, instruments may be good in one area [e.g., literacy] but wrong in another [e.g., age or language].)

Professional Insight 7.1: Program Improvement
Maurie D. Lung, MA

This simple interactive exercise addresses the idea of relevancy of the efforts and findings of an evaluation for stakeholder groups. For programs conducting internal evaluations or assisting with the data collection of an external evaluation, the quality of that data is, more often than not, dependent on staff, volunteers, and other stakeholder volunteers who may serve as data collectors. Training data collectors is the obvious technical fix, but how do you get staff to buy-in to the evaluation process? Successful staff training integrates tangible applied information and previous evaluation results as well as fun or meaningful activities that anchor the training points.

Title: Name Challenge
Topic Area: Will this data really help our program services? Uncertainty about applying information learned
Context: Practitioners who served as data collectors may not be sure why they are doing all of this work. Furthermore, they may struggle to make sense of data: How would they apply the data to what they do on a day-to-day basis? You want a training experience that includes them in the program improvement aspect as opposed to issuing staff a mandate: "Here is the form, make sure your client completes it on time."

Instructions:

1. Challenge the group (when you say "go") to say "hello" to everyone in the group using his or her preferred name in a certain period of time (about 2 seconds per person in the room, so a group of 30 would be challenged to complete this task in one minute).

2. After the time is up, ask the group to talk about the strategies and different greetings. Note anything else you noticed.

3. Share the information we have learned through research about the importance of a name. Research by Alford shows that our name is very significant to our identity and to how we socialize. Think about this: If you have a name that is not easy to pronounce, you probably have an emotional response when it is pronounced incorrectly. Or, if you go by your middle name instead of your first name, you know that the caller on the phone asking for you by your first name is probably a salesperson.

4. Now that you have shared this information, help the group make the connection to evaluation. Ask your group how knowing this bit of research might reinforce or change the way we work. When I work with people who oversee groups of youth, I usually hear, "Oh, now I know why we are told to learn all of their names on the first day, but I am also going to use their names more." This activity helps us to integrate and understand how the data we are to gather might help us to be more effective and thoughtful with the services we provide.

Alford, R. (1988). *Naming and identity: A cross-cultural study of personal naming practices.* New Haven, CT: Human Relations Area File Press.

VI. Title: *Picture This!*

Topic Area: Improve data accuracy (instruments, data source)

Context: To open the dialogue among the field staff collecting data and those in the office coordinating the evaluation, address concerns with current data source and create a more rigorous process for gathering information

Materials: markers (nonpermanent), 8 1/2" by 11" paper (10 to 15 sheets; one per group)

Participants: Large group

Time: 10 to 15 minutes

Flow:

1. Divide participants into groups of four to six, with everyone facing the front of their line. Give the person at the front of each line a marker and a piece of paper. Let the group know that part of the challenge is to complete this activity in silence; touch is the only form of communication.

2. Show only the person at the back of the line a simple picture (e.g., stick figure standing next to a simple tree with a sun in the sky) and tell him or her to draw on the back of the next person in line (moving toward the front) with his or her index finger. The picture can only be repeated once on a back (we have lots more to do than just enter data!).

3. Keep passing the picture up the line by drawing it on the back of the person in front of you until the front person receives the picture. The front person then re-creates the image drawn on his or her back onto the paper. Compare the drawing to the original.

4. Ask the group: "What happened?" "How accurate is the picture?" (The further from the source we were, the more diluted the information became along the way.) "How is this like data collection out in the field?" (To get accurate information, we need to get as close to the source as possible; sometimes the data doesn't get passed to the correct person, and data disappears.)

VII. Title: *Sort It!*

Topic Area: Data analysis; categorizing and organizing information (content analysis: emergent and predetermined)

Context: Introduce content data analysis and how to think about emergent and predetermined content analysis

Materials: A variety (six or more types) of small, wrapped pieces of candy (e.g., caramels, chocolates, hard candy). Look for variations in color, size, flavor, and so on. Prepare enough baggies of an assortment of candy (10 to 12 pieces) for each small group.

Participants: Small or large group. Adjust the amount of small stuff (candy) so the entire group can have a piece later.

Time: 30 to 40 minutes

Flow:

1. Divide the participants into groups of four or five or work together. One small group can do this exercise together. Give each group a baggie of mixed candy pieces.

2. Instruct the groups to categorize their candy in any way they like. In addition, ask them to write down the titles of each of their categories and be ready to report how they came to their decisions.

3. Have each group share their findings. "How did you sort the candy?" "Why?" Assumption: They will categorize the candy by size, shape, color, type of candy, etc.

4. Debrief: "Is one way better than another?" Link discussion with content analysis of open-ended questions. (There is no right or wrong way to group data; the appropriate way depends on the information needed.)

5. Ask the groups to quickly sort by color and size (or some other criteria). "What was different this time?" Discuss the differences between using emergent categories (sort according to what the data tell you) and predetermined categories (sort according to an already set plan of analysis).

References

Chemise, H. Proposal checklist (updated 2000). Office of Research, IUSB. Retrieved April 26, 2009, from www.iusb.edu/~reserach/Proposalcheck.html.

Cozzan, D. Internet Business Concept, Nafta Technology Trading, Inc. Write winning proposals: grant-writing checklist. Retrieved April 26, 2009, from www.writewinningproposals.com/checklist.html.

Kluge, D. Proposal preparation checklist. Retrieved April 26, 2009, from www.proporalwriter.com/chekclist.html.

Knowles, M. S. (1980). *The modern practice of adult education: Andragogy versus pedagogy*. Englewood Cliffs, NJ: Prentice Hall/Cambridge.

Renaissance Learning. Grant writing resources: grant writing checklist. Retrieved April 26, 2009, from http://kmnet.renlearn.com/Library/R004012303GG69E8.pdf.

The Web Center for Social Research Methods, Cornell University: www.socialresearchmethods.net.

8
Real-Life Samples

As with a puzzle, pieces of a grant proposal and an evaluation plan have been described and examples provided; however, the full picture has not been displayed. This chapter puts the pieces of the puzzle together so that examples of a complete grant proposal and evaluation plan can be seen.

Grant Proposals

This chapter provides two samples of real-life proposals that were submitted to a funding source with the hope of being awarded a grant. The names of people and places have been changed, but the proposal is in its original form when it was submitted. The two proposals demonstrate two different styles of proposal writing and formatting.

A Coordinated Approach to Youth: Prevention and Intervention Services in Sun Town

This proposal was developed by a local city police department and submitted to a community foundation, targeting youth who were at risk of being pulled into undesirable gang-type activities. This proposal demonstrates how a community need is established, the types of activities being proposed, and the anticipated outputs and outcomes to be measured.

Proposal
to the
Community Foundation
from the
Sun Town Police Department
Collaboration of Youth Services:
A Coordinated Approach to Youth
Prevention and Intervention Services in Sun Town
Date

I. Proposal Summary

The Community Foundation provided the Sun Town Police Department with a planning grant to conduct a needs assessment and asset inventory to enable us to develop a program proposal to prevent youth violence and gang membership in Sun Town. The results of the assessment indicated that Sun Town youth services are insufficient in meeting youth needs and providing alternative and positive pursuits. There are few programs that specifically target youth who are involved in the juvenile justice system, or high risk of entering the system. Of those programs currently in place, few include parental involvement, a key to youth success. In addition, programs that currently exist are, by and large, uncoordinated and referral systems are minimal. Gang-related activity, particularly among youth, has increased in recent years, high-school dropout rates remain high, teen pregnancies are high, and interethnic conflict has increased between youth. Our aim is to establish a program titled "Collaboration of Youth Services." This is modeled on the County Sheriff's Community Reclaiming Our Neighborhood (CRON) program, but within the specific context of the challenges and opportunities faced by the community of Sun Town. We propose to call together and facilitate a coalition of youth service providers to collaborate and to identify, prioritize, and address unmet needs of youth in Sun Town; develop and implement "parent involvement" models; develop and maintain a system to gather and analyze youth service information; and develop a comprehensive directory of youth services for Sun Town youth. The goal of the project will be to offer quality services to youth, including identifying the gaps in service delivery and filling those gaps.

II. Brief Description of Organization

The Sun Town Police Department was established in 1985. At present, the Sun Town Police Department operates a youth diversion program for youth within the Juvenile Services Unit. The Juvenile Diversion Program, modeled on the Redwood program, provides an alternative to taking youth into custody and imposing criminal penalties for first-time youth offenders. It is a voluntary program involving both parents and youth and includes mandatory family counseling, unannounced home visits, and jail tours.

III. Description of Proposed Project

A. Needs of Community   Current youth services in Sun Town are insufficient and underprepared in meeting the needs of high-risk youth. Within Sun Town itself there are approximately 20 community-based youth programs (see Attachments). Few of the programs currently in place deal specifically with gang/violence prevention or target youth who are already in crisis—already within the juvenile justice system. In addition, all of the community-based organizations in Sun Town serving youth currently report that they are either (a) understaffed—especially with staff that are culturally competent in dealing with diverse ethnic backgrounds of parents and youth; or (b) unable to provide service to all youth and families that request their services. In addition, youth service providers in general (c) have not networked with each other or have the knowledge of other youth resources in the area, making appropriate referrals and coordinated care of youth a difficult task. There is no continuity of services, access to health care is limited, and few partnerships are in place with mental health and health services at the county level. Another glaring need expressed by youth services providers is (d) the need for family support and parenting support—including parenting classes, family counseling services, and family social services in general. Involvement of parents has been minimal in most programs though parental involvement is critical to a child's success—in and out of school. Sun Town has no parent advisory committees or cooperatives. Finally, (e) Sun Town's geographic isolation from services provided by county services creates a critical barrier to accessing services. Furthermore, youth programs in general do not operate on weekends or early enough in the morning or late enough in the evening to accommodate parents' work schedules.

B. Purpose of Project   The long-term goals of the Collaboration of Youth Services are to:

> Strengthen the capacity of local community groups, schools and other organizations to provide effective programs to prevent youth violence and gang membership.
> Support promising methods of delivering youth gang/violence interventions at the community level.
> Focus on early interventions, particularly for youth, especially those in the 11 to 18 years age bracket.

> Mobilize the community, as a whole, to address youth gang/violence issues.

> Develop effective and appropriate systems (including web-based materials) to be able to share information on youth resources in Sun Town and in the County, best practices, and other topical areas of mutual interest such as funding sources and training opportunities.

Given the success of the County Sheriff's CRON project, the program proposed herein will borrow from its design and implementation phases. However, these will be customized to better meet the needs of the Sun Town Community and its youth. During this first phase, we share the goals of (1) developing partnerships with local community-based organizations to address the needs of the high number of youth in Sun Town involved in, or at risk of becoming involved in, the juvenile justice system, (2) increasing parental involvement in their child's activities and/or the youth service organization, and (3) developing systems of routine record keeping and information sharing and dissemination on youth programs. Finally, a useful byproduct of the program will be (4) the compilation of a comprehensive list of services for Sun Town youth; a directory that is much needed and can easily be distributed throughout the community.

In order to accomplish these goals, the first steps in Phase I of the program, for which funds are being requested in this proposal, are to:

> Develop a coalition of programs and people serving youth, specifically youth in the 11 to 18 years age bracket.

> Increase coordination among existing services.

> Develop both a coalition and steering committee that can identify, prioritize, and address unmet needs among the target population.

Currently, no one in the city of Sun Town has taken a leadership role in coordinating existing youth services, identifying gaps in youth services, and developing partnerships to expand and develop additional services for youth. The Project Coordinator, under the supervision and support of the Sun Town Police Department, will provide this leadership and begin this coordination process. By developing a coalition of key stakeholders, existing resources can be leveraged and synergy between programs can be developed. The Coordinator's role will be to develop relationships and trust with existing youth service groups identified in the needs and assets assessment, to form a coalition of stakeholders, and to coordinate youth services among existing youth service providers.

Kick-Off Meeting: The Coordinator will host a Youth Collaboration Kick-Off meeting with these youth service providers. The purpose will be to introduce the concept of a Collaboration of Youth Services effort, the advantages for forming and maintaining such an ongoing group, and develop a mission statement for this coordinating body. A draft mission statement to begin discussion will be:

To develop an infrastructure for the coordination of Youth Intervention Services so that existing youth services are used to capacity, quality youth prevention and intervention services are provided, and the youth service organizations collaboratively position themselves to pursue additional resources.

Monthly Youth Collaboration Meetings: After the Kick-Off Meeting, the Coordinator will host monthly youth service collaboration meetings for youth organizations to identify existing barriers to service delivery and how to solve them, how to include community members and parents as stakeholders or service beneficiaries of service providers, and the identification of mechanisms for sharing resources and information, as well as establishing means of ongoing collaboration. This will be a broad-based coalition of youth service program personnel representing 15 to 20 youth organizations from the community, city, and county levels. The main goal of these monthly meetings will be to develop an environment of youth service collaboration within the city of Sun Town and to begin developing an infrastructure for a Youth Service Providers Collaboration.

Steering Committee: From this group of participating youth organizations, the Coordinator will form a steering committee consisting of five to seven participants. The charge of this committee will be to explore additional resources to expand and/or develop new youth services, and to sustain project efforts. This committee will assist the Coordinator in developing a system for information gathering and a Sun Town Youth Services directory, as well as the dissemination of this directory to major stakeholders.

➤ Develop a model, with support and guidance of the Steering Committee, to increase parental involvement with their children and the community, including exploring the expansion of parent services offered by the youth service providers.

The needs assessment conducted in preparation of developing this proposal indicated that involvement of parents with youth issues has been minimal, including the lack of a parent voice (e.g., parent advisory committee or cooperative). This project will address this issue; however, it understands that a number of barriers exist, including the unavailability of parents due to their need to work long hours (e.g., having two jobs), as well as cultural barriers that may inhibit the parents willingness to "have a say" in community issues that affect their children. The Coordinator will work closely with the Steering Committee in developing models to increase parental involvement, including gaining support from the other youth service providers and encouraging them to pilot the models in their organizations.

➤ Develop systems for information gathering and dissemination for and on youth participating in youth programs, focusing on the juvenile at-risk population, ages 11 to 18.

Presently, there is no common receptacle of information about youth services. Most youth service organizations do not have information about the clients served, even in terms of numbers of youth served, and no systems are in place to follow-up on youth. Consequently, there are also no means by which to evaluate the success of youth programs. Better information collection mechanisms within and among community-, city-, and country-based youth programs and services will enable the Police Department and the City of Sun Town to document service delivery, evaluate service success, identify needs that remain unmet, and explore and leverage additional resources to strengthen youth services in Sun Town.

The Coordinator will develop a system to collect, document, and maintain information on youth services provided in the City of Sun Town. The specific type of information to be collected and maintained will be determined by the Steering Committee. The system will be reviewed at the first monthly Youth Collaboration meeting of the second quarter. The buy-in of the youth service providers will be critical because they will be providing the information that will be inputted into the system. The objective will be to get at least 60% of the youth coalition organizations to participate. The Coordinator will be responsible for demonstrating the benefits to the community organizations for their participation in this system. The coordinator will develop and maintain this information system, as well as disseminate the information to appropriate stakeholders.

Compilation of a comprehensive directory of services for Sun Town youth   A fortuitous byproduct of the project proposed will be the creation of a comprehensive directory of youth services that can be disseminated throughout Sun Town. At present, no such directory exists and even service providers are not aware of resources that could make a difference to the youth they serve. Parents are even less informed. The creation of such a directory will make referrals easier and enable more timely and appropriate services to youth in need.

C. Demographics of the Population and Number of Clients to Be Served   Youth (ages 0 to 17) in Sun Town comprise almost one-third of the total population and are of diverse ethnicities 40% Hispanic/Latino, 33% Afro-American, while the other 27% are Caucasian and Pacific Islanders. Most are living below federal family poverty levels. More than 10% of the youth (500) have disabilities or special education needs. Within the City of Sun Town, 60% of the young men have been to prison by age 25 and 75% of men and 20% of women, ages 15 to 35, have been under the control of the criminal justice system.

In Year 1, the focus is to generate a coordinated atmosphere of youth services. The primary beneficiaries will be approximately 20 youth organizations. Indirectly the youth, as secondary beneficiaries, will be affected, especially as organizations are better able to identify the needs of youth and match them with existing programs that address those needs. Thus, in Year 1, the primary level of effort will be the formation of a coalition, the identification and coordination of existing resources, and the initiation of a communitywide information and referral system. In the following year, we will be able to focus on more youth beneficiaries, once this basic and fundamental organizational structure is in place.

IV. Specific Geographic Area Served by Project and By Organization

The project focuses on the geographic area that constitutes Sun Town and on Sun Town youth who have already entered the juvenile justice system or are at risk of doing so, specifically youth between the ages of 11 and 13. At present, youth services for Sun Town residents are fragmented in character and many of these are outside the city of Sun Town. Since we begin the project by focusing on a coordinated effort with key stakeholders and service providers in youth violence prevention, the geographic area will be broadened to include those organizations that serve Sun Town Youth, regardless of their location. Crucial services for youth in Sun Town are received from other cities within in the County; these organizations will be invited to participate in the collaboration.

V. A Numbered List of Intended Outcomes

Three of the four objectives of this project have a direct impact on the indicators and outcomes identified in the Children's Report, *Children in Our Community: A Report on Their Health and Well-Being*. Each of these is addressed below:

A. Coalition of Youth Service Providers

1. *Desired Process Result*: Develop an infrastructure within the Sun Town Police Department to coordinate youth service providers throughout the city.

   Desired Outcome Result: Youth service organizations meet on a regular basis and coordinate service delivery efforts for youth.

2. *Desired Process Result*: Twenty youth service providers will actively participate in the Monthly Youth Collaboration Meetings.

   Desired Outcome Result: a) 70% of the providers participating in the monthly meetings will increase the quality of their services to youth and/or expand services to youth. b) Service providers will serve 100 additional youth, averaging five new youth per provider.

   Children in Our Community: A Report on Their Health and Well-Being
   Outcome 2: Children Are Healthy
   Indicators: Teen Births, Sexually Transmitted Disease, and Drug, Alcohol, and Tobacco Use

B. Parent Involvement

3. *Desired Process Result*: 50% of the youth service providers will, with the assistance of models developed by the Steering Committee, make an effort to involve parents in the program services or the lives of their children.

   Desired Outcome Result: Forty parents will see the value of becoming more involved with the lives of their children; 75% of these parents will actively participate in their child's programs or other services offered by the youth service providers.

Children in Our Community: A Report on Their Health and Well-Being
Outcome 5: Children Are out of Trouble
Indicators: Children Who Are Self-Supervised

C. Data Collection Information System

4. *Desired Process Result*: 60% of the coalition service provider participants will participate in the data collection system for information gathering among the youth service providers.

Desired Outcome Result: The information will be aggregated and analyzed for use in one proposal to expand existing youth services or develop new youth services.

Children in Our Community: A Report on Their Health and Well-Being
Outcome 5: Children Are Out of Trouble
Indicators: Children Who Are Self-Supervised

D. Comprehensive Directory

5. *Desired Process Result*: A comprehensive directory of youth services for Sun Town Youth will be developed and disseminated to youth service providers and institutions serving youth in the city of Sun Town.

VI. Evaluation of the Success of the Project

Both process and outcome data will be collected using a variety of instruments, including minutes of meetings, youth service provider surveys, parent surveys, and existing data (e.g., data collected for the Data Collection Information System).

A. Coalition of Youth Service Providers

Process: Minutes of the Monthly Youth Collaboration Meetings and the Steering Committee Meetings will be collected to obtain the dates of the meetings, participants, and agenda items discussed.

Outcome: A Youth Service Provider post-survey will be administered to measure the benefits the providers received from the monthly meetings, including the number of additional new youth they were able to serve because of the collaboration and information sharing.

B. Parent Involvement

Process: The Youth Service Provider survey will also ask providers whether they implemented a service component that encourage parents to become involved in the child's services or other programs within the organization, as well as how many parents participated.

Outcome: A brief Parent Survey will be administered to parents to determine how their involvement benefited their children as well as themselves.

C. Data Collection Information System

Process: Existing data will determine the number of youth service providers contributing data/information to the system.

Outcome: Existing data will be analyzed and results reported on the type of information collected, as well as how this information has been used and/or will be used.

D. Comprehensive Directory

Process: A list of organizations, institutions, and other stakeholders who receive the directory will be maintained. A log of how the directory is requested will also be maintained.

VII. Why Organization Is Uniquely Positioned to Serve the Target Population, Including Qualifications of Key Organizational Staff

The Sun Town Police Department is an integral part of the city's structure. It is viewed as a leader in addressing youth issues and currently oversees intervention (the diversion program) and incarceration (juvenile hall) of youth. At present, there is a great need for prevention efforts in the department in order to provide comprehensive services to youth.

Sun Town Police Department will hire a Project Coordinator that has strong administrative skills, including the ability to facilitate meetings, develop and maintain an information data system, collaborate and partner with a variety of organizations, and build and sustain a citywide infrastructure for the collaboration of youth service providers. The Coordinator will also need skills to interact with a variety of people with different cultures, professional status, and personalities.

VIII. How Is This Project Distinct from Similar Projects Offered by Other Local Agencies and How Project Will Collaborate with Other Projects?

A number of small, grassroots youth service organizations exist in Sun Town. However, the lack of resources has prohibited these agencies from taking a leadership role in the coordination of these services across the city. The Sun Town Police Department is interested in taking the lead in this effort because of its institutional strength, its support from the City of Sun Town, and its ability to work closely with the Sheriff's Office, the entity responsible for carrying out the CRON program, the model on which this project is based.

IX. A Detailed Timeline of Project

Quarter 1:

➤ Conduct one kick-off meeting with broad-based coalition of youth service program personnel from the community, city, and county levels to introduce program, solicit ideas and participation, set future agenda, and begin selection of the project's steering committee.

➤ Hold monthly Youth Collaboration Meetings to share, coordinate, and brainstorm.

➤ Begin the documentation process of existing youth service providers who serve youth, especially those that serve youth at risk of entering the juvenile justice system.

➤ Begin identification of data collection techniques and information sharing mechanisms.

Quarter 2:

➤ Continue monthly Youth Collaboration Meetings.

➤ Finalize selection of Project Steering Committee.

➤ Convene three Steering Committee meetings to: (a) establish detailed work plan for all project phases; (b) develop the Sun Town Youth Services and Program Directory and decide on its most effective means of dissemination; (c) continue identification of gaps in youth service delivery; and, (d) identify existing resources and funding mechanisms to sustain project in the future.

➤ Finalize the identification of data collection and information sharing mechanisms among youth service organizations and begin pilot testing the system.

➤ Begin developing models to involve parents with their children's youth activities.

Quarter 3:

➤ Continue monthly Youth Collaboration Meetings.

➤ Convene three Project Steering Committee meetings to: (a) identify plans for closing gaps in youth service delivery; (b) begin grant applications for further funding of project in Years 2 to 5.

➤ Continue pilot testing the data collection and information sharing system among youth providers.

➤ Begin implementation of mechanisms for parental involvement in youth prevention and intervention efforts.

Quarter 4:

➤ Continue Monthly Youth Collaboration Meetings.

➤ Convene three Project Steering Committee meetings to: (a) complete writing an application for funding process for Year 2; (b) finalize Sun Town Youth Services and Programs Directory and disseminate to stakeholders and community.

➤ Finalize the data collection and information sharing system.

Deliverables

➤ Quarterly Reports (3rd month, 6th month, 9th month)

➤ Final Quarterly Report (12th month)

➤ Final design of the data collection and information sharing/dissemination system for youth service providers (12th month)

➤ East Palo Youth Services and Programs Directory (12th month)

X. How We Plan to Sustain the Project in the Future

We are considering funding sources from a wide array of private and public sources. These include federal entities such as AmeriCorps Program and the Office of Juvenile Justice and Delinquency Prevention. State funds will be sought from Office of Criminal Justice and Planning (OCJP) gang suppression program, the Attorney General's Crime and Violence Prevention Center, and the California State Alcohol and Drug Department. We will also approach the Sun Town City Council for seed money/match money, and solicit funds from private foundations such as the California Wellness Foundation, the California Endowment Foundation, and the Irvine Foundation.

Mandarin Chinese Class in Your Schools Proposals

This proposal was developed by interested community stakeholders, including parents and local organizations. It was submitted to the school district requesting support and funding to implement Mandarin Chinese classes for students (see Tables 8.1 and 8.2).

Present to: YUSD Assistant Superintendent of Secondary Instruction

Principal, A High School

Principal, B High School

Prepared by: Chinese Class in Your Schools Working Group

Table 8.1 Mandarin Chinese Class in Your Schools (On Campus)

Proposed Course: Mandarin Chinese Class in Your Schools (On Campus)			
Start Date:	Fall 2009	**Teachers and support organizations:**	Certified Teachers: Ms. Y, Mr. N
End Date:	Spring 2011		Organizations: Chinese Classes in Your School's Working Group (Chinese School, Civic Club, Chamber of Commerce)

Objective:
A Mandarin Chinese course will be offered to students in Your High School or/and Vista High School beginning Fall 2009.

1. Identified Needs	Having knowledge of the Mandarin Chinese language has become an important skill for cultural and social exchange in this global society. It is evident by the demand for such skills in the job market and the increase of non-ethnic-Chinese students enrolled in this Chinese School. Several national surveys have reported an increase in offering Mandarin Chinese in schools of all levels. The City of Your School geographically stands at the frontline of contacts within the Asian Pacific region. The city also has a large number of residents who are of Asian descent, particularly ethnic Chinese, from countries other than China. These families, along with other non-Asian families, have expressed their desire to afford their children the opportunity to learn the Mandarin Chinese language through the school system.
2. Target Population	At least 35 students in A High School and 35 to 70 students in B High School. These students will have different levels of competency in Mandarin Chinese.
3. Desired Results	*Output:* Approximately 55 students in A High School and 55 in B High School will indicate interest in taking a Mandarin Chinese class. At least 40 students in each school will enroll in the Mandarin Chinese class during registration in February 2009. *Intermediate Outcome:* Mandarin Chinese classes (levels 1 and 2) will be offered in at least one of the high schools beginning in the Fall of 2009 with at least 35 students of different Chinese language competency enrolled. *End Outcome:* Mandarin Chinese language will become a regular World Language AP course in YUSD by 2011.
4. Activity/Curriculum	➤ An established Mandarin Chinese language curriculum meets the State Education Department A through G requirements and receives approvals for college credits transfer from state universities. ➤ Special activities such as recruitment fair, orientation, mentor/practice partners, and year-end celebration will be incorporated to improve learning and promote student interest. ➤ See attached Mandarin Chinese class curricular.
5. Measurement of Success	➤ Success of the class will be measured by students' class grade and participation. ➤ An advisory committee will be formed by school personnel and members of the working group to provide inputs and resources to ensure the success of the course. This committee will meet regularly and conduct a year-end review of the course.
6. Resources and Inputs	In order for this course to be successful, it needs the following resources and input: ➤ Support from the YUSD and principals of both high schools ➤ Support from parents of potential students ➤ Sufficient number of students interest in taking Chinese ➤ Chinese School ➤ Other local cultural and civic groups

Table 8.2 Mandarin Chinese Class in Your Schools (Off Campus at Chinese School)

Proposed Course: Mandarin Chinese Class in Your Schools (Off Campus at Chinese School)			
Start Date:	Fall 2009	**Teachers and support organizations:**	Certified Teachers: Ms. Y, Mr. N Organizations: Chinese Classes in Your School's Working Group (Chinese School), Civic Club, Chamber of Commerce)
End Date:	Spring 2011		

Objective:
A Mandarin Chinese course with credits transferable to the YUSD will be offered to students through the Chinese School [a 501(C)3 non-profit organization] *beginning Fall 2009.*

1. Identified Needs	Having knowledge of the Mandarin Chinese language has become an important skill for cultural and social exchange in this global society. It is evident by the demand for such skills in the job market and the increase of non–ethnic-Chinese students enrolled in Chinese School. Several national surveys have reported an increase in offering Mandarin Chinese in schools of all levels. The City geographically stands at the frontline of contacts within the Asian Pacific region. The City also has a large number of residents who are of Asian descent, particularly ethnic Chinese, from countries other than China. These families, along with other non-Asian families, have expressed their desire to afford their children the opportunity to learn the Mandarin Chinese language through the school system.
2. Target Population	At least 30 students in A and B High Schools who have different levels of competency in Mandarin Chinese.
3. Desired Results	**Output:** ➤ Approximately 50 high school students in local high schools will indicate interest in taking this Mandarin Chinese class at the Chinese School. At least 30 students will sign up for this class during registration at the Chinese School in April 2009. ➤ By March 2009, with assistance from YUSD School District, this class will meet all the educational requirements for high school credits. The Mandarin Chinese class curriculum will receive approval for college credits transfer from state universities. ➤ The class will meet after school in a local school. This course will meet the same requirements as an on-campus course. ➤ An MOU will be developed between Chinese School and YUSD School District prior to the offering of this course. This MOU will clearly describe the roles and responsibilities of Chinese School and YUSD. Fiscal, social, and educational implications will also be addressed. For example, the options a student would have if he/she is interested in taking the course as a regular high school course but could not afford the cost. ➤ Families of students will assume the nominal cost of the course. ➤ Fiscally and administratively, Chinese School will manage the implementation of this course. ➤ In coordination with YUSD, Chinese School will ensure the course will meet all the academic standards. **Intermediate Outcome:** High school course equivalent Mandarin Chinese classes (levels 1 and 2) will be offered in Chinese School beginning Fall 2009 with at least 35 students of different Mandarin Chinese language competency enrolled. **End Outcome:** ➤ If successful, YUSD takes over the classes from Chinese School in 2 years' time. By 2011, sufficient interest in taking the Mandarin Chinese language will be developed. It is expected that YUSD will absorb the course to become a regular World Language course. ➤ Additionally, if there are sufficient demands from the surrounding communities, Chinese School will continue to offer the proposed Chinese course. It is also expected that the course will be developed into an AP course.

(Continued)

Table 8.2 Mandarin Chinese Class in Your Schools (Off Campus at Chinese School)   *(Continued)*

4. Activity/Curriculum	➤ An established Mandarin Chinese language curriculum meets the State Education Department A through G requirements and receives approvals for college credits transfer from State universities. ➤ Special activities such as recruitment fair, orientation, mentor/practice partners, and year-end celebration will be incorporated to improve learning and promote student interest. ➤ See attached Mandarin Chinese class curricular.
5. Measurement of Success	➤ Success of the class will be measured by students' class grade and participation. ➤ An advisory committee will be formed by school personnel and members of the working group to provide inputs and resources to ensure the success of the course. This committee will meet regularly and conduct a year-end review of the course.

6. Resources and Inputs	In order for this course to be successful, it needs the following resources and input:
	➤ Support from the YUSD and principals of both high schools
	   ➤ Classrooms
	   ➤ Facilities support (janitor, bathrooms, etc.)
	   ➤ Class support (books, computers, etc.)
	➤ Support from parents of potential students
	➤ Sufficient number of students interest in taking Chinese
	➤ Chinese School
	   ➤ Managing and offering the Mandarin Chinese Course
	   ➤ Independently or in cooperation with YUSD, seeking appropriate grant funding support
	   ➤ Fundraising
	   ➤ In school and off campus activities
	➤ Other local cultural and civic groups
	   ➤ Visibility
	   ➤ Fundraising
	   ➤ Interactive learning programs

Evaluation Plans

Two evaluation plan samples (i.e., ABC Learning Kids, and Together with Services) are presented as follows. One was developed as an example of how grantees can design an evaluation plan to be submitted to the funding source. The second sample is a real-life evaluation plan that was submitted to a funding source to fund an evaluation.

Evaluation Plan Sample

This evaluation plan template integrates many of the key components discussed in this book and provides a comprehensive understanding of the use of these components. This helps grantee applicants organize and develop an evaluation plan. Programs of this funding source that are interested in reapplying for a second cycle of funding (i.e., three years) must include an evaluation plan that applicants intend to implement if they are re-funded.

Table 8.3 Evaluation Plan Sample (ABC Learning Kids)

I. Program Information

Date: December 15, 2009
Program Name: ABC Learning Kids
Program ID: 89-09-99-0H
Legal Applicant: MRB School District
Contact Person: Ken Francis, Program Director
Phone/e-mail: 888-888-8888 kfrancis@test.com

II. Program Summary

Program description and primary activities:
ABC Learning Kids provides reading tutoring to at-risk third graders using community volunteers in ten elementary schools in the MPD School District. The one-on-one reading tutoring occurs both during the school day and as part of the after-school program averaging three contacts per student per week for 20 minutes each session. Students are identified for participation in the program by teachers based on their reading proficiency and their resulting overall risk for academic failure.

III. Evaluation Plan Overview

1. Evaluation classification:

This evaluation will be conducted as an independent evaluation, using an external evaluator.

2. Role of the evaluator:

The external evaluator assisted in the development of this Evaluation Plan; she will also take a lead role in the actual evaluation process.

3. Evaluator qualifications:

Robin Smith, PhD, is an educational evaluation specialist. She has her own consulting firm, Aligned for Action, LLC, that works with educational organizations within the state doing strategic planning, grant writing, and evaluation design and implementation. She has five years' experience evaluating numerous grant-funded projects, ranging in size from $25,000 to $1,000,000, for such funders as the U.S. Agency for International Development, the U.S. Department of Education, the Library of Congress, and the Office of Juvenile Justice and Delinquency Prevention of the U.S. Department of Justice. Robin Smith was chosen because of her independent contractor status, excellent qualifications as an evaluator in the field of education, and good references from the U.S. Department of Education. She has no prior affiliation with the ABC Learning Kids Program and has certified that she has neither a conflict of interest nor vested interest of any kind in the outcome of this evaluation.

4. Evaluation timeline and completion of evaluation report:

Year One of the grant will be dedicated to further planning and taking the general evaluation approach outlined in this plan, operationalizing it, as well as finalizing our data collection tools and systems. The data collection portion of the evaluation will begin in the first quarter of Year Two and run through the full program year. The first quarter of Year Three will be focused on data analysis and the preparation of the findings and recommendations for the final report. The report will be completed by the independent evaluator during the last two months of the grant period. In the last month, this evaluation will be debriefed by the evaluator and stakeholder representatives; and then a post-evaluation action plan will be prepared by Ken Francis.

5. Participants who developed the Evaluation Plan:

Ken Francis—ABC Learning Kids, Program Director

Robin Smith—Aligned for Action LLC, Educational Evaluation Specialist

Mary Jones—MPD School District, Evaluation Specialist *(sponsoring organization's internal evaluator)*

6. This evaluation plan aims to serve the following purposes in addition to meeting the Major Funder requirements:

➤ To determine whether program targets are realistic

➤ To assess program output and program outcomes

➤ To report to other funders

➤ As a management and decision-making tool

(Continued)

Table 8.3 Evaluation Plan Sample   *(Continued)*

7. **Projected use of findings:**

The process evaluation findings will allow us to make more informed decisions toward continued improvement of ABC's reading tutoring services. We want to train our tutors (community volunteers) to more effectively provide high quality tutoring to our students. The outcome evaluation findings will enable us to decide whether the increased reading skills of students are, in fact, the result of our program services. The evaluation will provide us with information on causality. In addition to the Major Funder we will report our findings to other supporters/stakeholders, including funders and community partners. The evaluation findings will also be applied to improving promotion and outreach activities for recruiting new community volunteer tutors, nonprofit partners, and strategic business partners.

IV. Audiences

1. **Primary stakeholders for this evaluation:**

➢ Major funder

➢ Program staff and members

➢ Students tutored and their teachers

➢ Elementary school administrators

➢ Community partners

2. **Use of evaluation results for these primary stakeholders:**

As a competitively funded program, the Major Funder will require us to submit an evaluation report when we reapply for continued funds in 2010; therefore, the Corps Funder is an important stakeholder for our program evaluation. We also want to show our state commission that we are making a difference in our community, because we want their continued support assisting us in reaching out to the community to obtain matching funds. Our program staff members are, also important stakeholders, as outside feedback on how our program is really working will help us in future decision making and validation of our work. Lastly, our community partners are critical to our ability to provide services in the community; our continued collaboration allows us to place volunteers at their sites. Our partners have asked us for evaluation results of our program so that they can take this information to their institutional decision makers who determine whether to continue participation in our program.

V. Evaluation Questions

Key Evaluation Questions to be answered by this evaluation:

In consultation with our external evaluator, we identified the following key questions that our evaluation will address. Additional detailed questions will be determined when our evaluation plan is refined.

Process Evaluation Questions:

➢ Is our tutoring model being implemented with integrity by community volunteers? If not, why not?

➢ Do the sites' institutional infrastructure support the services provided by the volunteers to ABC Learning Kids? If so, how so; if not, why not?

➢ Are there any modifications that we need to make in our service delivery based on our outcome findings?

Outcome Evaluation Questions:

➢ Have students in the ABC Learning Kids Reading Tutoring Program improved in their reading ability as anticipated, after their participation in the program?

➢ If students improved in their reading ability, how much change occurred, in which areas, and in whom have these changes taken place?

➢ What ABC Learning Kids tutoring practices caused the reading ability changes in students?

➢ How will the outcomes of students enrolled in the ABC Learning Kids Reading Tutoring Program compare with similar students not served by any tutoring program?

➢ What other causal factors have an impact (positive or negative) on the desired program outcomes?

VI. Evaluation Design

Our evaluation approach will employ a variety of research designs, including exploratory, descriptive, and quasi-experimental designs. Based on these designs, appropriate data collection methods and instruments will be used to gather information for evaluating the attainment of the program objectives. These designs were identified in consultation with our external evaluator.

1. Summary:

Exploratory design: The evaluator will conduct a quick assessment to verify the need for tutoring services in the school district, which students need this service, and if students needing help are participating in the tutoring program. A literature review of program designs and results of similar scientifically based tutoring programs will be conducted and compared with ABC Learning Kids tutoring services. This review will inform us of the most effective program designs and performance measures to consider.

Descriptive design: The evaluation methods relating to the descriptive design will include service utilization studies, opinion polls, client satisfaction surveys, outcome surveys, and best-practice surveys. The descriptive design, along with information from the exploratory study, will respond to the process, intermediate outcome, and end outcome related questions.

Quasi-experimental design: The evaluator will select a number of students meeting specified criteria for evaluation. The established criteria will include, but will not be limited to, active participation in the program, ability to establish a stable baseline and to stay with the program, available school data, and willingness to be studied. The reading skills of the selected students will be measured at baseline (pre-tutoring phase), and after the tutoring starts, over several assessment points to monitor the changes. The quasi-experimental design will include case studies of the students to provide a human face highlighting the possible effects of the intervention (tutoring).

The ABC Learning Kids Reading Tutoring Program results will be compared with data gathered from existing records or reports of the general school/district data on students reading and/or with those students who are on the waiting list and have not yet received tutoring.

2. Data Types

We will collect two kinds of data. For the process assessment portion of our evaluation, we will collect data on the integrity of implementing our program model. This data will include the number of hours of reading tutoring provided per student, the number of tutoring sessions per week over what period of time, the tutoring methods used, etc. For the outcome assessment portion, we will utilize the data we currently collect for our annual performance measures, i.e., student outcomes including reading skill improvement and overall increases in reading proficiency.

There are several data sources for this evaluation.

➤ Information on ABC's program model implementation will be collected from community volunteer members and their supervising teachers.

➤ Data on student outcomes in the tutored group will be collected from school district staff and teachers.

➤ Data on the comparison group students/classes will also be collected from school district staff and teachers.

3. Ethical Considerations for This Evaluation:

ABC Learning Kids has established guidelines for protecting the confidentiality of all service recipient records. All ABC staff are required to complete training on participant protection and confidentiality.

Prior to participants' involvement in the program, procedures that safeguard their privacy and confidentiality will be presented both in English and if necessary in their primary language. The voluntary nature of their participation, their right to withdraw from the program at anytime without prejudice, potential risks, and the use of data collected through this project will also be discussed. Limitations on confidentiality for minors as well as adults will be explained. Risks are not anticipated, but we will inform the participants about the nature of instruments and the approximate length of time for completion.

Participants and their guardians will then be asked to review and sign the proper consent documents (i.e., consent to participate form, parental permission, or assent form). When appropriate, implied consent or verbal consent will also be used. However, no participants will be refused services if they are not willing to take part in the evaluation.

Human Subjects Review approvals will be secured from the ABC Learning Kids and the School District's Institutional Review Boards before the beginning of the evaluation. All safeguard procedures and documents are detailed in the evaluation plan and are on file for review. Memorandums of Understanding between School District and the ABC Learning Kids specify what and how information could be accessed and used.

(Continued)

Table 8.3 Evaluation Plan Sample   *(Continued)*

VII. Data Collection (Methods and Instruments)

1. Proposed data collection methods:
- Quasi-experimental methods: for outcome data
- Survey Questionnaire: for process/implementation data
- Secondary data analysis: for standard reading tutoring expectations and other program results

2. Instruments be to used:
➤ Instruments to collect process/implementation data about our program model will be developed by the independent evaluator in conjunction with program staff after we receive funding for the next three-year grant cycle.

➤ Secondary data summary tools will also be developed by our independent evaluator.

➤ We will use our existing performance measurement data collection tools to collect student outcome data from both the experimental and comparison groups.

3. Person responsible for data collection:
During the evaluation contract negotiations, we will work with our independent evaluator to identify specific roles in data collection for program, our legal applicant, site staff, volunteers, and the evaluator.

4. Data collection timeline:
The following data will be collected during Year Two:

➤ Student outcome data will be collected at the beginning of the school year, midterm, and end of the school year.

➤ Process data will be collected monthly.

VIII. Data Management and Analysis

1. Data management:
We plan to use the following data management methods:

➤ Paper-and-pencil hardcopy record

➤ Computer database (i.e., Excel, SPSS)

2. Data analysis strategies:
The following data analysis strategies are proposed:

➤ Basic display: frequency, percentage, charts

➤ Measurement of central tendency: mean, mode, median

➤ Comparisons using descriptive and inferential statistics (e.g., t-test, Chi-Square)

3. Person responsible for data analysis:
The data will be aggregated and analyzed by Robin Smith, our external evaluator.

IX. Strategies for Using Evaluation Findings

1. Reporting:
The external evaluator will compile a final report outlining all our process and outcome findings and the resulting recommendations for improvement. The complete report will be made available to our state commission/Corps Funder as part of our next grant application. We will compile a one-page fact sheet highlighting the results of our evaluation to share with other stakeholders (community partners, members, current and prospective funders, etc.), as well as participating teachers, school administrators and district staff. If our findings are strongly positive, we will also release a press release to our community paper, TV and radio stations to promote our work.

2. Evaluation debriefing:
ABC will hold an evaluation debriefing meeting after the evaluation report has been prepared to review the evaluation methodology, implementation, findings and recommendations with the evaluator and stakeholder representatives.

3. Post-evaluation action plan:
ABC will prepare a post-evaluation action plan based on recommendations made by the evaluator, participants of the evaluation debriefing meeting, and other stakeholders, such as Board members, staff members, partners, etc.

IX. Budget

Evaluation Staff/Consultant Salary/Benefits or Consultant Fee	$44,000
Travel	$1,000
Communications	$1,050
Printing/Duplication	$1,950
Supplies	$600
Indirect Costs	$6,000
Other: Data Entry	$5,400
Other:	0
TOTAL	**$60,000**

Budget Justification:

Our total evaluation budget, $60,000, is approximately 6 percent of the two-year annual budget for ABC Learning Kids.

Evaluation Staff/Consultant Salary/Benefits or Consultant Fee:

The independent evaluator will be responsible for implementation of the evaluation, including instrument development, monitoring data collection, analyzing the data, and reporting results. The estimated time over two years for this scope of work is 110 days (880 hours) at $50 per hour.

Travel:

Mileage to drive within the district: 520 miles @ $.445/mile = $750
Parking (50 days @ $5/day = $250)

Communications:

Cell phone, long distance, and fax charges (24 months @ $43.75/month = $1,050)

Printing/Duplication:

Duplication of data collections tools/report/evaluation materials @ $.10/copy = $1,500
Printing and packaging of annual and final reports: 30 reports @ $15/report = $450

Supplies:

Office supplies and miscellaneous material (24 months @ $25/month = $600)

Indirect Costs:

10% indirect costs (office space, utilities, accounting)

Other:

Data entry: 450 hours @ $12/hour = $5,400

Domestic Violence Prevention Program: Together with Services (TWS)

This evaluation plan was developed for a school-based domestic and sexual violence prevention project. This evaluation plan incorporates the major elements and concerns for developing a program evaluation plan by an outside evaluator. Similar to the previous example, this evaluation plan lays out all the important components of an evaluation plan. It also delineates important topics such as research designs, ethical considerations, responsibilities of parties involved, different types of results assessed, and the structure and function of program evaluation. This sample plan could also be used as a template for a detailed evaluation plan.

Prepared by Dr. Y, Professor and Dr. B, Assistant Professor, Division of Social Work, State University, Sacto.

Program Plan and Description   Together with Services (TWS) in North Lake and The Village is implementing and evaluating a 14-month, school-based domestic violence prevention education program. This demonstration project targets 100 tenth graders in two high schools and 430 seventh graders in two middle schools. TWS also plans to expand its services to one more high school and one more middle school at the end of this program period.

This project will test the efficiency and effectiveness of a set of theoretically based, innovative, and well-coordinated programs that are specific to gender, age, and culture of the target population. These programs aim to promote the current goals set by the Office of Community Services.

Through this Prevention Program, TWS hopes to provide the targeted students in our service areas (North Lake and Southshore in Wash County) an effective domestic violence and sexual harassment education program. TWS wants to facilitate the increase of the skills and self-confidence of teens by educating them to recognize abuse, understand the dynamics of power/control relationships, understand the actual threats to them physically, mentally, and emotionally. By doing this, we hope to empower these students to pursue and live healthy lives that are free from violence, abuse, and harassment.

The proposed interventions are based on social learning theory and the risk/protective factors applied to three domains: individual peers, and schools with strategies that are intended to improve targeted students' knowledge, resourcefulness, and life skills. The proposed Prevention Project has three main components: (a) Develop the service delivery system, (b) Provide school-based education program, and (c) Evaluate the effectiveness of the education program.

Program Evaluation

The objectives of the evaluation tasks are threefold:

1. Provide ongoing process data (output) for reporting and improvement. (Are we doing what we set out to do?)

2. Assess the intermediate outcomes or the effectiveness of program activities. (How well did we do? What changes have taken place?)

3. Assess the end-outcome or impacts of the program. (So at the end, what difference did it make?)

The results of evaluation will provide information for better understanding of key questions for the proposed project. These questions relate directly to Office of Community Services' requirements and to the proposed application's goals and objectives. They will serve as guiding principles for the evaluation of the program.

Could this school-based education approach lead to increased awareness of the problems of domestic violence and sexual harassment by target students? Will these activities contribute to the decrease of such problems? If so, what strategies or combinations of strategies produce the best results?

Process Evaluation (Output, Accomplishment)   Documenting and monitoring the planning, implementation, and interrelationship of the components of the proposed project are the focus of the process evaluation, which aims to: (a) describe program interventions' development, implementation, and activities; (b) provide quantitative and qualitative data on services delivered and their effectiveness; and (c) document the appropriateness and acceptability of the program within the target community. To achieve these results, there are three main components of the process evaluation: (a) program planning and development, (b) program interventions, and (c) database management system.

(a) Program Planning and Development

Planning and development is an ongoing process. The documentation of this process includes compiling information on administrative planning, staff meeting, staff recruitment and training, preparation for program activity, work schedule, organizational support, and community linkage. This information not only documents the progress of the project but also provides a basis for describing the resources and input for this project.

In order to document the process of program development and implementation, the project management will have records of meetings and other related documents. Staff or program collaborators may be interviewed, in addition to activity specific measures, to document satisfaction measures and other concerns. Staff training, workshops, and conferences will also be documented through records of participation and minutes of discussions.

(b) Program Interventions

The documentation of program intervention should provide both qualitative and quantitative description of the interventions. These documentation procedures include several elements and different data collection approaches. First, description or type of interventions will be recorded along with intervention products such as curriculum. Second, utilization and quantity of project services as well as the time and locations of these services will be documented through encounter forms, activity logs, and attendance sheets. Third, project staff and collaborators will be interviewed to provide feedback and assessment regarding the project. Fourth, some ethnographic observations of project activities will be used to collect qualitative information for the project. These process evaluation procedures provide a basis for the understanding of the operation and effectiveness of the project. The following are some of the measures and forms used to document these operations and their effectiveness.

Staff Recruitment, Hiring, and Training: Recruitment and hiring procedures as well as staff training and conferences will be documented.

Planning and Development: Meeting records will be used to reflect program development process, problems encountered, and alternatives and solutions to the problems.

Program Usage and Target Population: Activity logs, attendance records or sign-up sheets will be used to document the extent of service used, the achievements and barriers, student flow, students and school recruitment, and the characteristics of students.

Community Linkage: The Community Contact Form will track community meetings and other contacts with the community. These records will include the date, person contacted, organization, content, frequency, and results of these efforts to assess the extent and effectiveness. Other community collaboration efforts will also be tracked by meeting minutes, service contracts, and memorandum of understanding.

(c) Database Management Information System

A database management information system (MIS) provides the mechanism to store and compile quantifiable data to assess the development and effectiveness of the project. This system involves: (a) development of file formats and identification of appropriate software, (b) subsequent data entry, and (c) generating reports. With data collection and data analyses, the MIS forms the basis for evaluation.

If available, collective demographic information of participating students will be collected. All project forms and measures will be updated as needed; baseline and other project data will continue to be collected throughout the project years. Other data, which are available from local private and government organizations, will also be utilized for comparison.

Although the evaluation team has the primary responsibility for the development and maintenance of the MIS, it is a joint effort between evaluation and project staff to manage this system. Basic database software including Microsoft Excel and Statistical Package for Social Science (SPSS) will be used.

Process and Outcome Objectives Evaluation   Progress for each objective and its associated activities will be collected on a regular basis. In addition to the use of forms and self-reports from staff, participatory observation by evaluation team staff may also be used for data collection.

The Prevention Program will have the following three components during the project period:

I. Develop service delivery system:

1. Staff recruitment and training

2. Schedule school-based education activities

3. Involve a program evaluator

II. Provide number of presentations to 530 students in four targeted schools that result in some measurable changes in students' knowledge, attitudes, and behaviors:

1. Number of presentations

2. 530 students served

3. Four target schools involved

4. Changes in students' knowledge, attitudes, and behaviors

III. Outreach and community education:

1. Two new schools recruited

2. A total of two schools served

The attached Program Planning and Evaluation Worksheets detail each of the objectives (both process and outcome) and their evaluation strategies.

Data Analysis and Reports   On a regular basis, information including descriptions and data collected will be reviewed and analyzed. Data will be entered into a computer and be analyzed with updated database or spreadsheet software (Excel or SPSS). Appropriate descriptive statistics and inferential statistics will be utilized to measure program effectiveness and impact. These analyses will determine if there are significant differences between comparison groups (if available) and between pre- and post-tests. To assess overall program impact and its effectiveness, focus group or key-informant interviews will be used to evaluate the extent of the impact.

During the program year, a midterm and a final report to the project management will be submitted.

Evaluation Team   Two evaluators and two graduate social work research assistants make up the evaluation team. Dr. Y, Professor of Social Work at State University, Sacto, is one of the evaluation consultants. He has many years of experience in grant writing and program evaluation. His latest publication is: "How to evaluate programs." Dr. B, Assistant Professor of Social Work at State University, Sacto, also has many years of program evaluation experience. Her latest evaluation task was with the Stuart Foundation. The evaluation team also includes one or two part-time research assistants (RA) who are Master of Social Work students.

Together they will meet with the project management staff during the beginning of the project to further refine the following evaluation action plan. Project staff will then review this revised action plan to provide comments. Their input will help refine and further determine the focus of evaluation. The revised evaluation plan will be finalized in the second month.

Through the State University, Sacto Foundation, the evaluation team subcontract with TWS to evaluate this prevention project. The evaluation team will have regular meetings. It will also meet with project management and staff when needed. This may include the initial project planning and implementation meetings or selected program activities for observational measures.

The basic division of labor and responsibilities are as follows:

Program Evaluators:

➤ Develop an evaluation plan.

➤ Develop data collection instruments.

➤ Monitor the valuation process.

➤ Coordinate and monitor research assistants.

➤ Analyze program data.

➤ Generate midterm and end-of-program report.

Research Assistants:

➤ Develop data collection instruments.

➤ Collect, enter, maintain, and analyze program data.

➤ Coordinate the logistics of program evaluation with staff.

➤ Develop evaluation instruments.

➤ Generate drafts for midterm and final evaluation.

TWS Program Staff:

➤ Provide organizational support.

➤ Ensure collaboration with program evaluation.

➤ Prepare payment to University Foundation.

➤ Collect and enter project data.

Impact Evaluation   Based on the project objectives and their process and outcome evaluation results, program staff will identify and assess the areas and the extent of program impacts. This assessment will be further supported by information collected through end-of-the-year focused-group meetings or key informant interview with specific target populations including community representatives, service recipients, and staff members.

Sampling Plan and Analysis Plan

1. The evaluation plan for this project does not require sampling procedures. If necessary, however, sampling can be done on a three-tier level, if the program wishes to draw a sample to evaluate any portion of the program. This will

include (a) all participants for a particular activity, (b) participants who attend activities consistently, and (c) a percentage of the consistent participants who are selected by a random approach.

2. Basic to the analysis plan, the program needs to develop an information management system/database to store evaluation data. The program should update all process data on a regular basis. Process data will be collected and presented using single-variable analysis, measurements of central tendency and dispersion (e.g., frequency distribution, percentage, mean, mode, median, minimum, maximum, and range). Outcome data will also be collected through the above-mentioned forms. Assessments of changes are to be measured using quantitative descriptive and inferential statistics as well as qualitative analyses and comparisons.

Implementation of Evaluation

1. The program will involve its staff to assist in the data input and analysis.

2. The program should develop a functional database to store and compile quantifiable process and outcome data to evaluate the project.

3. The program will provide specific orientation sessions to staff members on the purpose and the implementation of evaluation. It will also schedule specific times during each week for staff to complete evaluation tasks.

4. Develop the sense of ownership and buy-in by the partner agencies, members, and volunteers.

Target Population, Participant Recruitment and Selection

1. The Prevention Program will target 530 seventh- and tenth-grade students in seven different classes at two different schools (one in Truck Ridge and one in Tahoville). It is expected that the program will be expanded to two more new schools and their students by the end of the Fall semester.

2. Project staff will conduct outreach to target schools. The agency's current client outreach and recruitment network will be used and revised for the project.

3. Participation in this project is strictly voluntary. Participants can withdraw from the prevention activities at any time.

4. Parental permission to participate in TWS program activities and their associated evaluation activities will be secured prior to the implementation of any TWS services.

Data Collection

1. Data will be collected from participants by the program staff by means of existing records, service logs, and data collection tools designed specifically for this project.

2. Copies of standard data collection instruments that will be used for this project are provided in the Appendix.

Confidentiality, Privacy, and Other Ethical Considerations   TWS has established guidelines regarding confidentiality of all records and charts of clients. Policies and procedures are written, reviewed, and subject to change following current requirements of the local Counties, the State, and other funding sources.

All information will be kept in the evaluation computer and in a locked file cabinet with access only by evaluation staff and the project director. All evaluation materials will be kept strictly confidential. Most forms will utilize numerical codes for identification. In order to track individual changes, each student will be given a number which they will use to print on the pre, post, as well as the quick list. Students are instructed to discard the number at the end of the post-test. Consequently, the evaluation is able to track individual student's performance in a given workshop but not the identity of the students.

Participation in the program and its evaluation is voluntary. Students will be informed verbally as well as in the evaluation form about their rights and the voluntary nature of their participation. However, no students will be refused for services if they are not willing to take part in the evaluation. Risks are not anticipated, but we will inform the participants about the nature of instruments and the approximate length of time for completion.

Protection from Potential Risks

1. Although potential risks are not anticipated, project staff and evaluation team members should adhere to the client confidentiality and protection procedures and policies to ensure the well-being of the clients.

2. Upon hiring, all project staff are required to be trained on confidentiality guidelines. Issues related to client protection and confidentiality will be discussed during staff training.

3. All agency staffs are trained to provide proper intervention in the event of adverse effects to participants. Additionally, they would seek consultations from local licensed clinical social workers, psychiatrists, and psychologists.

Consent Procedures

1. Prior to acceptance into the program, participants will be informed (both in English, and if necessary, in their primary language) about the nature and purpose of their participation in the program and its evaluation component. Procedures that safeguard their privacy and confidentiality will be presented. The voluntary nature of their participation, their right to withdraw from the program at anytime without prejudice, potential risks, and the use of data collected through this project will also be discussed. Limitations on confidentiality for adolescents will be explained.

2. Several considerations have affected the attainment of consent from project participants, particularly those who are under age 18. First, the proposed program evaluation is the agency's activity that aims to assess the effectiveness of the program activities. It is not a research project that aims to investigate the health and mental health well-being of the youth. Second, as part of the school districts' consent protocol, parents of students will be asked to sign an approval form that allows their children to participate in various educational activities (including the TWS domestic violence workshop) co-sponsored by the schools. Their approval indicates their understanding of nature of their children's participation in these program activities including the program evaluation component. Their rights to withdraw and the voluntary nature of their participation are clearly explained both orally and in writing.

3. Prior to any evaluation activities, students will be asked to review and sign an assent to participate form (see attached). The form will be worded in an age-appropriate language. Students will be informed that signing the assent form does not mean that they have to participate in the evaluation or to answer all the evaluation questions.

4. No students will be refused for services if they are not willing to take part in the evaluation.

References

Hudson, W. (1982). Index of Self-Esteem (ISE), in *The clinical measurement package: A field manual.* Homewood, IL: Dorsey Press.

Yuen, F. K. O., & Terao, K. (2003). *Practical grant writing and program evaluation.* Pacific Grove, CA: Brooks/Cole–Thomson Learning.

9

Application of Information Technology

Information Technology

Information technology has become a way of life both personally and professionally. Technology is becoming a necessary tool for planning programs, writing grants, and implementing evaluations. Those in the grant-writing field who do not know how to, or are not willing to, learn the use of technology will be at a disadvantage when searching for funding opportunities, applying for grants, or implementing a program and evaluation.

Funding Sources

Whether the task is searching for information to formulate a program design or searching for evaluation instruments, software, or examples to design a program evaluation, surfing the Web is an easy and quick process to access this information.

Technology is also becoming the norm to find information on funding opportunities. Funders, from government to private foundations, are using the Internet as a means to announce Requests for Applications (RFAs) and to provide information on the application process.

Government   Federal government departments provide opportunities for community organizations and institutions to apply for funding to address various types of issues, including education, public health, public safety, and environment. Many federal departments publish a list of RFAs that they hope to release sometime during each program year and place these lists on their web site. This allows applicants to plan and strategize funding opportunities before an RFA is released. Generally, applicants have six weeks from the time the RFA is released to the time the proposal is due; therefore, having advance notice of funding opportunities can be an advantage. Applicants can find RFA announcements for various federal departments on the following web site, http://gov.org, which provides links to a variety of government departments that plan to release RFAs.

Local governments are also following suit with the federal government by using the Internet to announce RFAs. For those interested in applying for funds at the local level, conduct a search for the city, county, parish, or state and look at the Web sites for possible funding opportunities.

Foundations   Foundations can be categorized as corporate, community, and family foundations. What they all have in common is that they are philanthropic organizations that provide funding resources to organizations and institutions that are interested in providing services that supports the foundation's mission. Where they differ is that each foundation (1) has a different mission statement; (2) focuses on an issue area of interest that it wants to support; (3) may limit where services are to be implemented (e.g., local, domestic, global); (4) varies in its level of financial support; and (5) has different methods of applying, including timelines when applications are due.

Before the advances of technology, applicants had to visit a foundation office and scroll through several binders to find this information. With the Internet, applicants can now search for foundations that support specific issue areas and provide the information needed to apply for a foundation grant. There are hundreds of foundations that fund a variety of causes. Here are examples of a few foundation Web sites or Web site resources available:

> **Foundation Center**—http://foundationcenter.org Established in 1956 and today supported by close to 600 foundations, the Foundation Center is a national nonprofit service organization recognized as the nation's leading authority on organized philanthropy, connecting nonprofits and the grant makers supporting them to tools they can use and information they can trust. (Retrieved May 2009)

Ford Foundation—www.fordfound.org/grants Our overall mission is to reduce poverty and injustice and to promote democratic values, international cooperation, and human achievement. (Retrieved May 2009)

Bill and Melinda Gates Foundation—www.gatesfoundation.org To increase opportunity and equity for those most in need. Our belief that every life has equal value is at the core of our work at the foundation. We follow 15 guiding principles, which help define our approach to our philanthropic work, and employ an outstanding leadership team to direct our strategies and grant making. (Retrieved May 2009)

The Robert Wood Johnson Foundation—www.rwjf.org/grants Provides grants for projects in the United States and U.S. territories that advance our mission to improve the health and health care of all Americans. (Retrieved May 2009)

Applicants interested in applying for funding through a foundation are encouraged to invest the time to search for opportunities on the Internet. Obviously, the key word to use when searching on the Internet is "foundations."

Grant Applications: Going Green

In October 1998, the federal government passed a bill, the Government Paperwork Elimination Act (GPEA), which was instituted to improve customer service and government efficiency through the use of information technology. The purpose of this Act is to make transactions between the field and government quicker and to provide a vehicle for information access to be more easily tailored to specific questions critical to the issue needing to be addressed.

In addition to this Act, the environmental movement for recycling and waste reduction, both nationally and internationally, has encouraged federal departments to use less paper. Therefore, grant information, grant applications, and grant reporting requirements have been increasingly moved from paper documents to online information technology (Office of Management and Budget, 2009).

Application Submittal Increasingly, funders are requiring grant proposals to be submitted on CDs or online via e-mail or a Web-based system. In the past, many funding agencies, especially government funding sources, requested proposals to be submitted both by paper document and electronically. More recently, funders are requiring that applications be submitted for proposals online by getting onto the funder's web site and placing an application on an online template. This application process is meant to make the submittal of proposals more efficient and to support the Paperwork Elimination Act. The advantages to the applicant include the ability to submit a proposal the day before, or on the same day, that the proposal is due. This process can also be more efficient in knowing that the proposal was received within the deadline.

However, the use of technology for submitting proposals also places several challenges on the applicant. Does the applicant have the know-how to get into the system to submit the proposal? Did the applicant use the guidelines in formatting the proposal so that when cutting and pasting it into the online system, the technology used by the funder will not reformat the text and make the proposal difficult to read? If the applicant waits until the last day of the due date, will the system become overloaded because other applicants are trying to submit their proposals online at the same time, resulting in the proposal being kicked back and requiring the applicant to try at a later time to submit the proposal? Is the person submitting the proposal computer literate? Following Internet instructions and finding where to go within the system can be confusing for a person who is not Internet savvy. The following describes a real-life example of the challenges an applicant faced when writing a proposal and submitting online:

When applying for a federal grant with the National Service Department (NSD), a federal department that oversees the allocation of grants for community service programs, the applicant wrote the proposal in a Word document. This was advised by the funder because placing the proposal into the online application system is time limited (15 to 30 minutes). There is always a chance that the system may crash or malfunction when the applicant is cutting and pasting the proposal online. The application may need to be reentered but the original proposal file is not affected.

It was also important that the applicant follow the guidelines when writing the proposal, so that when it came time to cut-and-paste the proposal into the online application system, the proposal would not be reformatted. For example, in certain applications, the applicant could not use italics, bold font, underlined text, bullets, symbols, or charts or tables. The only organizational tactic the applicant could use was capital letters and spacing. If the applicant did not follow these guidelines, the proposal may have been difficult or not possible to read.

The sections of the proposal also had to be entered in separate text boxes in the Internet application system. The challenge of the applicant was to write the proposal so that it transitioned from one section to the next when each section was read like a separate document. In addition, as part of the application process, NSD wanted an organizational chart and timeline chart that did not follow the written guidelines. Therefore, organizational charts and timelines had to be submitted to NSD as paper documents.

These limitations place challenges on the applicant. Not only did the applicant need to develop and write up the program design and evaluation plan, but he or she also had to learn how to write the proposal so that it met the online application requirements. Formatting the proposal according to the online application guidelines, as well as writing the sections of the proposal so that they read as one document (even though the sections are in separate online text boxes), made it challenging for the applicant. No doubt these challenges will be addressed and online application and reporting will improve and become more user friendly. Knowledge and proficiency in the use of computer software and Internet technology have become required skills for program staff, grant writers, and evaluators.

Referencing Information Technology Sources

As applicants increasingly use the Internet to obtain information in writing proposals, they will need to reference where they obtained the information. Referencing Web sites of where information is obtained is a new task for many applicants. What are the standard methods for referencing information that is obtained from the Web site? How long will the information that was obtained online remain online? Will the institution/organization take down the information or revise it? Many grant writers face these questions and challenges. Therefore, it is important to document the date when the information was retrieved from the Web site. A common method to reference information from the Web site is to state the author (if appropriate), the original publication date (if known), the name of the article, the name of the organization (if applicable), the date when the information was retrieved, and the URL address. Different writing styles cite online references differently. For example the APA (American Psychological Association) reference to information retrieved from a web page may look like this:

Trochim, W. (2006). *Research methods knowledge base*. Retrieved January 16, 2009, from www.socialresearchmethods.net/kb/qualdeb.php.

Proposal Review   After proposals are submitted electronically to the funders, information technology is increasingly being used as part of the process for proposal reviews, especially by federal government agencies. A standard method of reviewing proposals is to identify community members who are knowledgeable about the issue area and have them review and rate the proposals, making recommendations about which proposals should be awarded grants. In the past, funders have sent the proposals to community member reviewers as paper documents. It has been common practice for a reviewer to receive a large box containing up to 10 or more proposals. But now, more funders are sending the proposals to the community member reviewers electronically. Reviewers may no longer be viewing the entire proposal document, only screen shots of the pages as they are being reviewed. Using technology in the review process does not affect the applicant directly; however, the applicants should be aware of how proposals may be reviewed, as this may help determine how proposals are written and submitted electronically.

Progress Reports   The use of information technology is becoming full circle for the entire grant process, from submitting proposals to the funder to submitting progress reports after being awarded a grant and implementing service activities.

Once services begin, most funders require programs to provide quarterly, semi-annual, and/or annual reports. Funding sources, especially government grants, are beginning to require progress reports to be submitted electronically. Grantees most likely will face similar advantages and challenges when submitting progress reports electronically as they did when submitting grant proposals to the funder. Progress reports can be submitted the day before or on the same day that the progress report is due and still meet the deadline due date. However, the formatting guidelines (e.g., no use of italics, bullets, bold font) most likely will be the same, restricting creativity when grantees tell their story of progress to date. After being awarded a grant, be aware of how the progress reports will need to be submitted, and be prepared for the challenges faced if the reports are to be submitted electronically.

Evaluation Methods and Technology

Information technology continues to play a critical role in program planning, program implementation, and evaluation, especially in the area of data collection. Access to personal computers and connections on the Internet has become the norm. Social service organizations and institutions have become dependent on this technology, not only for word processing and budgeting, but also for communication (e.g., e-mails, Web sites, list serves, social networking). The continued advances in technology and development of new software have begun to intersect with how evaluators can plan for and conduct their evaluation.

Electronic Surveys

One area of research technology that has become popular is online surveys. In most cases, software or Internet services are user friendly and cost effective. Not only do these Internet services allow evaluators to develop electronic surveys and disseminate the surveys quickly and at low cost, but these software/services also will aggregate and, in most cases, analyze the data, saving evaluators time and expense.

The strengths of using electronic surveys are described in Table 9.1. However, information technology also comes with disadvantages. Table 9.2 points out the potential challenges if an evaluator chooses to use an electronic survey.

Table 9.1 Strengths When Using an Electronic Survey

Cost savings	Less expensive to send questionnaires online
Easier to edit	Easy to make changes to the survey
Ease of analysis	Depending on the software, easy to sort data
Fast dissemination	Surveys delivered to participants quickly
Respondents can respond quicker	Generally, it is easier for respondents to take a survey electronically than it would be to take a paper survey

Table 9.2 Challenges When Using an Electronic Survey

Access limitations	Some populations may have limited access to a computer that is connected to the Internet.
Limited confidentiality	Online networks limit the evaluators to guarantee anonymity or confidentiality.
Format of survey limited	Formatting a computer survey is limited to the design options of the software.
More instructions needed	More instructions may be needed for the participant on how to complete an electronic survey.
Potential technical problems	There is always a risk of encountering technical problems when using technology.

Database Software

Computer and information technology are also making data aggregation and statistical analysis more efficient for evaluators. Database software is now available for evaluators to aggregate data using cross-tabs. For example, after administering a survey with adults at a health fair and then entering the data into a database, an evaluator may want to know how many males stated they have diabetes as compared to the number of females who stated they have diabetes. The evaluator may then want to know the average age of those males who do not have diabetes as compared to the average age of those males who have diabetes; also the same for the females. If the evaluator had 30 to 40 surveys, calculating the data by paper and pencil may not be a challenge, but if the evaluator had 500 to 600 surveys, this task would take a tremendous amount of time and expense. Data that are entered into a preprogrammed database allow easy access to this information within seconds. In addition, the database can produce a variety of data combinations quickly, depending on how the database software is programmed.

The advantage of a database is that it is an organized collection of data. A *database management system* is a specific type of software that can organize data in a flexible manner. It has the ability to add, modify, or delete data from the database, ask questions (or queries) about the data stored in the database, and also summarize selected contents.

The disadvantages in using a database are few, but extreme. The cost of database software can be expensive. Also, it takes a great deal of planning and preparation at the front end before data can be entered and an analysis is conducted. For example, program staff, stakeholders, and/or the evaluator must first determine what kind of data they want aggregated and in what combinations they want the data retrieved (e.g., cross-tabs). Next, a person who knows how to program the software must program the database according to the specifications identified, so that the database can retrieve the data as desired. In most cases, a professional programmer who specializes in the database software being used must program the database. This task can be costly. Lastly, ongoing maintenance by a programmer may be needed to ensure that the database is working properly.

Finding the Information Technology

New electronic surveys and database software are continually being improved at a rapid pace. What is new today can be obsolete next year. If specific software were named in this book, by the time readers determined the type of software needed, that software may no longer be the most effective technology system. Therefore, when it comes time to determine the type of electronic survey to use or the type of database to purchase, use technology: search on the Internet to see what is on the market. Key words to use for the search can be "electronic survey" or "database software." In addition, talk with other community organizations and universities and see what they are using or recommend. After learning the "techie" language, in most cases the dominant information technology begins to surface.

References

Bill and Melinda Gates Foundation. Retrieved May 1, 2009, from www.gatesfoundation.org.

Ford Foundation. Retrieved May 1, 2009, from www.fordfound.org/grants.

Foundation Center. Retrieved May 1, 2009, from http://foundationcenter.org.

Office of Management and Budget. Retrieved April 21, 2009, from www.whitehouse.gov/omb/fedreg/gpea2.html.

The Robert Wood Johnson Foundation. Retrieved May 1, 2009, from www.rwjf.org/grants.

EFFECTIVE GRANT WRITING AND PROGRAM EVALUATION FOR HUMAN SERVICE PROFESSIONALS

Author Index

Subject Index

CPSIA information can be obtained at www.ICGtesting.com
Printed in the USA
BVOW03n1339200116

433556BV00007B/8/P